AIRBORNE ESPIONAGE

INTERNATIONAL SPECIAL DUTIES OPERATIONS IN THE WORLD WARS

DAVID OLIVER

SUTTON PUBLISHING

First published in the United Kingdom in 2005 by
Sutton Publishing Limited · Phoenix Mill
Thrupp · Stroud · Gloucestershire · GL5 2BU

British Library Cataloguing in Publication Data
A catalogue record for this book is available from the British Library.

ISBN 0-7509-3870-6

Typeset in 11.5/15pt Garamond.
Typesetting and origination by
Sutton Publishing Limited.
Printed and bound in England by
J.H. Haynes & Co. Ltd, Sparkford.

Contents

Acknowledgements

Of the many people who assisted me in writing this book by providing personal anecdotes and photographs, I would like to extend particular thanks to the following individuals and organisations:

François Prins, who provided me with a constant stream of contacts, information and photographs; the late Bruce Robertson, who, as always, was a vital source of information and photographs – he will be sadly missed; Sir Lewis Hodges, Reginald Lewis and Roy Buckingham, who flew with the RAF 'moon' squadrons; Ron Clarke of the Carpetbagger Museum at Harrington; Ian Frimston, Cliff Knox, Richard Riding, Andy Thomas, Richard Chapman and Bo Widfeldt for providing photographs; Bill Stratton's International Liaison Pilot and Aircraft Association; Peter D. Evans's Luftwaffe *Experten* Message Board; and the Royal Australian and Royal Norwegian Air Forces' excellent archives.

Introduction

The twentieth century witnessed not only man's first flight in a heavier-than-air machine, but also the use of that machine as a powerful weapon of war. First as an airborne scout, then for dropping bombs on the enemy, it became a platform for shooting down enemy scout and bomber aeroplanes; and last but not least, and perhaps surprisingly, it became as a mode of transport for men and equipment.

There were plenty of opportunities for developing these roles in a century that will go down in history as witnessing the outbreak of no fewer than two world wars and countless local wars. These times of conflict and intrigue also brought an awareness of the value of another weapon – intelligence: in particular what we now know as HUMINT (human intelligence) but which was previously known as 'spying'.

At the start of the First World War, the transport by aeroplanes of spies across enemy lines was not seen as a priority by the combatants, but this would change as the conflict dragged on into its second year. At the beginning, there was no organisation for these flights, no reception teams at the drop zone and – most importantly – no communications network between the air forces and the agents, apart from homing pigeons or an occasional snatched telephone call.

The situation had not improved to any great extent by the outbreak of the Second World War in 1939. Although dedicated 'Special Duties' air units had been established to fly the spies, or 'agents' as they were then known, their aircraft were hand-me-downs and the role of their aircrews was considered a poor third to the more glamorous fighter and bomber operations.

However, the results ultimately achieved by these men and their aircraft were in many ways more hazardous and demanding than any other type of wartime flying. Finding a drop zone behind enemy lines at night, or actually landing in a remote field they had probably never seen before, with the only landing aids being the moonlight and a few hand torches, required a special type of expertise. Often flying an unarmed aircraft, and with the knowledge that being shot down and captured might end in summary execution, also called for a particular type of dedication and courage. Operating in all weathers, at low level and without escort, the Special Duties units paid a heavy price in aircrew killed and missing. By the very nature of these operations, their exploits were unreported during wartime, and for some considerable time thereafter; in fact, to this day, the official records of many of their flights have never seen the light of day and may never be released.

What is still relatively unknown is the fact that nearly all the Second World War combatants carried out clandestine flights to a greater or lesser extent. In the following chapters the exploits of British, Commonwealth, American, Free European, Soviet, German, Italian and Japanese airmen and units are recorded. The role played by the long-suffering ground crews who kept the Special Duties aircraft in the air, often in appalling conditions, must also be recognised as an integral part of the unsung backroom team which supported the individual agents and special forces who chose to operate in that most dangerous of war-time environments – behind enemy lines.

CHAPTER 1

Behind the Lines

On a crisp moonlit night in the third winter of the Second World War, a dozen people took up their positions around a snow-dusted field in central France. Among them were local farm workers, a storekeeper, a pharmacist and a teacher. They had broken the six o'clock curfew to risk local police and German checkpoints, travelling by foot, bicycle and delivery van to their windswept rendezvous. A few were armed with ancient shotguns, while others carried only battery-operated pocket torches. Two of the men and a young woman clutched battered suitcases.

Here they waited in silence, listening for the sound of an approaching engine. If it came from one of the roads leading to the nearby farm, they would be in mortal danger and would have to flee for their lives. But it came from the air, and soon a small, single-engined aircraft circled the field while the reception committee's *chef de terrain* aimed his torch in its direction and flashed a code letter in Morse. When the pilot flashed back the agreed code letters with his landing light, the reception committee laid out three pocket torches in the shape of an inverted L shape 150 yards long. The aircraft, a black-painted, high-wing Royal Air Force Lysander, touched down at the first torch, bouncing on the frost-hard earth and kicking up flecks of snow in its wake.

It ended its short landing run between the two torches that marked the end of the flarepath. Here the pilot gunned the engine, swung the Lysander around in a 180-degree turn and taxied back to the first torch. The plane came to a halt facing into the wind, with its engine idling. The rear cockpit canopy slid open and a figure in civilian clothing climbed down the short, fixed ladder and jumped to the ground. A second passenger passed down two suitcases and a bundle of packets, while the three figures waiting in the shadows moved forward and passed their luggage up to him. He quickly stowed it and climbed out. When the new passengers were aboard and the sliding canopy closed, the *chef de terrain* passed a string bag of bottles to the pilot and gave him the 'thumbs up' to take off.

As the aircraft lifted off after a run of less than 50 yards, the remaining men, all members of a local resistance network, melted into the winter night to make their hazardous journeys to homes or safe houses. Having been on the ground for less than five minutes the unarmed Lysander, carrying three Special Operation Executive (SOE) agents, faced a dangerous two-hour night flight over occupied France towards the safety of an airfield in southern England.

*   *   *

The Second World War was not the first time that intelligence agents had been flown behind enemy lines. A quarter of a century earlier, soon after the outbreak of the First World War, one of France's most remarkable pioneer aviators became the first pilot to fly these dangerous special missions.

Jules Védrines, born to working-class Parisians in 1881, grew up with an interest in all things mechanical, becoming a chauffeur/mechanic before learning to fly at Pau after witnessing Wilbur Wright's demonstration flights at Le Mans in 1908. The ill-mannered, bad-tempered Védrines proved to be a natural flyer, and in 1911 he embarked on an extraordinary series of record-breaking flights. He began by winning the Paris to Madrid race in a Morane-Borel monoplane, flying over the Pyrenees to arrive in the Spanish capital after being airborne for a total of 15 hours, spread over three days. With no instruments, Védrines narrowly missed winning the Circuit of Britain race in July 1911, but over the following year he was to make the World Absolute Speed Record his own.

Flying a revolutionary Déperdussin monoplane with a highly polished, wooden monocoque fuselage, Védrines pushed the speed record from 90 to 108mph in seven separate attempts, becoming the first pilot to break the 100mph barrier at Pau on 22 February 1912. He also won the prestigious Gordon Bennett race of that year in the United States, and in November 1913 made the first overland flight from France to Egypt – a total distance of 2,500 miles – in a two-seat Blériot XI.

When war was declared Védrines was one of the first to volunteer to join France's Aviation Militaire (the French Air Force). However, hardly had the war begun when the French authorities ordered that the fragile Blériot and Déperdussin monoplanes be withdrawn from service, leaving many experienced pilots, including Védrines, without aircraft to fly. Adding insult to injury, at the age of 33 he was also considered to be too old for front-line service. Undaunted, his navigation skills and experience of flying over unknown terrain were soon in demand to fly secret agents to and from behind enemy lines. Védrines was also one of the few pilots who had experience of flying by moonlight, another pre-requisite of a special mission pilot. Early flights were made using a two-seat

Déperdussin monoplane, the pilot risking not only capture by the Germans, but also being fired upon by French soldiers when crossing the lines.

Two experimental Blériot monoplanes were delivered to the Aviation Militaire in late 1914, one of which was acquired by the French intelligence service for Védrines to fly. Powered by a 160hp Gnome rotary engine, the Blériot had a bulky, streamlined fuselage made of papier mâché covered with linen fabric, prompting Védrines to christen it *La Vache* (The Cow). Unusually, the engine and two tandem cockpits were protected by 3mm-thick chrome-nickel armour plating, and a door was fitted on each side of the fuselage under the wing to enable the observer to fire at targets on the ground. When used for special missions, however, these doors proved to be a convenient method of entry and exit for an agent in a hurry.

In 1915 Védrines taught a young pilot, Georges Guynemer, who would later become France's second most successful air ace, the skills required to fly behind the lines. Serious, ascetic and frail, Guynemer was the exact opposite to the assertive and bombastic Védrines, but he was never lacking in courage. Posted to Escadrille MS3 in May 1915 soon after gaining his wings at Pau, he carried his first 'spy' across the lines in a two-seat Morane-Saulnier Type L parasol monoplane. The experience led him to acknowledge the dangers faced by those who flew regular special missions, such as Védrines, and others who would remain unknown. However, one of these anonymous heroes left a graphic account of the dangers faced by these early adventurers well behind enemy lines.

I had flown to the outskirts of Laon. There was a deserted corner, a sort of hollow basin where an aeroplane could stay without attracting too much attention. It was also an excellent strip for taking off. No main road passed nearby, and the only roads around were seldom used. It was impossible to find a better place to land for an operation of this kind. My mission was to pick up a passenger. The agreed signals were given and I let myself down to the ground to let him come aboard. He was late, and you can imagine the anguish that gripped me. I risked capture at any moment and could not stay there indefinitely. He was, however, the bearer of precious and compromising documents, and had no other means of safety than my aeroplane. What would happen to him if I were forced to abandon him?

A half an hour passed by, which seemed like half a century. I expected to see him come out of a clump of trees located nearby. The full moon was shining over the entire terrain, and under its pale light, objects seemed to come alive and move. Attentive to the slightest noise, I watched the horizon at the same time. Suddenly I heard steps, and behind the thickets two shots followed in quick succession. A man was running. Nervously I triggered my carbine, which never left my side, and, ready for anything, I awaited the fight. I finally saw my man appear.

He was running with all his might, and behind him several shapes were already in view. Without a doubt he had been followed, and I, for my part, fired away in order to take the pressure off him. I owe him this, that in such great peril he thought only of me. Still out of breath from his running, he shouted to me, 'Quick, leave! There they are!' I told him to get in, and with a gesture, I showed him the empty seat. There was barely enough time. I realised, once in the air, that several metal plates had been pierced. Fortunately, the petrol tank was intact, but my companion was wounded. 'That's all right,' he said. 'I am not ready to go back there again. I wouldn't go back to that place for 100,000 francs.'

Special missions were not the sole preserve of the Aviation Militaire, and the longer the war continued, the more important human intelligence became to all sides in the conflict. A few weeks before British and French armies began the battle of the Somme on 1 July 1916, a Royal Flying Corps (RFC) two-seat aeroplane landed at an airfield a few miles north-east of Amiens on the Western Front. Lahoussoye was the base for No. 3 Squadron, equipped with a varied collection of French Morane single- and two-seat reconnaissance machines; but the visitor was an anonymous BE2c, an artillery observation biplane that had been among the first British types to be deployed to France two years earlier. The BE2c taxied up to the furthest hangar away from No. 3 Squadron's crew hut and parked, with its engine idling. A few minutes later a 'civilian' hurried out of the hangar and climbed into the empty observer's position in front of the pilot, who turned the aircraft into wind and took off from the grass airfield, heading east. The 'civilian' was a French spy who was being flown across the lines and landed in enemy territory.

A few miles north of Lahoussoye at Boubers-sur-Canche near Arras, the home of Naval Airship Detachment No. 4, a young Royal Naval Air Service (RNAS) midshipman, Victor Goddard, was preparing for clandestine, long-range operations to insert and extract secret agents to and from behind enemy lines. Trials had been taking place at RNAS Polegate near Eastbourne, using Submarine Scout (SS) airships powered by a wingless BE2c suspended beneath in which the crew sat. Its young crew, led by Sub-Lt W.P.C. 'Billy' Chambers with Goddard assisting, conducted a series of trials with a new airship, SS 40, specially designed for its clandestine role; it was painted with a matt-black overall finish and had a silenced engine. These trials impressed the War Office so much that SS 40 was sent to France on 6 July 1916.

After a protracted flight to Boubers due to a broken oil-pipe, a Lt C.R. Robbins parachuted safely from 1,500ft, along with a number of homing pigeons in baskets, on 13 August. Several high-altitude, night-reconnaissance flights were made across the lines, of between three and four hours' duration, but night landings without the aid of a handling crew met with less success. During the summer of 1916 the Somme was being lashed by storms that turned the battlefield into a quagmire, and Chambers and Goddard were forced to abandon their attempts to carry any spies over the lines. SS 40 was flown back to England in October, never to return.

Meanwhile, the more conventional way of inserting secret agents – by aircraft – continued. On 3 August 1916 Lt C.A. Ridley of No. 60 Squadron who – according to British ace James McCudden VC, DSO, who had flown with him as an observer the previous year – was 'a dashing and enterprising pilot', picked up a French spy at Vert Galand, north of Amiens. Soon after crossing the German lines, the Le Rhône rotary engine of his Morane BB two-seater failed. Having made a successful forced landing, Claude Ridley and the agent managed to avoid capture for more than three weeks before making their way towards the Belgian border. There, the Frenchman left him to his own devices; speaking neither French nor German, and by now wearing civilian clothes, Ridley himself was liable to be shot as a spy if captured.

By bandaging his head and smearing it with iodine and blood from a cut in his hand, Ridley pretended to be an injured deaf mute. He managed to board a train travelling towards the Dutch border, but was arrested for having no papers or tickets. As it slowed down, he knocked out his captor and jumped from the train. He hid during the day and walked another 50 miles at night, navigating by the stars, having little food and being in constant danger of capture. Almost eight weeks after he took off for his two-hour mission, he was discovered asleep by a sympathetic Belgian, whom Ridley persuaded to find a ladder so that he could climb over the electrified border fence into neutral Holland. On 9 October he rejoined his squadron, which had by then moved on to Savy on the outskirts of Arras, bringing with him much valuable intelligence.

Lt William Harold Haynes of Military Intelligence was a British agent who had been flown behind the lines, and who had also escaped across the Dutch border on more than one occasion. After a year as an agent in the field he transferred to the RFC, learned to fly and in 1917 joined No. 44 Home Defence Squadron, flying Sopwith Camel night fighters from Hainault Farm in Essex. Its role was to intercept German Zeppelin airships and Gotha bombers carrying out night raids on major cities in south-east England. Flying aeroplanes at night was then in its infancy and, after much trial and error, the home defence squadrons devised a simple but effective flarepath. It comprised several two-gallon petrol tins cut in half and filled with cotton waste soaked in paraffin; these were placed in an inverted L, with the long arm pointing downwind and the short arm marking the limit for the landing run. They were lit when the returning fighter was heard over the airfield.

Bill Haynes's training as an agent stood him in good stead, and so when a 'well-connected' Norwegian joined the squadron and soon became notorious for the lavish entertainment of his fellow pilots, his suspicions were aroused. After Bill had alerted his former colleagues in Military Intelligence, the Norwegian was posted away and later charged with espionage and imprisoned. But by then Capt Haynes had met a tragic end, just two months before the war ended. Serving with No. 151 Night Fighter Squadron, he had climbed out unhurt from his overturned Camel after clipping a ditch during a night landing at Vignacourt, and was standing in front of the wreck, when his mechanic accidentally fired a round from the Lewis gun while checking it to make sure it was safe. William Haynes was 23 years old.

Although by no means a common practice, the RFC and RNAS undertook many ad hoc clandestine flights at the behest of the Secret Intelligence Service (SIS), or Military Intelligence Department 6 (MI6). There were no dedicated units or aircraft assigned to the role, but it is interesting to note that when RFC Commander-in-Chief, Maj-Gen Hugh Trenchard, asked for parachutes to be made available for RFC trials in France, the request was refused. However, twenty Calthorp parachutes were authorised to be issued for dropping agents behind the lines. The most popular type of aircraft used for clandestine flights was the obsolete BE2c, whose main virtues were its inherent stability and docile handling, both important factors when attempting night landings on unprepared surfaces. During the last year of the war the rugged and adaptable two-seat Bristol F2B Fighter (Brisfit) was favoured. With pilot and observer positions close enough for easy communication, the Brisfit's rear cockpit was large enough for agents to parachute from in safety. By this time a special duties flight had been established under the command of Lt Jack Woodhouse, a pre-war motor cycle racing champion.

The British and French were not the only First World War combatants to carry out clandestine flights into enemy territory. In May 1918 an Italian Air Corps observer, Tenente Camillo de Carlo, was dropped behind Austro-Hungarian lines from a Voisin two-seater. He then spent three weeks sending back information, in the form of ground signals that were photographed by Italian reconnaissance aircraft flying overhead, during the build-up to the decisive Battle of Piave River in northern Italy.

Later in the war the French used at least one captured German aircraft for over-the-lines reconnaissance and for dropping agents. A Rumpler two-seater in German markings was retained at Toul for clandestine flights, during one of which its French-Alsatian crew landed at a German airfield, demanded that the plane be refuelled, and departed for home undiscovered. The Germans replied in kind when Leutnant Hans Schroeder, an Air Service observer and intelligence officer, used a French two-seater to visit a number of RAF airfields on the Western Front in mid-1918. The aircraft was a Breguet 14B2 reconnaissance bomber, flown to the German lines by a defecting French pilot in May 1918; serialled 1333 and wearing the markings of Escadrille BR 117, it was a new machine he had collected from a delivery park near Paris.

Schroeder, a former infantry officer who had joined the German Air Service after being wounded in the knee, served as an air observer on the Russian front before training as an intelligence officer in February 1918. Speaking excellent English and French, he was flown by the French deserter to British airfields, where he posed as a French officer, and to French airfields where he posed as a British officer. He would visit the local town or village before departing at dusk, having dined as a guest of the officers' mess. While interrogating a captured RAF pilot in September 1918, Schroeder claimed to have dropped in on No. 5 Squadron at Acq, No. 56 at Valheureux and No. 60 at Boffles, all within a few weeks of the last Allied push on the Western Front.

The Eastern Front was the preserve of another British spy who was also an intrepid aviator. A pre-war businessman in Russia, George Hill was on holiday in Canada when war was declared. Having joined a Canadian army unit, he was sent to France as an interpreter, but after being wounded while serving in the trenches, Hill was posted to Military Intelligence at the War Office to be trained in the gathering of espionage. Being fluent in several languages, including Russian and Arabic, he was sent to the Balkans in June 1916. While attached to the British Intelligence Headquarters at Salonica in Greece, he persuaded the local RFC unit to teach him to fly in order to be able to drop spies into enemy territory. With very little flying experience, he managed to 'borrow' a BE2e aircraft for his clandestine adventures. Hill later recalled:

Nico Kotzov was one of my first passengers. He was a Serbian patriot who had been in the enemy's country nine or ten times and always brought back valuable information. We wanted information from an inaccessible part of the country, and as this information was urgently needed it was decided to drop him by aeroplane. I took him up for a couple of trial flights, and although he did not enjoy the experiences very much, he was quite determined to go. He knew the country where we were going to land, and I explained to him I wanted the landing ground to be as much like our aerodrome as possible.

As we climbed into the machine at dawn on the day of the drop, the sergeant in charge of the pigeons brought along a little cage with six of our best birds in it. I ran up the engine. Everything was all right. I signalled the sergeant to pull away the chocks and we taxied out into the dark aerodrome. I opened the engine full out and we were away. I had to do a stiff climb in the air in order to be able to cross the mountain range, and the higher I got, the less I liked the job before me.

The flight was uneventful. I picked out the various objectives that were serving me, together with a compass, as a guide, and got over the country that we were to land upon in the scheduled time. It was getting light as I throttled back my engine, so that it was just ticking over, in order to land. We lost height rapidly and I could faintly make out the ground before me, which seemed fairly suitable. As a precautionary measure I made up my mind to circle it just once more.

Suddenly I noticed that the whole of the field selected by Nico for our landing was dotted with giant boulders. To land in the field would be suicide. I climbed into the air again, and when I had got sufficiently high, switched off my engine to be able to make Nico hear me and I told him that his selection was no good as a landing ground. He said simply that I had told him nothing about boulders, and that he imagined we would hop over them. All hope of landing that morning had to be given up, but as it was rapidly getting light I hoped to be able to pick out a suitable landing ground for the next day and through my glasses located a dry river bed which promised to be the best place for landing, and back we went to the aerodrome.

Next morning we made the trip again and I safely landed my passenger. Within ten days he had dispatched all six pigeons and on the return home of the last one, I took over a further cage of pigeons and dropped them by parachute over the spot where I had landed Nico. These also returned home safely. In all, I dropped Nico three times over the line.

On one occasion, Hill had landed a man called Petrov behind the lines when his aeroplane hit a furrow which jarred the BE2 and stopped the propeller. While Petrov climbed out to swing the propeller, an enemy cavalry patrol spotted them on open ground. 'I think at first they thought it was one of their own machines. Then they must have got suspicious, for they started trotting towards us. Suddenly the engine fired and Petrov raced round to the fuselage and leapt into his seat. The cavalry patrol broke into a gallop and called upon us to stop. I opened the throttle and we were away, but before we left the ground the patrol opened fire. Their shooting was good, as we found when we got back to the aerodrome with half a dozen holes in the fuselage.'

In July 1917, Capt G.A. Hill was ordered to join the RFC mission at Petrograd in Russia, but before he had a chance to resume flying special missions the aeroplanes were withdrawn to Archangel, and so he travelled overland to Moscow as imperial Russia descended into anarchy and revolution. As the monarchy collapsed and the Bolsheviks seized power, George Hill continued his career as a spy, which he considered as a 'joyful adventure'.

Another officer renowned for his subterfuge in the field was T.E. Lawrence, whose Arab irregulars were harrying the Turks in Palestine and Trans-Jordan. Attached to the British Military Intelligence Department in Cairo called MO4 in December 1914, Capt Lawrence spoke excellent Arabic and had built up close contacts with various Arab leaders during his pre-war archaeological and mapping expeditions to the region. His brief was to contact and encourage Arabs in Turkish-controlled Sinai, Syria and western Arabia to carry out a campaign of guerilla warfare in support of the Allies. Lawrence realised very

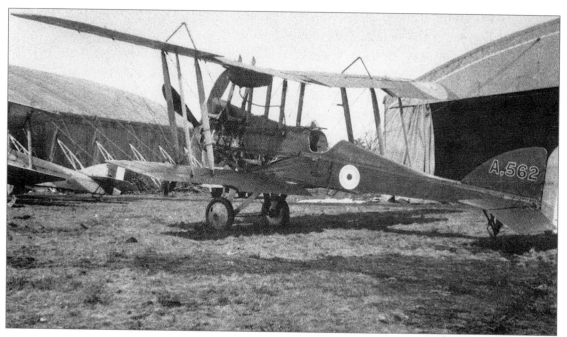

A BE12a of the Australian Flying Corps, the type used by 'X' Flight, a detachment of No. 14 Squadron AFC, to support Col T.E. Lawrence's Arab irregulars fighting the Turks. (Bruce Robertson)

early on the value of air support in order to keep in touch with his Arab irregulars, and to gather accurate intelligence from behind the Turkish lines.

The first experience of British aircraft operating behind enemy lines in the region fell to the RFC air unit in Mesopotamia (Iraq), when British troops captured a Turkish garrison at Kut el Amera on the banks of the River Tigris, midway between Baghdad and Basrah, in September 1915. A Turkish counter-attack cut the British supply lines, and by the beginning of 1916 the garrison was surrounded and under siege. The one and only way to ensure the survival of the 10,000 soldiers was to supply them by air, something that had never been done before, and No. 30 Squadron, based at nearby Ora, was allotted the task.

Its ubiquitous BE2c aircraft braved German Fokker Eindekker monoplane fighters and Turkish ground fire to cross enemy lines carrying food, medical supplies and ammunition to the besieged force, and flying out their sick and wounded. Three RNAS Short 827 and Farman floatplanes that could operate from the River Tigris joined No. 30 Squadron at the end of February to drop supplies from low level, without parachutes, to the British troops below. During the 143-day siege, more than 13 tons of supplies were delivered in the world's first airlift, half of which was delivered over a 14-day period; but it was not enough and General Townsend's garrison was forced to surrender on 29 April 1916.

However, it was not until the end of 1916 that No. 1 Squadron Australian Flying Corps (AFC) arrived in Egypt and T.E. Lawrence first met one of its flight commanders – Lt Ross Smith, an ace with twelve confirmed kills – and plans could be made to set up an air base behind enemy lines at Jauf, in western Arabia. Supplies and fuel had been stockpiled en route when irregulars of Emir Feisal, one of Turkey's staunchest allies, captured Wejh on the Red Sea and plans for the covert air base had to be abandoned.

In 1917 a detachment of No. 14 Squadron AFC moved to Aqaba equipped with three BE12 reconnaissance aircraft, a development of the BE2c. Manned by Australian pilots Lts Ross Smith and C.H. Vautin and observer 2/Lt L.W. Sutherland, who had been credited with seven kills, the unit became known as 'X' Flight and was put at the disposal of Lawrence and his Arab irregulars. His Arabs being prone to inaccuracy or exaggeration, Lawrence himself regularly flew over the Turkish lines to carry out his own assessment of enemy positions, especially along the Hejaz Railway that stretched for hundreds of miles across the desert between Medina in the south and Damascus in the north.

The railway was crucial to the Turks and a constant target for Lawrence's guerrilla fighters. His spies were also dropped behind the lines by 'X' Flight, while its pilots often landed in enemy territory to pick up agents or rescue downed aircrew who were in danger of capture – the Turks offered £40 in gold for every Allied airman delivered – or worse, were dying of thirst. In August 1917 Lawrence and his Arabs prepared an airstrip at Kuntilla in the Sinai as a forward operating base for RFC aircraft based at El Arish. On 18 September General Allenby launched an offensive against the Turks at Beersheba in Palestine, and six weeks later Jerusalem fell to British troops, ending 730 years of Muslim rule.

Ross Smith, now flying Bristol F2B Fighters with No. 1 Squadron AFC, was based at Guweira, flying reconnaissance missions over the Turkish stronghold at Jurf el Derwish on the Hejaz Railway. In May 1918 he flew Lawrence, now a lieutenant-colonel, to Allenby's headquarters in his Brisfit to discuss the preparations for a final push to chase the Turks out of the Middle East. The attack was launched on 19 September and within five weeks British and Arab armies were within sight of the Turkish border at Aleppo, having taken Damascus and Beirut.

Two Bristol Fighters were assigned to Lawrence in support of his Arab irregulars behind Turkish lines, one of which went unserviceable; the other, flown by Lt Junor, fought a number of dogfights with Turkish aircraft. Ross Smith flew spares and fuel for the Brisfits into Emir Faisal's headquarters at Umm as Surab in a twin-engined Handley Page 0/400 long-range heavy bomber. The giant aircraft, the only one of its type in the Middle East, did much to reinforce the Arab irregulars' belief that Allah was, indeed, on the side of the Allies.

On 30 October 1918 Turkey signed an armistice with the Allies, and 12 days later the First World War was over. The aftermath of the Great War saw most of Europe in turmoil. The victors wreaked economic and political vengeance on the vanquished, and on Germany in particular. The Austro-Hungarian and Ottoman empires imploded and nationalism and revolution spread from eastern Europe to Asia Minor. New countries were carved out of old – Czechoslovakia, Yugoslavia, Iraq and Saudi Arabia. Civil wars broke out in Russia and Poland, while Finland declared war on Russia and Greece attacked Turkey. As Great Britain and France battled to hang on to their empires, monarchs were deposed and fascists vied for power with communists. The seeds of another 'great' war in the twentieth century were being planted.

By the 1930s Russia had become part of the Soviet Union, ruled by a communist dictator; Italy and Germany had fascist dictators; and Japan had a fascist government under an emperor without an empire. All were looking to expand beyond their borders, as the world slid into economic depression following the Wall Street Crash of 1929.

The first to move was Japan. On 18 September 1931 the Japanese Army invaded Manchuria, and a year later attacked Shanghai. Europe's meltdown began when the Italian dictator, Mussolini, invaded the African kingdom of Abyssinia in October 1935 and, less than a year later, civil war broke out in Spain. Suddenly government intelligence departments were working overtime to recruit agents from wherever they could be found, in a frantic effort to cut through the confusion of world events. It was a time of unprecedented opportunity for the freelance spy, who could sell his or her services to the highest bidder. However, there were a few who passionately supported one side or the other for ideological reasons, while many were gentleman spies who craved only the excitement and danger they expected from the murky world of espionage. Some of the latter also had the advantage of having another skill then in great demand, that of being a qualified pilot.

Many of the founder members of the select band of special mission pilots were now dead. Jules Védrines died in August 1919 when his Caudron G4 crashed near Lyonss during an air race from Paris to Athens. Three months later Capt Ross Smith and his brother Keith won the first air race from England to Australia, when they flew their Vickers Vimy bomber from Hounslow to Darwin in 11 days to claim the £10,000 prize – and a knighthood. Sir Ross Smith was killed in a flying accident near Brooklands aerodrome on 13 April 1922. There was, however, no shortage of adventurous pilots prepared to pick up the gauntlet. One such was a Swedish aristocrat, Count Eric von Rosen, whose aunt Karin was married to German First World War fighter ace, Hermann Goering. Von Rosen was earning his living as a stunt pilot when Italy invaded Abyssinia in 1935. He volunteered to fly for the Red Cross delivering doctors and medicines to remote mountain passes, risking Italian anti-aircraft fire in the process. After the fall of Addis Ababa, von Rosen had stopped in Cairo on his way back to Sweden to raise money for the Abyssinian resistance when he was contacted by British intelligence officers. For the next few months, von Rosen agreed to fly arms and supplies, using his single-engined Fokker F VIIa, from British airstrips in Egypt to Abyssinian guerrilla fighters.

Cecil Bebb, a captain with Olley Air Service Ltd flying charter flights from Redhill aerodrome in Surrey, was another adventurer pilot. In June 1936 he was asked to fly a DH.89 Dragon Rapide, a rugged, eight-seat, twin-engined biplane, to the Canary Islands to pick up a passenger for a clandestine flight into Spanish North Africa. After flying to Las Palmas via Bordeaux, Lisbon and Casablanca with three decoys aboard – a well-known member of the British hunting and fishing fraternity and two of his young so-called lady friends – Bebb was met by two Spaniards, codenamed Mutt and Jeff after well-known

The Olley Air Service's Dragon Rapide used by Capt Cecil Bebb to fly Franco from Las Palmas to Spanish Morocco in July 1936 at the beginning of the Spanish Civil War. *(Richard Riding)*

cartoon characters of the time, with secret instructions about the mission. These included the name of a contact in Las Palmas, but after landing there the mission was nearly compromised when Bebb was accused of entering the Canaries without official permission from the local governor. However, his contact was able to defuse the situation and Bebb's special passenger, introduced as a prominent Rif leader of the Berber Arabs, finally boarded the Rapide on the afternoon of 18 July 1936. The following day it flew on to Agadir and Casablanca before touching down at Tetuán in Spanish Morocco at dusk, where the mysterious passenger, codenamed Father, was greeted by a throng of excited Spaniards. Father was in fact Generalissimo Francisco Franco. The Spanish Civil War was about to begin.

On his return flight to Croydon, Bebb was questioned about his flight to Tetuán by the French authorities at Biarritz, and was given permission to take off only after assuring the French Air Ministry that he was no longer working for Franco's agents. Many years later Gen Franco awarded Cecil Bebb the Spanish Order of Merit, and Dragon Rapide G-ACYR is today exhibited at Madrid's Military Museum.

The Civil War unleashed a frenzied search by Nationalist and Republican agents for aircraft and aircrew to fly them, and these were often bid for by both sides at the same time. When the British and French governments prohibited the export of aircraft to either side, Spanish emissaries resorted to begging, borrowing or stealing anything that would fly. More than 500 civil aircraft were clandestinely imported into Spain, many of them by a weird collection of agents of spurious companies extending from Mexico to China. One of the most popular types was the Dragon Rapide, which was flown by both sides, some being converted into bombers; another was the fast Airspeed Envoy, an eight-seat, twin-engined light transport monoplane. Four of the latter had belonged to the French airline Air Pyrenées, which maintained a regular service between Biarritz and Bilbao during the war until two of its Envoys were shot down by Nationalist fighters in 1937. The surviving aircraft were taken over by the Société Française de Transports Aériens, which was owned by agents for the Republican government.

A Beechcraft B17R 'staggerwing' single-engined biplane, also a former Air Pyrenées aircraft, was used in an abortive Italian plot to kidnap the Abyssinian emperor Haile Selassie in 1935. Two years later it was used by the defeated Basque President Aquirre to escape to the south of France, and was impressed into the Luftwaffe after the fall of France in 1940.

The Spanish Civil War attracted volunteers and mercenaries from all over the world and from many backgrounds and persuasions. Acclaimed French writers who rallied to the cause included André Malraux, who raised money to buy French aircraft and pay pilots to fly with the Republican Escuadrilla España, with which he himself flew several missions over central and southern Spain; and Antoine de Saint-Exupéry, who flew with Air Pyrenées. Airspeed's co-founder N.S. Norway, subsequently better known by his pen name Nevil Shute, became involved with emissaries from both sides who were offering large amounts of cash for his company's Courier, Envoy and Viceroy airliners. The American writer Ernest Hemingway flew in and out of war-torn Spain on several occasions and claimed to have based his best-selling book *For Whom the Bell Tolls* on his exploits as a soldier for the Republican cause.

Numerous members of Europe's aristocracy played their part in stirring the Spanish cauldron. The Anglo-Hungarian racing driver and amateur pilot, Count Zichy, flew British agents out of Burgos in his DH Puss Moth G-AAXY and was reportedly rewarded with a flight in a Nationalist Fiat CR.32 fighter. Polish Count Lasocki was killed at Biarritz while trying to smuggle one of four former British Airways Fokker F XII airliners to the Nationalists at Burgos. His tri-motor was attempting to land at the French airfield during a violent thunder-

Racing driver Count Zichy's Puss Moth G-AAXY, in which he claimed that he flew a British spy out of Spain during the Civil War. *(Richard Riding)*

storm. After three aborted landings the Fokker stalled, crashed on approach to the airfield and caught fire. Lasocki died in the flames. The Fokkers had been subject to rival bids soon after the war began and sold to one of Franco's agents, the Marqués de Rivas de Linares, for £38,000 in gold pesetas! The other three aircraft were prevented from flying out of Bordeaux airfield by Republican sympathisers.

At the time, the marqués was being flown between Burgos and Lisbon in a Puss Moth piloted by the 1934 Mac-Robertson England-to-Australia air race winner, Tom Campbell Black. Black also assisted Spanish aircraft designer Don Juán de La Cierva to buy aircraft in England on behalf of the Nationalist Gen Emilia Mola, and to fly them from Heston to Burgos. Cievra had excellent contacts in England, owing to the fact that his unique C-30A autogiro was being built for the RAF under licence by Avro in Manchester as the Rota 1.

Taking a more active role in the war was a titled Belgian, the Comte Rodolphe de Hemricourt de Grunne, a private pilot who flew Nationalist Fiat CR.32 fighters and became one of the few non-Germans to fly Messerschmitt Bf 109Ds with the famed Condor Legion. Known by his colleagues in Spain as 'Dolfo', he claimed to have shot down fourteen Republican Polikarpov I-16 Rata fighters in less than a year, and was destined to meet his former colleagues again in the next European conflict.

As the Nationalists tightened their stranglehold on Spain during the spring of 1938, Adolf Hitler's troops were marching into Austria to force a union, or *Anschluss*, between the two nations. Threats to invade Czechoslovakia provoked the Munich Crisis in September 1938 that culminated in the Munich Agreement, signed by Britain, Germany, France and Italy. Under its terms, the Sudeten territories of Czechoslovakia would be ceded to Hitler in return for his assurances that he would renounce claims to other disputed regions of Europe. In reality the agreement did nothing to curb Hitler's appetite for enlarging his empire, but it did buy time for the four signatories to build up their forces for the inevitable conflict to come. During and following the crisis commercial aviation continued without interruption, shuttling agents of various national intelligence agencies between European capitals. Deutsche Lufthansa (DLH) services to London's Croydon aerodrome and British Airways flights from Heston to Berlin's Tempelhof were fully booked by 'commercial travellers' and 'tourists', both excellent but obvious covers for agents seeking to make new contacts or simply go sightseeing.

One such commercial traveller was in fact just that. Sidney Cotton came from a wealthy Australian family and served with the Royal Naval Air Service (RNAS) during the First World War, flying BE2cs and Sopwith Pup scouts. He had an inventive mind, one product of which would benefit his fellow aviators when he had military tailors Robinson and Cleaver of London make him a one-piece flying suit to his own design. Lined with fur and silk, with the outer covering made from material supplied by Burberry's, he registered the suit as 'the Sidcot', using the first three letters of each of his names. Cotton's invention was taken up by his fellow officers and soon became standard equipment for the RFC and RNAS pilots.

Having crossed swords with the RNAS chief of operations, Cdre Geoffrey Paine, about the practicality of flying photographic missions over the German naval base at Wilhelmshaven in DH.4 bombers, Cotton resigned the service. The Admiralty reacted by issuing a report that stated, 'He is of a difficult temperament and unsuitable for employment in a uniformed service.'

After the war Cotton became a mail and survey pilot in Newfoundland, and by 1923 had five aircraft operating for his own flourishing seal- and timber-surveying business. Having made and lost a fortune in Canada he played the New York stock market in the late 1920s, again losing as much as he made. Cotton then returned to England. While indulging his wife's interest in expensive fast cars – she took part in four Monte Carlo rallies – he had a chance meeting in France with a Madame Durand, the widow of a film manufacturer who had developed a new colour film called Dufay-Chromex, the first tri-pack transparency material generally available to the enthusiast.

Cotton acquired the marketing rights to the process, but when he tried to break into the lucrative United States market he came head to head with the giant Eastman Corporation that produced the rival Kodachrome colour transparency film – and he lost. By the beginning of 1938 Sidney Cotton was once more back in England and again facing bankruptcy. However, another chance meeting in France would change his fortunes, and his life.

During a conversation with Parisian businessman Paul Koster, Cotton told him of his attempts to get the German Agfa company to use the Dufay negative, involving frequent visits to Germany and contacts with important trade officials. Koster sounded him out on the Nazi menace, something that Cotton had given a great deal of thought to during his trips to Germany, and these conversations led to his being approached by Wg Cdr F.W. Winterbotham, head of the Air Section of the British Secret Intelligence Service (SIS). Fred Winterbotham was a former RFC pilot who had learned fluent German as a PoW after being shot down over the Western Front. He had also travelled extensively in Germany in the early 1930s, gathering intelligence on German rearmament following Hitler's rise to power. One of his many European contacts was Paul Koster, who mentioned his meeting with the Australian pilot who had more than a passing interest in aerial photography, knew Germany well and who was looking for a new adventure. In September Winterbotham asked Cotton to meet him at his Whitehall office to discuss a 'project of mutual interest'.

Winterbotham had discussed the importance of monitoring the mounting threat with his French counterpart at the Deuxième Bureau, Georges Ronin. They agreed that covert aerial photography of Germany's military build-up was vital, but their respective air forces were unwilling to undertake such missions, which could be construed as acts of war. The answer was to use high-performance civil aircraft and it was agreed that two should be ordered in early 1939, one each for the French and British intelligence agencies. They chose the American Lockheed 12A Junior Electra, a sleek, all-metal, twin-engined monoplane seating six people. It had a top speed of over 200mph, faster than many fighters of the day, and a maximum range of nearly 1,000 miles. In order to disguise their real purpose, the contract for the two aircraft was placed under the cover of British Airways, which was subsidised by the British government. The Deuxième Bureau paid for its aircraft in cash. The first Lockheed, G-AFKR, was delivered by sea and assembled in great secrecy at Heston aerodrome.

This was a former private airfield near Southall in West London, which had recently been acquired by the Air Ministry and where a company called the Aeronautical Research and Sales Corporation was formed as a front for the operation. Once the Lockheed had been flight tested by Cotton, he was asked to train a French pilot to fly it. However, as the Frenchman did not speak any English, and in Cotton's opinion was not a competent pilot anyway, Sidney insisted on flying the first Deuxième Bureau missions himself. These were flown at 10,000 feet along the Franco-German border and carried a French fashion photographer who operated a large plate camera. When Cotton was finally allowed to see the results of this first mission he considered the photographs next to useless, so when the French refused to let him overfly Germany at higher altitudes, he left the Lockheed at Le Bourget in Paris. Cotton then set about converting the second Lockheed 12A, G-AFTL, as a 'spy in the sky'. Ironically, three German 35mm Leica 250 cameras were fitted in a recess hidden behind a sliding panel in the floor of the fuselage. These were fitted with large film magazines which took 10 metres of film stock taking, as the name suggests, 250 exposures. Known as 'the Reporter', the Leicas also had electric motors to advance the film, a tremendous bonus for the planned operations.

During trials it was discovered that warm air from the cabin's efficient heaters flowed across the lenses and prevented condensation. Although 35mm frames

One of Sidney Cotton's two Lockheed 12A Junior Electras registered to the Aeronautical Research and Sales Corporation, at Orly Airport. *(David Oliver)*

were acceptable, finer detail was required. Winterbotham, with the assistance of Gp Capt Laws, head of the RAF Photographic Section, obtained three F.24 cameras and lenses of different focal lengths. Fitted with an automatic timing device to take photographs in sequence according to the height and speed of the aircraft, these were installed in the Lockheed's fuselage.

It was important to disguise the cameras and a special cover was made in the form of a spare fuel tank, so that anyone looking under the floorboards should have no reason to suspect anything out of the ordinary. An additional Leica was fitted in each wing, pointing downwards and rearwards. All the Leicas could be operated by the pilot from the cockpit, and the F.24s by an operator in the cabin. Trials with the camera installations from 20,000ft produced spectacular results, better than had been so far obtained by the RAF. Cotton had discussed with experts the camouflaging of the Lockheed, but came up with a solution by chance. He was at Heston when the Maharajah of Jodhpur's private aircraft, painted a pale duck-egg green, took off and was lost to sight a few seconds into the climb. Cotton seized on the colour and had the G-AFTL painted the same shade, which he patented as 'camotint'.

Winterbotham agreed to the hiring of a Canadian former bus driver, Robert 'Bob' Niven, as second pilot/navigator, and Cotton himself recruited his mistress, 23-year-old Patricia Martin, to act as camera operator. The blue-eyed blonde daughter of a wealthy landowner, Pat Martin had always been something of a tomboy. She had been born with a club foot, which Cotton later paid to be operated on, but her strong-minded independence and her love of horses had attracted her to Cotton, who was twenty years her senior.

After a series of trial flights over Germany, during which Cotton met with his German business contacts, his team prepared for their longest mission yet. On 14 June the Lockheed, with extra fuel tanks fitted in the cabin, flew to Malta and then to Algiers where, with the help of Ronin, permission had been granted to fly up the coast to Tunis and on to Tobruk, ending up at Djibouti in French Somalia. During the 15,000-mile round trip Italian military facilities in Eritrea, Italian Somalia, Sicily and the Italian mainland were photographed. In the event of being questioned, Cotton had been given papers by SIS to show that he was a feature film-maker looking for suitable European locations.

When the new Lockheed first visited Berlin, without cameras, it had been searched, but afterwards Cotton was allowed to come and go as he pleased. He would refuel at various points en route to Berlin so that he could vary his flight to cover new airfields, factories and installations and photograph them. Cotton was welcomed by the Nazi hierarchy and on 28 July attended the Frankfurt Air Rally, where the Luftwaffe's latest aircraft were on display. There was even a suggestion that he fly Reichsmarshall Hermann Goering to Britain to meet with Lord Halifax, the Foreign Secretary, to avert a war; but Winterbotham was unimpressed by the scheme and distanced the SIS from an obviously ill-conceived and impractical mission.

However, Cotton and Niven had already flown to Berlin when the covert mission was cancelled. Initially, the Germans would not allow the Lockheed to take off; it was 24 August 1939 and tension was rising, but they relented and Cotton set course for home. This time he flew over Wilhelmshaven, where the German battle fleet was at anchor, but unfortunately Niven was armed only with a single, hand-held camera and a golden opportunity was missed on the eve of war.

A few months later, Sqn Ldr, acting Wg Cdr, Sidney Cotton was in command of the RAF's first dedicated photo-reconnaissance unit at Heston.

CHAPTER 2

Lighting the Flame

Operation 'Weiss' began when Hitler's forces invaded Poland on 1 September 1939, and two days later Britain, Australia and New Zealand declared war on Germany. The Second World War had begun. Although it had been obvious that war was inevitable since well before the Munich Crisis, the security services of both Britain and Germany were caught almost totally unprepared.

Adm Wilhelm Canaris, head of the Abwehr, the intelligence arm of the German Armed Forces High Command, had a number of Kriegsorganisationen (KO) operating clandestinely in foreign countries, including Britain. The small number of agents planted in Britain were, however, pre-war sleepers, mostly German nationals and a few Irish citizens; virtually all were interned at the outbreak of hostilities.

Canaris had been recruited by the German intelligence service in 1915 following his dramatic escape from a Chilean internment camp on the desolate island of Quiriquina, near Valparaiso. He was one of the few survivors from the naval battle of the Falkland Islands in December 1914, when the British fleet destroyed Adm Graf Spee's squadron. After undertaking spy missions in Switzerland and Spain, Canaris finished the war as a successful U-boat captain. He rejoined the German Navy in 1931 and was appointed head of the Abwehr four years later.

At the outbreak of war Hitler was reluctant to allow agents to be sent to the British Isles, as he still clung to the hope that Britain would agree to peace talks. This left the Abwehr with little choice but to attempt to establish networks within the Irish Republican Army (IRA) and the Welsh Nationalist movement. The problem was that members of both these dissident organizations were well known to Britain's SIS and Military Department 5 (MI5), and only a handful of such agents were to prove of any value. What was less obvious was whether the Irish Free State, which declared neutrality in 1939, would allow Germany to set up U-boat refuelling bases along its remote west coast.

Rear Adm John Godfrey, the Director of Naval Intelligence, was aware of Sidney Cotton's pre-war covert spy flights over Germany and arranged for his personal assistant, a young Lt Cdr Ian Fleming, to meet him at his Mayfair flat. Fleming asked Cotton if he was prepared to fly the Lockheed on a photographic mission over neutral Ireland. He agreed. Ten days after Britain declared war on Germany, Cotton and Niven left Heston, refuelled at Liverpool's Speke airport and crossed the Irish Sea, heading for the southern tip of the Republic. With cameras clicking, the Lockheed flew along the entire Irish coast, transited Northern Ireland and landed at RAF West Freugh on the west coast of Scotland, short of fuel.

Here Cotton and Niven were promptly arrested, as private aircraft were then banned from landing at RAF stations. It took a call to Whitehall to secure their release, and prior to any further flights over Ireland Cotton was issued with a letter of passage addressed to the commanding officer at RAF Aldergrove in Northern Ireland. Ignored by the Irish, the photo flights revealed nothing of interest, but impressed the Naval Intelligence Directorate, which suggested that Cotton, a former RNAS officer, be offered a commission in the Royal Navy. However, he was soon to accept the rank of squadron leader, acting wing commander, in the RAF.

Britain's oldest ally and another neutral country, Portugal, had become a magnet for the intelligence agencies of more than a dozen countries since the outbreak of the Spanish Civil War. During the opening months of the Second World War the SIS station in Lisbon compiled a list of hundreds of known and suspected German agents. Britain's secret services also relied heavily on their own network of agents and informants in Lisbon and in the capital of another neutral state, Stockholm.

During the so-called phoney-war period that followed Poland's defeat on 5 October SIS worked closely with the intelligence services of other European governments, including those of France, Belgium and Holland, and it soon became evident that inserting and communicating with British agents in Germany was becoming an almost impossible task. As the Allies and Germany faced each other, waiting for the next offensive, a short sharp campaign broke out on 30 November between the Soviet Union and Finland in what became known as the Winter War. Foreign volunteers from several countries, including Sweden, Britain and the United States, boosted the small but well-trained Finnish armed forces.

Among them was Count von Rosen, who had donated his faithful Fokker to the Finnish Red Cross and was now flying a former KLM Douglas DC-2 airliner converted into a bomber by the Finnish Air Force. Eric von Rosen flew the makeshift bomber on several long-range missions in harsh winter conditions to bomb targets deep in the Soviet Union. With only limited international assistance, the Finns more than held their own against the overwhelming numbers of Soviet attackers, whose offensive was halted by mid-December. The Soviets then resorted to airborne assaults and to dropping commandos and saboteurs behind Finnish lines by parachute, the first time such operations had been used in the Second World War. Owing to poor planning and communications, these airborne assaults proved little more than a nuisance to the Finns and by March 1940 an armistice brought the fighting to a temporary halt.

There might have been more international support for the Finns had Germany not decided to invade Norway and Denmark, ostensibly to protect supplies of Swedish iron ore that was shipped to Germany from the Norwegian port of Narvik. Operation 'Weserübung' began on 8 April, with Denmark falling within days, but Norway proved to be as hard a nut to crack as its neighbour, Finland. A 30,000-strong Anglo-French force, already assembled for a possible expedition to Finland during the Winter War, was sent to support the Norwegian Army along with a handful of RAF Gloster Gladiator biplane fighters. The task of finding a suitable base for the veteran British fighters, when the Germans had already captured or destroyed most of the Norwegian airfields, fell to the American-born Flg Off W.W. Straight.

Whitney Willard Straight was a man of independent means, a private pilot at 16 and Grand Prix racing driver at 20. He joined No. 601 (County of London) Squadron, Auxiliary Air Force, at Hendon – known as the 'Millionaires Club' – in 1936, the same year that he became a British citizen. A graduate of Trinity College Cambridge, he had studied German at Munich University, and later turned down an offer to join the all-conquering German Auto-Union Grand Prix racing team as a works driver. Having started the war flying obsolete Bristol Blenheim IF fighters with No. 601 Squadron at Biggin Hill, Whitney Straight was sent on a secret mission to Norway in April 1940 as an Air Liaison Officer to the Norwegian High Command. Acting Sqn Ldr Straight's mission was to find an airfield in central Norway that could be used by the Gladiators of No. 263 Squadron, now only a day away. He selected a frozen lake at Lesjaskog and with the help of 200 local inhabitants set about clearing a runway through the two-foot-deep snow on the frozen surface. The Gladiators were flown off the carrier HMS *Glorious* on 24 April, but their arrival was soon discovered by German reconnaissance aircraft. With no protection for the Gladiators, most were destroyed on the ground within a few days when the lake was repeatedly bombed by Luftwaffe Heinkel He 111 bombers. Whitney Straight was badly wounded during one of the raids, before making a hasty escape by RAF Sunderland flying boat from Romsdal fjord on 27 April. Norway finally fell to the Germans on 9 June, by which time Straight had been awarded the Military Cross for his mission.

As Norway fought a losing battle for its freedom, Hitler's forces unleashed their long expected Blitzkrieg against France and the Low Countries on 10 May. During Operation 'Fall Gelb', more than two million German troops smashed their way from Rotterdam to the outskirts of Paris within a month. One of those caught up in the battle for Amsterdam was the redoubtable Count von Rosen, now a captain with the Dutch national airline, KLM. Hours before the Germans overran Schiphol Airport on 13 May, a DC-3 was loaded with military and state papers and KLM's chief pilot Captain Parmentier took off for England. His co-pilot was von Rosen. On arrival at Heston the Swede, who had flown KLM's Berlin route, was regarded with suspicion and about to be interned, before a member of the security service for whom he had worked in Abyssinia was able to vouch for him.

Eric von Rosen caught a Finnish boat to Sweden the following day, from where he travelled back to Holland searching for his wife, a former KLM stewardess, but he was arrested by the Gestapo on the border. After mentioning his family's relationship with Hermann Goering, he was released on the understanding that he would leave Holland as soon as he found his wife, but when he located her she insisted on staying in Holland. To avoid his own arrest von Rosen returned alone to Stockholm, spending the duration of the war as an ABA Swedish Airlines pilot on the vital courier run between Stockholm and Berlin. He never saw his wife again. She joined the Resistance, was later arrested and sent to Dachau concentration camp, where she committed suicide.

As the German advance continued almost unchecked, the British Expeditionary Force (BEF) Air Component fought over France to the last, losing almost 1,000 aircraft in the process, while some 300,000 Allied troops were snatched from Dunkirk's beaches during Operation 'Dynamo' between May 26 and 3 June after the fall of Calais and Boulogne. Winston Churchill, Britain's new prime minister, made a last-ditch effort to prevent the fall of France. On 13 June he flew from Hendon to Tours on a No. 24 Squadron DH Flamingo to meet French Prime Minister Paul Reynaud for the last time. Churchill's mission failed to delay the inevitable and on 22 June France sought an armistice with its German invaders.

During this period a series of official and unofficial clandestine flights to and from French territory was launched. Sidney Cotton flew the unofficial flights in his faithful Lockheed 12A. In uniform since October 1939, with his faithful co-pilot Flt Lt Bob Niven at his side, he commanded the RAF's first photo-reconnaissance unit, known as the No. 2 Camouflage Unit – later the Photographic Development Unit (PDU) based at Heston.

While most of the PDU's specially adapted Spitfires and Blenheims were deployed to France, and one of its 'civil' Hudsons was based in Iraq secretly to photograph Stalin's oil fields in the neutral Soviet Union, Sidney Cotton was spending much of his time in France. This made it very convenient for him to fly his own Lockheed to French airfields either on Air Ministry or private company business. Now assigned to the PDU, the aircraft was under the control of the Directorate of Intelligence (Air Ministry), ultimately the responsibility of Wg Cdr F.W. Winterbotham, head of the Air Intelligence Branch (AI1(C)), the air component of SIS. He had already expressed his disapproval of Cotton's earlier freelance mission to fly Goering to Britain, and was well aware of his current conflicting business enterprises. As the Germans approached the outskirts of Paris in June 1940, Winterbotham tracked Cotton down to a military airfield at Le Luc in the south of France and instructed him to fly directly to Orly airport to pick up 'essential equipment and personnel'.

One of the most important British intelligence coups of the war was the breaking of Germany's Enigma code, used to transmit top-secret operational information to Hitler's army, navy and air force. It was discovered almost by accident when a German cipher clerk in the pay of the Deuxième Bureau passed on documents detailing research for a new code system, called Enigma, in the late 1930s. Thanks to the Franco-Polish Treaty, copies were sent to the Polish Intelligence Service, whose cipher department even managed to build their own Enigma encoding machines from the information contained in the German documents. They were helped by Polish Jewish scientists who had worked in the Berlin factory where the Enigma encoding machine was produced, and who had been expelled to Warsaw in 1938. One of them contacted Polish Intelligence, then in close touch with SIS as well as the Deuxième Bureau. Charles Steinmetz bought with him the key to the device's secret code, which was passed on to SIS by an aide to the Polish foreign secretary, who had been 'befriended' by the wife of an official at the British Embassy in Warsaw.

Amy Elizabeth Pack was a vivacious American blonde who quickly became the centre of diplomatic cocktail parties and receptions in the summer of 1938. Any information that passed her way at these functions and at several 'private' meetings with foreign military officers was passed on to SIS, who had given Pack the codename Cynthia. Col Stewart Menzies, then deputy director of SIS, took personal charge of the Enigma project, codenamed Operation 'Ultra', and its safe delivery to Britain. However, in an act of great generosity Poland presented a complete Enigma machine to the governments of both France and Great Britain only two weeks before Hitler unleashed his Blitzkrieg on the country. Although Menzies had a machine, more work had to done on breaking the codes.

Richard Lewinski, one of Steinmetz's fellow scientists at the Berlin factory, had been smuggled out of Warsaw to Paris via Stockholm by the SIS as the Germans overran Poland in October 1939. For £10,000, a British passport and a passage to England for himself and his wife, he had offered to build a replica Enigma machine and help crack the codes. The Lewinskis and their SIS handler in Paris, Cdr Wilfred Dunderdale, were the 'essential personnel' that Cotton was ordered to fly to Heston. Biffy Dunderdale was a secret-service character straight out of the pages of *Bulldog Drummond*. Born in Odessa in Russia, Biffy served as a midshipman in the Black Sea Fleet in 1917. Settling in England after the Revolution, he later joined up with a former colleague in the Black Sea Fleet, Cdr Vladimir Wolfson, who was working for British Naval Intelligence. Being fluent in Russian and Polish, Dunderdale was soon recruited by SIS.

On arrival at Orly, however, Cotton found the airport full of French business-men and their families offering large sums of cash to anyone who could fly them out of the country. Among them was Marcel Broussac, a wealthy Jewish racehorse owner and textile merchant, who would later found the Dior fashion house and who was a good friend of Cotton. As there were spare seats in the Lockheed, Sidney offered two of them to the Frenchman, who was prepared to pay handsomely, but Dunderdale would have none of it and immediately contacted London for advice. After a one-sided telephone conversation with Winterbotham, Cotton had to refuse Boussac's generous offer and took off forthwith with only his official passengers on board, heading for England. Fog over the Channel forced an unscheduled landing at St Helier in Jersey, where the party spent the night before completing their flight the following day.

On arrival at Heston, Cotton was handed a letter from the Air Ministry informing him that the Photographic Development Unit was to be taken out of his hands, along with the Lockheed. The words of the Admiralty report penned 23 years earlier – 'He is of a difficult temperament and unsuitable for employ-ment in a uniformed service' – had come back to haunt him. Although he continued to work on various experimental projects with the RAF until 1944, his days as a free-ranging SIS agent were over.

The official clandestine flights were both flown by No. 10 Squadron Royal Australian Air Force, posted to Britain in mid-1939 for training on the new Short Sunderland flying boat. The British Dominion Office requested that the squadron should remain in England following the declaration of war. In action from the onset, flying anti-submarine, air–sea rescue and transport sorties, the squadron was also equipped with a Supermarine Walrus amphibian for training and communications duties.

As the Battle of France drew to a close, General Charles de Gaulle, an ambitious French tank commander who had been appointed under-secretary for war only days earlier, was flown to Heston from Bordeaux via Jersey on 17 June aboard an RAF Flamingo. The day after his arrival an urgent request was received by the Naval Intelligence Directorate (NID) to pick up a member of de Gaulle's family, plus a trunk full of important state documents from the relative's house in Brittany.

At very short notice No. 10 Squadron's Walrus L2312, a four-seat, single-engined amphibious biplane, affectionately known in service as the Shagbat, was selected for the mission to be flown on the evening of 18 June. Its crew comprised pilot Flt Lt J.N. Bell, navigator Sgt C.W. Harris and Naval Intelligence officer Capt Norman Hope. Neither of the flight crew had experience of flying the Walrus at night, and their charts and briefing were lacking in detail. Nevertheless, the amphibian took off after midnight from the squadron's base at Mount Batten, Plymouth for the 100-mile flight to Carantec Bay near Roscoff, on the north Brittany coast.

It never reached its destination, and at 0400 hours on 19 June wreckage was found some miles east of its track. All on board had been killed in the crash, the two Australians being the first RAAF casualties of the Second World War. Although the cause of the accident was never officially disclosed, the short time allowed for planning the flight and the crew's unfamiliarity with the Brittany coastline were accepted as contributing factors.

Only days later, No. 10 Squadron RAAF Sunderland P9602 was sent on a secret mission to North Africa. On 25 June the giant four-engined flying boat, which was developed from Imperial Airways luxury Empire 'boats', left Mount Batten for Calshot near Southampton. There it made a brief stop to pick up Viscount Lord Gort VC, the former C-in-C of the BEF in France, and Duff Cooper, British Minister of Information, for a flight to Rabat in French Morocco. Their mission was to make contact with French minister Georges Mandel, who had left Paris after the armistice and who it was thought might rally to the Allied cause and secure Free French cooperation in North Africa.

After 8 hours in the air, the flying boat's captain, Sqn Ldr J.A. 'Dick' Cohen, made a hazardous landing on the narrow River Bouregrea, touching down amongst a fleet of native fishing boats at dusk — no mean feat bearing in mind that the Sunderland wing span was over 112 feet. The British VIPs were met by French Air Force officers who took them to the British Consulate, but the mission almost failed there and then when the harbourmaster told the crew to move the Sunderland out of the shipping lane. When they refused, the local police were called to prevent the crew from coming ashore or anyone boarding the flying boat.

A Short Sunderland Mk I flying boat of No. 10 Squadron RAAF carried Lord Gort and Duff Cooper on a secret flight to French Morocco on 25 June 1940. *(François Prins)*

This coincided with a coded message being delivered to the crew by hand, asking for Cohen to collect Lord Gort. As strict radio silence had to be maintained on the aircraft, the situation soon became more confused. Drastic measures were called for. The co-pilot, Plt Off D.A. Stuart, decided to capture the policemen in the guard boat with his service revolver. After re-establishing contact with the consulate's representative, Dick Cohen went ashore and was driven to Lord Gort's hotel, only to find that he and Duff Cooper were being prevented from leaving by the local police chief. However, they managed to bluff their way back to the flying boat, but without ever having made contact with the French minister. In the meantime the co-pilot had prepared the aircraft and crew for an immediate departure. As a French naval gunboat deliberately circled the Sunderland, Cohen fired up its engines and began a fast taxi towards the open water. He lifted the flying boat off the river at 0300 hours on 26 June heading for Gibraltar, where his distinguished passengers disembarked 5 hours later. After refuelling, the flying boat and its crew returned to Mount Batten without mishap. Sqn Ldr Cohen was awarded the Distinguished Flying Cross (DFC) in September.

There followed a brief period of respite while Britain braced herself for the German onslaught. The Battle of Britain was about to begin. For Britain's security services, reeling from their earlier mistakes, Hitler's occupation of most of the Continent was to prove a double-edged sword. On the downside had been the capture of two SIS agents at Venlo on the Dutch–German border at the end of 1939. Capts Henry Stevens and Sigismund Payne Best belonged to the top secret 'Z' Section of SIS, which was fronted by bogus commercial companies and had its headquarters at Bush House in London. Stevens and Best had been instructed to meet some German officers who were reportedly involved in a plot to overthrow Hitler. In fact these officers were members of the Sicherheitsdienst or SD, the SS's own security service. Unbeknown to the British agents, one of them, codenamed Schaemmel, was in fact Walther Schellenberg, chief of the Foreign Intelligence section of the SD. On their third meeting at Venlo, they were apprehended and a Dutch Army intelligence officer accompanying them was shot dead. Taken to Gestapo headquarters in Berlin, Stevens and Best were to reveal so much information about Allied intelligence networks in Europe that most of them had to be closed down, including the discredited 'Z' Section. On the plus side was the fact that most of the European governments now in exile in Britain, including those of Belgium, Czechoslovakia, France, Holland and Poland, had brought with them details of their respective intelligence networks. The files of these networks were made available to the British government and became an invaluable source of information for SIS and MI5, the British counterintelligence organisation, during the crucial months ahead.

Alarmed at the state of Britain's security services when France fell, Winston Churchill established the Special Operations Executive (SOE) to create 'economic sabotage' within occupied Europe 'by any means possible'. Churchill wanted SOE to 'set Europe ablaze', using an undercover army of resistance fighters supported by a clandestine supply-and-communications network. Established on 16 July 1940, SOE was to be a powerful civilian body independent from MI5 or the now-compromised SIS. Headed by Dr Hugh Dalton, the Minister of Economic Warfare, SOE was free to headhunt staff from any government department, civil or military, without recourse to higher authority. While SOE set up shop at 64 Baker Street, several German agents were being dropped into Britain prior to Hitler's planned invasion, with mixed fortunes.

Two Danish Abwehr agents, Hans Schmidt and Jorgen Bjornson, were parachuted over Hampshire in July 1940 from a Luftwaffe He 111 bomber based at Rennes in France. Bjornson, who landed near Winchester in the dark, breaking his ankle in the process, was soon arrested and narrowly escaped execution. Schmidt was luckier. After a safe landing, he met a Welshman named Arthur Owens in the waiting room of Winchester station and Owens gave him the address of a safe house in Salisbury; from there he transmitted to Hamburg reports of troop movements and locations in the southern counties.

A Luftwaffe Heinkel He 111 of Kommando Rowehl, the forerunner of KG 200, about to leave for a night-drop mission over England. *(ww2 images)*

Arthur Owens was a Welsh Nationalist who had volunteered his services to the Abwehr in 1937. His job as an electrical appliance salesman enabled him to make frequent visits to the Continent, and Germany in particular. After September 1939 Owens' main point of contact with his German handlers was Lisbon, while funds were made available through the Japanese Embassy in London. The Welshman was an important contact for many of the Abwehr agents dropped into the British Isles, including one from Sweden.

On 6 September 1940 a farm worker near Denton in Northamptonshire noticed a stranger asleep under a hedge and mentioned it to his boss, a member of the Home Guard, who decided to investigate. Dressed in grey flannels and a sports jacket cut in the Continental style, when awoken the man said he was Gosta Caroli from Sweden and had arrived by parachute during the night. His candid answers took them by surprise, and when Caroli produced a loaded pistol and £300 in banknotes they telephoned Northampton police station. At no point did Caroli try to escape; indeed, while waiting for the police he showed them where his parachute, suitcase with a wireless transmitter, and food were hidden. Maps of the Banbury area were also found, indicating that Caroli had been dropped in the wrong place. When he was searched the police found his

Swedish passport and a genuine Alien's Registration Certificate, dated 15 May 1939 and issued in Birmingham.

Caroli was taken to Latchmere House, a former mental hospital near Richmond in Surrey, MI5's Camp 020, to be questioned about other agents who might have landed in Britain. Again the Swede hid nothing. The Abwehr had approached him in 1938 while he was living in Germany and had asked him to visit Britain as a 'travel writer'. They offered good money and Caroli agreed; hence his visits to Birmingham the following year. Once war had been declared the Swede was trained in radio procedures and prepared for the flight back to England. His task was to radio back the results of German air raids on the Midlands.

Caroli had also been flown to England by an He 111 from Chartres, with instructions to contact Arthur Owens. Unknown to him or the Abwehr, Owens was in fact a double agent working closely with SIS and MI5, under the codenames Johnny and Snow respectively. He was, however, unaware that Caroli had landed, and since time was of the essence and the Abwehr would be waiting to hear from the Swede, MI5 arranged for him to transmit a message. Caroli told them that he had been injured in the drop, had lain low and would be going on to London as a refugee. The Germans were unhappy with that and told him that they would arrange for Owens to meet him at High Wycombe station and take him to London.

Meanwhile his captors had given him the codename Summer and a chance to save his life. They told Caroli to give them as much information as possible on agents that might be on their way, or be already in the country, and in return they would not commit him to trial in a court, where he would be found guilty and sentenced to death. Caroli agreed and told MI5 about two agents, Hans Rysen and Wolf Schmidt, who were on their way. MI5 were keen to use Summer for their own benefits; he agreed to help with wireless transmissions to his paymasters in Germany and under supervision send spurious messages to the Abwehr.

Wolf Schmidt parachuted from an He 111 piloted by Hauptmann Karl Gartenfeld on 19 September and landed in a field near Willingham, in Cambridgeshire. The next morning he walked into the village and bought a cheap pocket watch, as his own wristwatch had been smashed in the fall. He then bought a copy of the morning newspaper and had breakfast at the only café in Willingham. By 1000 hours he decided to go back to the field and collect his belongings, which included the statutory wireless in a suitcase. On his way he was stopped by a member of the Home Guard and escorted to its local headquarters, in the Three Tuns public house. Here its commanding officer, Col Langton, questioned him and had him searched. All they found was an identity card and a few personal belongings. Schmidt offered the usual story of being a Danish refugee but, unhappy with this story, Langton telephoned the police in Cambridge.

It was obvious by now that he was an enemy agent and MI5 was called in. Although told by Col Stephens at Camp 020 that he faced certain execution, Schmidt refused to talk; he even suggested that as the invasion of England was about to take place, he would soon be free. Stephens and his team continued their interrogation every day for two weeks; then early in October Schmidt suddenly agreed to work for MI5 and to use his radio to send messages to Germany. MI5 gave him the codename Tate, and although he had been silent for over two weeks the Abwehr accepted his story that he had been ill and unable to contact them earlier. While Schmidt was at Camp 020, his fellow agent arrived in England.

Near Yardley Hastings in Northamptonshire, not far from where Caroli had landed, another He 111 dropped Hans Reysen early in October. After burying his wireless transmitter and other items in a rabbit warren he took refuge in a barn, where he was discovered by a farmer who accused him of stealing eggs. Reysen denied this by saying he was simply visiting the area and staying with a local farmer named Walter Penn, who was in actual fact a real person.

When told of the encounter by his neighbour, farmer Percy Keggin, who knew Penn, set off in the direction taken by the stranger, caught him up and offered him a lift in his van. Keggin invited him back to his house for tea before continuing the journey; and once inside telephoned Walter Penn, who said he knew of no one staying with him or coming to see him. They smelled a rat and decided to act. Penn arrived at Keggin's house with a member of the Home Guard, who took the man to Bozeat police station. Reysen offered no resistance and when questioned showed his identity card in the name of Frank Phillips of Southampton. It was obviously forged, and when he realised the game was up he admitted being a German agent and agreed to show the police where he had buried his parachute, wireless and £500 in notes.

He was held at Wellingborough police station overnight and later moved to Camp 020. Col Stephens's team conducted the interrogation and, after the threat of execution, Reysen informed them that he was to report back to the Abwehr any general military intelligence he could glean from the north-west of England. Under MI5 control he reported his findings, suitably censored, to Hamburg which again appeared to accept the transmissions. He continued to send doctored messages until December. As with the other agents captured and 'turned' by MI5, he was sent to prison for the duration of the war and released soon after VE-Day.

Most Abwehr agents proved less than successful at merging into the local community. Soon after Adolf Hitler called off Operation 'Sealion', the invasion of Britain, three spies were sent on a fool's errand to Scotland. On 30 September the Regional Security Liaison Officer (RSLO) in Edinburgh was telephoned by the Chief Constable of Banffshire, informing him that two suspects, a François de Deeker from France and a Vera Erikson from Denmark, had been detained at Buckie on the Moray Firth. The couple had been spotted earlier by the Portgordon stationmaster who was suspicious of their damp appearance, especially as there had been no rain. He called the local police, who questioned the pair. They claimed to have come ashore the previous day and spent the night at a hotel in Banff. The truth was that they were landed in the Moray Firth by a Luftwaffe He 115 seaplane from Stavanger-Sola in Norway.

When they were searched several items were discovered, including a loaded Mauser automatic pistol, a wireless set with codebooks and two forged National Registration Cards with addresses in London. Now suspected of being spies, they were taken to Buckie police station and the Chief Constable, George Strath, was contacted with the news. Strath was not new at the game of seeking fugitives and following information extracted from Erikson, instigated a search for a third man. A clerk at Buckie Station said he had sold a one-way ticket to Edinburgh to a young man early that morning. What had aroused the clerk's suspicions was the fact that the man then boarded the train to Aberdeen, and so the authorities were told to meet the Aberdeen train and the third man, now known as Werner Waelti, using the information imparted by Erikson.

Unfortunately the police reached the station after Waelti had left. However, a damp suitcase was found at the left luggage office, and inside it were a wireless transmitter and batteries. The police then waited for someone to claim the case. Later that day Waelti returned to the left luggage office and, producing his ticket, was immediately apprehended and searched. A loaded Mauser was found. Waelti then produced a switchblade knife, a short struggle took place and he was disarmed. Other items discovered included a codebook, a list of airfields in eastern England and a passport issued in Switzerland. He also had a National Registration Card giving an address in London, the same address as the Buckie couple. He too was taken to Camp 020.

After both men and the woman had been questioned for several days, it emerged that de Deeker was a German named Theodore Druecke who had been working for the Abwehr for some time. Waelti insisted he was a Swiss national and gave no other name. His passport was suspect, even though it looked genuine. Investigations by the Swiss authorities later showed that Waelti's passport was genuine, but had not been issued to him; it had been obtained in

1937 by a Swiss national, a totally different man. Waelti's real name was never confirmed, but subsequent evidence pointed to his being a German national called Robert Petter. Both men were tried at the Old Bailey and sentenced to death; following an appeal, which was rejected, they were executed at Wandsworth Prison on 6 August 1941. Erikson, whose real name was Vera de Cottani-Chalbur, languished in Holloway Prison until after the war; her subsequent life is unknown.

As Britain was finding it equally difficult to infiltrate agents into Germany, its long and close relationship with neutral Portugal was to pay dividends, particularly when Britain stood alone and virtually surrounded in 1940. The only lifelines open to Britain were the sea and air. Not only was Lisbon the espionage Mecca of western Europe, but it was also the terminus for the Pan American Airways transatlantic Clipper service to the River Tagus. This service was much in demand by politicians, arms dealers, wealthy refugees, and intelligence officers from almost every country in Europe, and with every German victory the traffic increased.

To meet passengers from the giant Boeing 314 flying boats, several European airlines, including Deutsche Lufthansa (DLH) and BOAC – which set up offices next door to each other at Lisbon's Sintra airfield – were available for onward flights. BOAC, formed on 1 April 1940 by merging the fleets of Imperial Airways and British Airways, used a fleet of four former KLM Douglas DC-3 airliners on the Heston-to-Lisbon route. Flown by Dutch crews who had brought their aircraft to England when Germany invaded the Low Countries, the weekly, seven-hour flights took the DC-3s via the Isles of Scilly to head south across the Bay of Biscay, well west of the Brittany coast.

This service was used extensively by SIS and its agents, two of whom were on the passenger manifests during the autumn of 1940. Dusko Popov was a wealthy Yugoslav playboy who, with his brother Ivo, had been persuaded by a German schoolmate to join the Abwehr in 1939. However, Dusko also offered his services to the SIS in Belgrade. When the Abwehr sent him to Lisbon in November 1940, he already had a contact at the SIS station and a few weeks later was on the BOAC flight bound for London. There he was recruited by both MI5 and the SIS, and given the codenames Scout and Tricycle.

On his return to Lisbon, Popov provided valuable and accurate intelligence for the British over a long period, despite being branded as a double agent by MI5 operative Guy Liddell, himself a Soviet agent. In August 1941 Popov flew to America by PanAm Clipper with vital information about Japanese plans to attack the US Navy, gleaned from his Abwehr contact in Lisbon. However, America's Federal Bureau of Investigation (FBI) chief, J. Edgar Hoover, dis-

approved of the Yugoslav's dissolute lifestyle and recommended that his information be treated as unreliable. Popov spent the rest of the war in a South
American backwater.

An even more unlikely spy, flown to Lisbon at the end of 1940, was leading
Belgian fighter ace Rodolphe de Hemricourt de Grunne, who had fought along-
side the German Condor Legion against the Republican Air Force during the
Spanish Civil War. On his return to Belgium, de Grunne joined the Belgian Air
Force and was converting to the new, British-built Hawker Hurricane fighter as
Germany overran the Low Countries. Sous-Lt de Grunne flew air defence patrols
from March 1940 with the 2nd Squadron at Schaffen, but only three days after
Germany's invasion of Belgium on 10 May all its Hurricanes had been destroyed,
most of them on the ground. The squadron's personnel evacuated to France as
the German forces advanced. With a group of fellow pilots, de Grunne made his
way south in a 'borrowed' staff car, arriving on 23 June 1940 at Montpellier's
Port Vendres, where they managed to board a ship bound for Gibraltar. Another
ship took the group on to Liverpool, where they disembarked on 7 July.

The Battle of Britain was at its height, the RAF was desperate for experienced
fighter pilots and, after a quick refresher course, de Grunne was posted to No.
32 Squadron at Biggin Hill, flying Hurricanes. He had time to claim only two
confirmed kills and one 'probable' during the fierce fighting in the days before
and after Eagle Day, Goering's planned annihilation of the RAF, before he was
shot down by his former colleagues on 18 August. Suffering from serious burns,
he spent several weeks in hospital before being invited by the SIS to convalesce
in Lisbon.

With his Spanish Civil War background, he was encouraged to make contact
with his old Condor Legion comrades-in-arms in neutral Portugal and find out
which of their units were now facing the RAF across the English Channel. After
some weeks in Lisbon, de Grunne returned to England on a BOAC DC-3 flight
sporting a healthy suntan, although his wounds were not yet fully healed. He
was eager to return to action and at the end of April 1941 was posted to No.
609 Squadron, again stationed at Biggin Hill. On 21 May his Spitfire was shot
down over the Channel by a Bf 109 and although he was seen to bale out over
the sea, his body was never found.

Meanwhile, the emerging SOE was beginning to be seen by SIS as a potential
rival and the seeds of discontent between the two agencies were already being
sown. When Churchill ordered the formation of SOE he also appointed a
Canadian businessman to head both SOE and SIS operations in the United
States. Born in Manitoba in 1896, William Stephenson joined the Royal Flying
Corps in 1917 after being gassed twice in the trenches.

Shot down in February 1918 while flying a No. 73 Squadron Sopwith Camel, he spent five months as a prisoner of war in Karlsruhe camp before escaping. He returned to his squadron and ended the war credited with twelve victories. Between the wars he built up a million-dollar industrial company and travelled extensively to Europe. Alarmed by Hitler's rise to power and the subsequent rearming of Germany, Stephenson became involved in espionage as a private citizen, first coming into contact with SIS in 1938.

His British Security Coordination (BSC) office in the RCA Building in New York, which vetted passport applications under the guise of a British-based commercial company, was a front for several SIS agents. One of his operatives was Amy Pack, who had moved from Warsaw to Washington when the Germans invaded Poland. Stephenson asked her under her codename Cynthia to prise information out of German, Italian and Japanese diplomats stationed in Washington. She had particular success with an anti-Nazi Vichy French press attaché, Capt Charles Brousse, who passed on information about the French fleet in North Africa. Pack became Brousse's mistress and later married him, after her husband Arthur had committed suicide.

Stephenson, meanwhile, was instrumental in developing a close relationship between the SIS and a new US intelligence agency. As the bulk of the British Army in France was being plucked from the Dunkirk beaches, Stephenson was persuading the agency's American lawyer chief that Britain would not only survive, but with US help could defeat Hitler's Germany.

William Joseph Donovan was born in 1893 of Irish extraction, and had studied law before joining the US Army to fight Pancho Villa in Mexico. He then fought the Germans in France during the First World War, and was awarded the Medal of Honor and the Croix de Guerre. He had much in common with Stephenson. Both were millionaires, anglophiles and passionately opposed to the United States' isolationism. Acting as an unofficial advisor to Roosevelt's Secretary of State for the Navy, W. Frank Knox, and with help from Stephenson, Donovan arranged to fly to England on a fact-finding mission. On 15 July 1940, as the Battle of Britain began, he flew to London via PanAm *Lisbon Clipper* and BOAC DC-3. Donovan stayed at Claridges, met Winston Churchill and Col Stewart Graham Menzies, the urbane head of SIS, and then was entertained by Lady Astor before returning to New York on 3 August aboard the BOAC Empire flying boat, *Clare.*

This visit reinforced his firmly held view that the United States should become more actively involved in the European war, and he was soon planning a second and more comprehensive visit to England and its overseas bases. On 17 December, the Battle of Britain having been won by the RAF, Donovan and

Stephenson – nicknamed 'Wild Bill' and 'Little Bill' – were again crossing the Atlantic. Early in the new year Donovan boarded an RAF Sunderland for the first leg of a three-month tour of the Mediterranean and Middle East, fortified for the trip by a hamper from Claridges. Beginning at Gibraltar, the American lawyer flew to Malta, Egypt, Iraq, Libya and Yugoslavia before returning to the United States via London.

Brig Sir Colin McVean Gubbins MC, the fledgling SOE's recently appointed Scottish director of operations, had also met Donovan, who had expressed more than a passing interest in the concept of covert warfare. Gubbins had fought with the Royal Artillery on the Western Front throughout the First World War; in the Russian Civil War in 1919; and in Ireland during the Nationalist revolt two years later. All this experience gave him a thorough grounding in guerrilla warfare. In the 1930s he had a spell with the Soviet section of Military Intelligence at the War Office, later building links with Polish and Czech resistance movements after their countries collapsed.

At the outbreak of hostilities, Major Gubbins was in Section D, Military Intelligence (Research) of SIS, which was absorbed into SOE in 1940. In common with his SIS counterpart, Fred Winterbotham, he had excellent connections within the Establishment and appreciated the importance of air power to deliver and supply agents in the field, so he made it his business to seek the RAF's assistance from the very outset.

ACM Sir Charles Portal's reaction, as Chief of the Air Staff, however, was less than enthusiastic. He considered that dropping spies to kill enemy forces was 'not an operation with which the Royal Air Force should be associated'. Nevertheless his deputy, AVM Arthur Harris, later to become C-in-C Bomber Command, was tasked by the Air Ministry with supporting SOE, although he would continue to argue that it took assets away from his main task, that of bombing Germany into submission.

As SOE agents were being recruited and sent to remote country houses to be trained in 'ungentlemanly warfare', No. 419 Flight was established at RAF North Weald at the end of 1940, equipped with a brace of elderly Armstrong-Whitworth Whitley Mk V twin-engined, long-range bombers. Part of No. 3 Group Bomber Command, the unit would initially be used for parachute training at nearby Stapleford Tawney, but subsequently for dropping agents into occupied Europe.

While this unit was working up, a Westland Lysander of No. 2 (AC) Squadron had undertaken the first clandestine flight to the Continent carrying a secret agent. The Army Cooperation unit had been part of the BEF until June 1940 when it was evacuated from France, eventually setting up residence at

Sawbridgeworth airfield in Hertfordshire, a few miles from North Weald. It was equipped with the slow, single-engined, two-seat Lysander, which was vulnerable to enemy fighters but had an excellent short take-off and landing capability, making it ideal for operating from unmade fields. The squadron was tasked with flying an SIS agent into France, a mission that was officially recorded as a 'long-range air test'. Wg Cdr Andrew Geddes, the squadron's commanding officer, flew the unidentified SIS agent from Newmarket to meet a reception committee in a remote field at Tours, in western France, on the evening of 3 September 1940. A few weeks later an RAF aircraft was to make the first official pick-up of an agent from France.

Phillip Schneidau, born in Paris in 1903 to British parents, played international hockey for France before volunteering to join the RAF at the outbreak of war. With the rank of sergeant, he had acted as an interpreter to the commander of the British Air Forces in France (BAFF), AM Sir Arthur 'Ugly' Barratt, during the Battle of France, when he also came in contact with Sidney Cotton and his PDU. He was commissioned as a pilot officer and recruited by SIS on his return to London after the fall of France.

Schneidau arranged to be flown back into France by Barratt's personal pilot using the Air Marshal's DH.89B, a four-engined development of the Dragon Rapide biplane, and to be picked up at the same spot a few nights later. His scheme was dismissed out of hand by his RAF superiors, who arranged for him to be dropped by parachute from a No. 419 Flight Whitley. After four aborted attempts due to bad weather, Schneidau, who had been given the field name of Felix, was dropped into France by Flt Lt Jacky Oettle on the night of 9 October carrying with him a brace of homing pigeons in his haversack, his only means of communication. One of these birds arrived at East Grinstead ten days later carrying an encoded message from Felix saying he was waiting to be picked up.

Flt Lt W.R. Farley of No. 419 Flight was tasked with collecting Schneidau on 19 October and had borrowed Lysander R9029 from No. 2(AC) Squadron for the mission. After a frustrating delay due to heavy rain, Wally Farley eventually took off from Tangmere, a fighter station on the south coast of England, and with the aid of clear weather and a full moon successfully landed in a field at Montigny, south of Fontainebleau, where Felix was waiting. He had instructed Schneidau to use three lit torches laid out in an inverted L-shaped pattern as a flarepath, the system originally used by First World War night-fighter squadrons.

Their take-off at 0100 hours on 20 October was uneventful, but Farley soon ran into more bad weather; driving rain poured into the rear cockpit which had been left open for easy access, putting his radio out of action and soaking his passenger. After battling gale-force winds and being out of sight of land for more than 5 hours, it was Felix who spotted cliffs through the clouds. With fuel tanks registering empty, Farley had little alternative but to crash-land on the clifftop, not knowing whether he was in the Irish Republic or occupied Europe. In fact they had arrived near Oban in north-west Scotland! Farley and Schneidau both survived the landing unscathed, but the borrowed Lysander was a write-off.

By the end of the year No. 419 Flight was equipped with three Whitley Vs, P5025 having been lost on 11 October during a training sortie, and two Lysander Mk IIs under the command of Flt Lt Keast. Wally Farley had been replaced after breaking his leg when he crashed another borrowed aircraft, this time a Hurricane fighter at North Weald. Experienced pilots were being recruited from widely varied backgrounds. Flt Lt E.V. 'Teddy' Knowles was a former Battle of Britain fighter pilot from North Weald, while 22-year-old Plt Off F.M. Gordon Scotter belonged to No. 2(AC) Squadron, which was responsible for training the flight's Lysander pilots in night-time, short-field landings and take-offs at Sawbridgeworth. Several more were former No. 24 (Communications) Squadron pilots. Based at Hendon and tasked with transporting VIPs, who included members of the Royal Family and the Prime Minister, No. 24 was the only RAF squadron to be given authority to fly at any time and in any weather – often without radio and normal navigational aids; thus its pilots were well qualified to undertake clandestine flights to the Continent. Most were self-sufficient individuals who were trusted to get their VIP passengers to their destination in one piece, whatever the conditions. Among those who would make the move from Hendon to the 'moon' squadron were Keast, Boris Romanov, Ron Hockey and later, Edward Fielden.

The qualifications for pilots volunteering for Special Duties were demanding. First, they had to be commissioned. They needed to have at least 1,000 flying hours, 500 of which must be night flying; had to be above average at 'dead reckoning' – navigation without visual, radio or astronomical aids; and be fluent in French. The Air Ministry also stated that no former PoWs would be allowed to fly operationally again in the same theatre. This latter stipulation was later rescinded.

Far away from 'fortress Britain', two separate but soon-to-be related incidents in the Mediterranean were to play a part in shaping future SOE support operations. Days after Royal Navy Swordfish and Skua aircraft from the carrier HMS *Ark Royal* attacked Vichy French warships at Algerian ports in July 1940, a three-seat Laté 298B reconnaissance floatplane of Escadrille 2HT, flown by Premier-Maitre Réne Duvauchelle and radio operator/observer Quartier-Maitre Jacques Mehouas, defected from Bizerta and flew to Malta. Initially attached to a Sunderland squadron based at Kalafrana, No. 230, the Laté was tasked with the carriage of agents to North Africa. On the night of 10 September the floatplane, flown by its French crew, landed Commandant Robert, a Free French agent, in a small isolated bay near Bizerta. The seven-hour mission was flown with great skill in bad weather conditions, the Laté returning to Kalafrana during a spectacular thunderstorm at 0514 hours.

Two months later Sergeant Fred Robertson of No. 261 Squadron, the first Hurricane squadron to arrive in Malta, was vectored to intercept an unidentified aircraft approaching from the south-west. It was a three-seat Vichy Navy Loire 130 communications flying boat from the battleship *Richelieu* that had escaped during a ferry flight between Bizerta and Dakar. Two aircraft had attempted to defect on 10 November but one crashed on take-off from Lake Bizerta; its crew were captured and court-martialled. The surviving Loire, piloted by Deuxième-Maître Georges Blaize with his observer Raoul Gatien, was escorted into Malta's Kalafrana harbour to moor alongside their French colleagues' Laté 298B.

Two thousand miles south-east of Malta, British and South African forces were preparing to invade the Italian colonies in East Africa, including Abyssinia, which had been annexed by Mussolini in 1935. Playing a major part in planning the Allied campaign was a veteran of guerrilla warfare in Palestine, Maj Orde Wingate, who had formed a successful band of resistance fighters in the Abyssinian Mountains known as Mission 101, or more commonly 'Gideon Force'. Although nominally under the control of FM Wavell's GHQ in Cairo, Mission 101 was in fact SOE's first active unit, with a budget of £2 million.

On 20 November 1940 Wingate was flown from Khartoum in Sudan to a remote mountain airstrip at Sakala, near Lake Tana, to meet local resistance leaders led by Col Dan Sandford. He flew in a three-seat Vickers Vincent III general-purpose biplane of No. 47 Squadron's 'B' Flight, fitted with a 120-gallon extra fuel tank. Flown by Flg Off Collis and with his navigator Flt Lt Bavin Smith, Vincent K4683 refuelled at Rosieres on the Blue Nile and picked up a local guide before flying on to the guerrilla encampment, where it remained for two nights. It was the RAF's first successful pick-up operation for SOE, for which Collis was awarded an immediate DFC.

On his return Wingate asked No. 47 Squadron's commanding officer, Wg Cdr James Pelly-Fry, if he would arrange for a series of covert supply drops to Force 101. Using its Vickers Wellesleys – large, obsolescent, single-engined long-range bombers – the squadron flew several missions during December dropping arms, fuel and food for the guerrilla force, and whisky for the Brigadier. Flying from Khartoum, these long-range supply missions took their toll and at least one Wellesley force-landed in the desert and had to be abandoned by its crew. However, the supply drops enabled the Gideon Force to become a thorn in the Italians' side in the period leading up to the planned Allied invasion.

By the end of 1940, all the elements of Churchill's 'ungentlemanly warfare' campaign were about to spring into action.

CHAPTER 3

The Cloak and Dagger Mob

In its first year, the Special Operations Executive had established research and training establishments at country houses in the home counties and Scotland (SOE was said to stand for the 'Stately 'Omes of England'), had devised its own cipher codes, and was recruiting agents from the British Isles – many with dual nationality – and from all over occupied Europe. These included businessmen who had managed to cross the Channel before the borders of their defeated countries were sealed, or who had been stranded in the British Isles unable to travel back to their home countries. All government departments, both civil and military, and the old boys' network were trawled for young men and women who were fluent in a language other than English and who were willing to volunteer for an 'adventurous' future overseas, without being told exactly how adventurous it would be.

Initially its equipment was definitely of the hand-me-down variety. For communications, it had to rely on bulky Mark XV radio sets designed before the war for SIS agents. Contacts with agents in the field were broadcast by the BBC in the form of news items and family messages, which were repeated at hourly intervals until the reception committee was activated. Department STS 33 was responsible for parachute training, then seen as the best way of inserting agents behind enemy lines, with drops being made into Tatton Park near Manchester using two elderly No. 78 Squadron Whitley bombers based at the city's Ringway airport.

Col Maurice Buckmaster, a former executive with the Ford Motor Company in France and an Army information officer, and Anglo-Dutch diplomat Maj R.V. Laming headed two sections, 'F' (France) and 'N' (Netherlands) respectively. Each section had its own system of codenames for agents and operations: 'F' Section used English occupations, while 'N' Section used vegetables!

The few agents dropped into occupied France during 1940 had been recruited by SIS, while further afield No. 47 Squadron's covert supply flights to SOE's Gideon Force in Abyssinia were continuing. In February 1941 one of its Wellesleys delivered Major Orde Wingate to Mission 101's mountain base.

The first SOE agents used elderly Whitley V bombers of No. 78 Squadron for parachute training at Ringway. *(ww2 images)*

A few days later Flg Off Collis made another hazardous flight behind enemy lines to the hilltop town of Belaiya, carrying a young, 6ft 5in tall Grenadier Guards captain, Douglas Dodds-Parker. There he picked up Col Sandford and Maj Wingate, who were about to take part in the final Allied campaign to liberate the East African country from its Italian occupiers. Seven weeks later Wingate and his Gideon Force fighters accompanied the country's ousted ruler, Emperor Haile Selassie, into the liberated Abyssinian capital Addis Ababa. Their experience and expertise in irregular warfare and covert air support would take both Dodds-Parker and Wingate to other theatres of operations in the coming years.

In the spring of 1941 more operations to occupied Europe were flown by the Special Duties (SD) unit, now renumbered No. 1419 Flight and based at Stradishall in Cambridgeshire. During the February moonlight period the first mass drop from a Whitley of SOE agents took place, not in France but in Poland, the first of the occupied countries to raise an organised resistance force. Undertaken in the depths of winter, in skies ruled by the Luftwaffe, the 14-hour flight was a triumph of navigation and endurance. Six agents landed safely and although they were some 50 miles from their planned drop zone, the operation was hailed as a success.

The flight lost its first Whitley, Z6728, when acting flight commander Flt Lt Keast was shot down over Belgium on 18 February while returning at low level from an SIS operation to occupied Europe, this time Belgium. He and his crew survived to become the flight's first prisoners of war. A month later Anglo-French agent Phillip Schneidau, now using the name 'Flt Lt Phillipson', was again dropped near his home in Fontainebleau from a Whitley flown by Jacky Oettle. Carrying a radio, he was sent crashing into a tree at the edge of a nearby forest by a strong wind. With a damaged leg and several broken teeth, Schneidau took more than hour to extricate himself and his equipment from the tree before making his painful way to the house.

The next moon period was to see both success and failure for the flight. On the evening of 11 April Whitley T4165 crashed on landing at Tangmere, after an operation to Bordeaux flown by Jacky Oettle and carrying six Polish agents was aborted owing to engine trouble. Two of the crew were killed and three others injured. At the same time Gordon Scotter, the former No. 2(AC) Squadron pilot, was taking off from Tangmere near Chichester in a specially equipped Lysander II V9287 to pick up an agent in France. Fitted with a long-range fuel tank and a fixed ladder to the rear cockpit, his Lysander narrowly escaped a German night fighter as it crossed the French coast. Nevertheless, Scotter was able to identify the landing ground to the north of Châteauroux, where he saw the signal letter being flashed. Almost as soon as he landed a 'Lt Cartwright' climbed aboard, telling Scotter to take off immediately as he thought the Gestapo were close on his heels. Members of the reception committee were already making their escape as Scotter accelerated over the bumpy field to hedge-hop his way out of danger. The Lysander arrived back over Tangmere during a German air raid on the airfield and was almost shot down by the defending anti-aircraft guns as it landed without lights. Scotter became the second RAF pilot to be awarded an immediate DFC for a covert operation.

Georges Bégué, codenamed George Noble and an 'F' Section wireless operator, became the first SOE agent to be dropped into France. The only survivor of four SOE trainees lodging in a Knightsbridge flat that had suffered a direct hit during a German air raid a few weeks earlier, Bégué was dropped 'blind', with no reception committee to meet him, on 5 May. He landed north of Châteauroux, close to where Scotter had earlier picked up 'Lt Cartwright'.

Scotter himself returned to France on 10 May, this time to pick up Phillip Schneidau who, with the financial backing of his father-in-law Paul Schiffmacher, established one of the first French resistance networks. The importance of the SIS agent can be gauged by the fact that RAF Hurricane night fighters patrolled the area while Scotter landed on the edge of Fontainebleau forest, successfully to pick up the limping 'Flt Lt Phillipson'.

By mid-year No. 1419 Flight had moved to Newmarket Racecourse airfield, which had been requisitioned for Bomber Command at the outbreak of war. Conditions were far from ideal. Aircrews were billeted in draughty corridors and jockeys' changing rooms in the racecourse's main grandstand, while its groundcrews maintained the aircraft in temporary hangars on the grass airfield. A few Nissen huts were made available for planning operations, briefing crews, packing parachutes and receiving and equipping agents. As operations increased in tempo the Lysander flight was deployed to Tangmere, but the search for a permanent base was on.

While the Whitley had its limitations, the Lysander proved to be the ideal aircraft for transporting agents, or 'Joes' as they were known to the pilots, to and from France. Although slow – its long-range cruising speed was 120 mph – it had a range of 750 miles and could carry a pilot and up to three passengers in an emergency. After the fall of France, the Lysander had lost its front-line role as an artillery spotter and was relegated to second-line air–sea rescue and target-towing duties.

Its pilot sat forward and below the high, shoulder-mounted wing with a relatively unrestricted view all round, a great asset when searching for the flash of a torch from a remote field in blacked-out France. The positions of its vital but cluttered selector switches, control knobs and fuel cocks had to learned by heart if they were to be used with any confidence at night with a gloved hand. A large elevator trim wheel was prominently mounted on the left of the cockpit, the Lysander being susceptible to marked changes in trim with any change in power or movement of the flaps and slats.

The aircraft's ingenious leading-edge slats and trailing-edge flaps opened and closed automatically, governed by the speed of the aircraft. The lower the speed, the more the flaps and inboard slats opened, giving the Lysander an excellent short take-off and landing capability. With power on, the aircraft was almost impossible to stall and safe landings could be made at between 40 and 45mph. A steep angle of climb could be obtained at only 60mph, although the pilot's notes recommended that this should be used only as an emergency procedure. The maximum permissible speed for diving was 300mph, a speed that more than one Special Duties pilot would learn to appreciate while being chased by enemy night fighters.

Following the success of the in-unit modifications made to Donald Scotter's Lysander, the Air Ministry issued a Special Contract Westland (SCW) for the more extensive modification of new and low-hours Mk III aircraft. Work was undertaken by Fairfield Aviation's production line at Odhams Press, near Watford. The aircraft were stripped of their armament; two forward-firing .303in machine guns were mounted in the wheel fairings, plus one manually operated gun in the rear cockpit; and the detachable stub wings were used to carry six light bombs or a rescue dinghy. A 150-gallon De Berg fuel tank from a pre-war Handley Page Harrow bomber was installed between the undercarriage legs to increase the range to over 1,000 miles, giving the Lysander III a maximum endurance of 10 hours.

A permanent external ladder was fitted to the port side of the fuselage below the rear cockpit and the rear cockpit canopy was mounted on rails for easy access. The bulky 1133/1134 radio telephone (R/T) receiver and transmitter mounted in the back of the rear cockpit were replaced by a smaller 1154/1155 set, and the variable-pitch propeller was later replaced by a constant-speed unit from the Blenheim light bomber, which used the same 890hp Bristol Mercury XII radial engine. An extension was fitted to the floor of the rear cockpit, with a fixed locker installed under the agent's rear-facing, two-man bench seat for the stowage of essential equipment or luggage. There was also a shelf across the rear of the cockpit that could be used as an additional seat if necessary. The modified Lysanders, known as the Mk III (SD) in service, were given a paint scheme of matt black overall, although some had a green/grey camouflage scheme applied to the upper surfaces. A total of some forty Lysanders were eventually modified to Mk III (SD) standard and were test flown from Fairfield's Elstree airfield in Hertfordshire.

While dedicated air support for SOE was slowly expanding, the insertion of German agents into the British Isles had virtually ground to a halt. Since the outbreak of war, this had been the responsibility of the Aufklärungsgruppe der Oberbefehlshaber der Luftwaffe, a reconnaissance wing equipped with Dornier Do 17s, Do 215s and He 111s. It was commanded by Oberstleutnant Theodor Rowehl, who was the Luftwaffe's equivalent of Sidney Cotton. His Gruppe, which became known as the Kommando Rowehl, dropped one of the few German agents into England in 1941, Josef Jakobs.

On the morning of 1 February two farm workers near Ramsey, in Hunting-donshire, heard a shot. They dropped to the ground. Earlier they had heard a low-flying aircraft and had recognised the distinctive desynchronised engine sounds peculiar to German twin-engine bombers. Another shot rang out and a figure was spotted lying in a field nearby. As they approached, the man began to wave but remained lying down, obviously injured. When challenged he said he was a parachutist from Germany, had hurt his leg on landing and had fired his

Night-camouflaged He 111s based at Rennes in France were used by the Luftwaffe for dropping Abwehr agents into the British Isles in 1940. *(ww2 images)*

gun to attract help. Harry Coulson volunteered to stay with him while his friend went for help. The man told him that he was from Luxembourg and that under his Luftwaffe flying suit he was wearing civilian clothes, a smart suit of Continental cut, as was the felt hat which lay nearby. While looking through the man's pockets Coulson found an identity card in the name of George Rymer and an unused ration book; both proved to be forged.

Coulson soon led a policeman and a member of the Home Guard to the field and the German was taken to the police station on a farm cart, along with his suitcase containing a wireless transmitter and batteries. At Ramsey police station the German was thoroughly searched; £500 in sterling banknotes was discovered, along with other items that indicated he was certainly not a refugee. He was taken to MI5's Camp 020, where he told Col Stephens that his name was Josef Jakobs, born in Luxembourg on 30 June 1898 and, although well over service age, he had been called up by the Wehrmacht as he had been on the reserve lists. In September 1940 he was transferred to the Abwehr for training in receiving and sending Morse code. Moved to Holland early the following year, Jakobs awaited news of a mission. He told his interrogators that all he had wanted to do was to get to England and contact the Jews, so as to organise a resistance movement against the Nazis.

He was committed for trial as a spy, but as a member of the German Army he was entitled to a military hearing, which took place at the Duke of York's Head-quarters in Chelsea. The hearing lasted two days; Jakobs was found guilty of espionage and sentenced to death. In his defence he mentioned that a Dr Burgos had suggested he join the Abwehr as an agent for a secret Jewish society, but had not given him any further details. As his story could not be substantiated, the verdict stood. Josef Jakobs was taken to the Tower of London, where he was incarcerated in a cell at Waterloo Barracks while his appeal was heard by HM King George VI. It was unsuccessful, and on 14 August Jakobs was taken out to the small courtyard and seated in a chair, blindfolded, to face a firing squad. He was the only spy to be executed at the Tower during the Second World War.

Within weeks of Jakobs's arrival in England, two Norwegian Abwehr agents, Olaf Klausen and Jack Berg, landed in Scotland. They had flown from Stavanger on 6 April in a Luftwaffe He 115B twin-engined long-range floatplane of Küstenfliegergruppe 106 based at Borkum, but owing to high seas the pilot had aborted the landing. The pair returned the following night, when the Heinkel made a successful landing in the Moray Firth – where a year earlier the three Abwehr agents now under arrest and facing execution had also arrived. When the two agents rowed ashore at Crovie in a rubber dinghy, they gave themselves up to the local police as German spies. They surrendered their radio transmitter and revolvers before being escorted to Camp 020, where their true identities were discovered.

Berg was John Herbert Neal Moe, who had been born in London to an English father and a Norwegian mother. He had been working in Oslo when the Germans invaded and went to work in the puppet government's censorship office with his friend Tor Glad. Their job for the Germans was to intercept subversive mail, but when they found any they would surreptitiously warn the correspondents. Learning of Moe's British background, Oslo's Abwehr com-mander, Ernst Mueller, thought that he would be an ideal agent to send to England. Moe and Glad, who had joined the Nazi party to get the job in the censorship office, were recruited and sent for intensive training in sabotage tech-niques. Given the cover names of Berg and Klausen, the pair were flown to Scotland with orders to sabotage any sites vital to Britain's wartime defences. At Camp 020, they convinced MI5 that they wished to become double agents, the fact that Moe's father was imprisoned in Norway for having denounced the German occupiers, adding weight to their argument.

This was accepted and they were given the popular codenames Mutt and Jeff before transmitting misinformation to their former Abwehr bosses from a safe house near RAF Hendon. Within weeks of their arrival Berg and Klausen were sending back reports to their Abwehr controllers saying that they had arranged a series of sabotage operations on factories in southern England causing widespread damage, stories that were supported by local newspaper reports fed to them by the SIS. So began the career of two of the most successful 'turned' agents.

By coincidence, the Heinkel seaplane used to carry the Norwegian to Scotland was the only German aircraft to be successfully used for clandestine missions by both British and German security services. A few days after the fall of Norway in June 1940, four Norwegian Naval Air Service He 115A-2 floatplanes of No. 3 Squadron, plus an He 115B-1 captured from the Luftwaffe, escaped to Finland and from there were flown to Sullom Voe in the Shetlands by their Norwegian crews. One ran out of fuel and was sunk by its crew, who were rescued by a British warship. The remaining Heinkels landed safely before being sent to Helensburgh on the Clyde for evaluation by the Marine Aircraft Experimental Establishment (MAEE), where their exceptional water-handling qualities, good stability at low speeds, long range and spacious cabin led to their being evaluated for use on BOAC's vital link to neutral Sweden.

Luftwaffe Heinkel He 115B long-range maritime reconnaissance floatplanes based in Norway flew a number of Abwehr agents to the Moray Firth in Scotland during 1941. (*ww2 images*)

Designed as a three-seat, long-range torpedo bomber in 1936, the large, twin-float seaplane, powered by two 865hp BMW 132N radial engines, established a series of speed records in 1938 over 1,000 and 2,000km courses at an average speed of 205mph. Having entered Luftwaffe service later that year the He 115, which had a maximum range of over 2,000 miles, was exported to Norway and Sweden before the outbreak of the Second World War. Initially delivered to BOAC at Hythe, the He 115s were never issued with civil registrations, but were given RAF serials and modified for clandestine operations by Scottish Aviation at Prestwick in February 1941. The modifications comprised the removal of much of the cockpit transparency and replacement of the two-forward firing 7.9mm MG 15 machine-guns by eight .303in Browning machine-guns in the wings, four of them firing aft! Painted in RAF camouflage with matt black undersides, He 115A BV185 was ferried to Calshot, near Southampton, by its Norwegian pilot, Lt Håkon Offerdahl, on 14 June and one week later left for Gibraltar.

Offerdahl slipped into Malta's Kalafrana Harbour at dusk on 23 June to join 'Z' Flight, which had been formed at the end of 1940 with the former Vichy Loire 130 and Laté 298 seaplanes in RAF markings. Tasked with transporting agents into and out of North Africa, their French crews had moved into No. 261 Squadron's sergeants' mess. Although the Laté was well suited to long-range covert flights, Duvauchelle and Mehouas left to convert to Martin Maryland reconnaissance aircraft in early 1941. Both the French seaplanes were powered by the same 880hp Hispano-Suiza V12 liquid-cooled engine, but spares soon became a problem and when the Loire was damaged by shrapnel while moored at Marsaxlokk Bay, the He 115 was sent out to replace them. Its first two clandestine missions to North Africa took place on the nights of 2 and 3 July, both of some two hours' duration. Only a week later, the Heinkel was damaged when its hangar at Kalafrana was hit during an Italian air raid. Offerdahl returned to England and, following repairs, the floatplane was test flown by Georges Blaize and Raoul Gatien on 3 September.

The RAF's 'Z' Flight was not the only unit transporting agents across the Mediterranean. With the Heinkel out of action, Malta's AOC, AVM Hugh Pughe Lloyd, requested that a detachment of 830 Squadron Fleet Air Arm, comprising a single Fairey Swordfish biplane, be based at Hal Far airfield to transport French agents to North Africa.

Affectionately known as the 'Stringbag', the single-engined, three-seat torpedo bomber first flew in 1934 and equipped a dozen front-line Fleet Air Arm squadrons at the outbreak of the Second World War. Despite a maximum speed of little over 100mph, the Swordfish's ability to absorb punishment, fly in

A rare shot of the former Vichy Navy Latécoère 298B used for clandestine flights from Malta to North Africa in 1941, attached to No. 230 Squadron at Kalafrana; one of its Sunderlands is seen here. *(NWMA)*

all weathers and stay in the air for up to 8 hours made it almost irreplaceable. Designed to operate from small escort carriers, this extraordinary aircraft had a short take-off and landing performance to rival that of the Lysander.

Col Bertram Ede, the local SOE spymaster based in Valletta, briefed the Swordfish's pilot, Lt Charles Lamb, and his observer, Sub-Lt John Robertson, for a covert operation to North Africa on the night of 28 August. Their precise mission was to fly to the small Tunisian coastal town of Enfidaville, near the Gulf of Hammamet, to pick up two agents who were being pursued by Vichy authorities, and fly them back to Malta – a round trip of over 500 miles.

This was at the extreme of the Stringbag's range so it was decided to carry ten five-gallon cans in the air gunner's rear cockpit, refuel on landing and drop the empty cans into the sea during the flight back to Malta. At the last minute Lamb was told that he would have to carry two agents out to Tunisia, both of whom had to be shoehorned into the rear cockpit of the three-seat Swordfish along with the petrol cans. They had a long, uncomfortable flight from Hal Far to a field on the outskirts of Enfidaville. As the two agents disappeared into the darkness, Lamb and Robertson poured the petrol into the Swordfish's main tank mounted behind the hot Pegasus engine. They then began an agonizingly long wait before their passengers eventually arrived. As soon as they were spotted in the distance, Lamb fired up the engine and taxied towards them. Robertson hauled them into the rear cockpit and, despite sinking up to the wheel hubs in the soft sand, the Swordfish made a successful take-off and return flight to Hal Far. Less than two years later a large airfield was built at Enfidaville for RAF Baltimore medium bomber squadrons of the Desert Air Force.

Lamb and Robertson subsequently flew several other covert missions, but on 16 September they were briefed for what would be their last clandestine flight into Vichy North Africa. It was to land a French Arab leader, and his bicycle, on a dry salt lake near Sousse, 25 miles south of Enfidaville. For this trip the Swordfish carried an underslung long-range tank, similar to that fitted to the Lysander Mk III (SD), and after collecting the crew's escape gear – which included Tunisian money and a first-aid kit – and the agent, they took off from Hal Far at 0200 hours on 17 September. The salt lake proved easy to spot as it glowed in the moonlight and, despite Lamb's reservations about how dry the lake actually was, he decided to land.

As it touched down, the Swordfish promptly slithered to a halt on the anything but dry surface. As its wheels dug into deep mud the biplane almost somersaulted, but stopped with its tail waving in the air and nose buried in the slime. The three occupants managed to scramble clear to dry land, where the agent was met by a group of armed Arabs and made a hasty retreat – without his bicycle. Lamb and Robertson crawled back through the mud to set fire to the slime-covered aircraft. They failed and set off to rendezvous with a rescue seaplane that would be dispatched to pick them up in Hammamet Bay, some 25 miles from the salt lake, if they had not returned to Malta on time. That rescue aircraft was 'Z' Flight's He 115. Tired and hungry, as they had inadvertently left their escape rations in the aircraft, Lamb and Robertson walked into an Arab village where they were given food and drink. However, while they were enjoying the local headman's hospitality, their arrival was being reported to the local Vichy police. The pilot and observer were quickly arrested and escorted to a prison cell in Sousse, from where they listened to the Heinkel circling over-head several times during the following night.

After lengthy and often painful interrogations by the Deuxième Bureau, Lamb and Robertson spent 18 months in Vichy prison camps, without revealing the nature of their ill-fated last mission. During their internment they learned that the 'Z' Flight Heinkel had been lost while setting out again to search for the missing British airmen at Hammamet Bay. After taking off from Kalafrana at midnight on 21 September, the He 115 lost power and crashed into the sea some 20 miles off the Maltese coast, breaking up in the high seas. Georges

Blaize, his observer Robert Gatien, and FAA observer Sub-Lt Reg Drake all lost their lives in the accident. On the night of 29 October, Lt Offerdahl returned to Malta with Lt Bibbie in another former Norwegian He 115. BV187 was flown from RAF Mount Batten in two days, a total flight time of 19 hours 5 minutes. After flying its first operation to North Africa in November, Offendahl left Malta for the last time on 23 December in a No. 138 Squadron Halifax.

While 'Z' Flight was starting its clandestine operations in the Mediterranean, other German agents were continuing to be parachuted into England. SS Oberst Karl Richard Richter was dropped by a Kommando Rowehl He 111 from Chartres on 14 May and landed near Tyttenhangar Park in Hertfordshire, close to Salisbury Hall at London Colney where the ultra-secret prototype DH Mosquito was being built. A local reserve constable found him in a telephone booth, after a lorry driver had reported that he had been stopped by a man who had asked him directions in a foreign accent. Constable Alex Scott was shown an Alien's Registration Card in the name of Fred Snyder and suggested that the man accompany him to the police station, as it was approaching 2300 hours, when all aliens were required to be at their registered addresses.

Twenty-nine-year-old Snyder was searched at the police station and found to be carrying a Swedish passport in the name of Karl Richter. MI5 was alerted and the next day Richter was taken to Hatfield police station to be interviewed by several MI5 officers, including Col Stephens. He soon caved in, admitted his real name and offered to show them where he had hidden his parachute and other items. Accompanied by policemen and MI5 personnel, Richter took them to the hedge in Tyttenhangar Park. Apart from the parachute they found a loaded Mauser pistol, a quantity of money, documents, a wireless transmitter, batteries and some spare valves. Also a Czech passport in the name of Karel Richter was discovered. His story was that he had been trying to make his way to the United States, but was captured in Sweden and deported to Germany, where he was recruited by the Abwehr and sent to England as a courier. The tall, thin, red-headed Richter was tried at the Old Bailey on 21 October 1941 and executed at Wandsworth prison on 10 December, without ever having revealed the true nature of his mission.

Apart from providing convenient cover for Abwehr agents, neutral Sweden was of vital importance to the British war effort and air links between the two countries had to be maintained at all costs. In 1941 former Norwegian NAS crews joined BOAC to fly hazardous missions transporting 'diplomats' to the important SIS station and, after June 1941, to the Soviet NVKD network in Stockholm, and provide access for British newspapers to counteract German propaganda. Sweden was also one of the world's leading producers of high-quality ball bearings, a product much in demand by all the combatants. After a number of false starts, a regular courier service was opened from Leuchars in Fife to Stockholm's Bromma airport in February 1941, using converted Armstrong-Whitworth Whitley V bombers. At the same time the Swedish airline ABA established a risky courier shuttle between Stockholm and Aberdeen, using Douglas DC-3s taken from the regular airline service. They transported mail, crucial war materials and passengers, among them industrialists, diplomats and agents.

The limited range of the BOAC Whitleys and the ABA DC-3s forced them to choose a direct flight path over the heavily guarded Skagerrak Strait between occupied Norway and Denmark. Although the distance between Scotland and Sweden was less than 1,000 miles weather conditions often ranged from bad to impossible, while the unarmed transports were forced to run the gauntlet of German fighters based in Denmark and Norway. To avoid detection, the unpressurised aircraft flew at night and as high as the passengers could endure to arrive at Bromma at dawn; but it was soon clear that passenger aircraft with a better performance were required. Initially these proved to be five Lodestar airliners owned by the Norwegian government in exile and contracted to BOAC. The Lockheed 18 Lodestar, a larger, faster development of the pre-war Super Electra used by Sidney Cotton's PDU missions over the Soviet Union, had accommodation for three crew and fourteen passengers, a top speed of 250mph and a range of almost 2,000 miles.

Flown by former Naval Air Service crews, including Cdrs Finn Lambrechts and Håkon Jorgensen – the latter having flown one of the NAS He 115s to Sullom Voe – the Lodestar was introduced into service on the Scotland-to-Sweden run on the night of 18 August 1941. Although never a Special Duties unit, the Norwegian Lodestars would also provide a vital lifeline for SOE agents and RAF SD aircrews who had escaped to Sweden after being shot down over Norway.

In order to cope with growing demand for its services from both SIS and SOE, the RAF's only unit tasked with the carriage of secret agents, No. 1419 Flight, became No. 138 (Special Duties) Squadron on 25 August as part of No. 3 Group, Bomber Command. Commanded by Wg Cdr Farley, the new squadron had an establishment of two Lysander IIIA (SD)s, ten Whitley Vs, an American Martin Maryland II, and three newly delivered, four-engined Handley Page Halifax II bombers.

Sqn Ldr John Nesbitt-Dufort, the commander of 'B' Flight's Lysanders, flew the new squadron's first pick-up from France on the evening of 4 September. Son of a French father and a Scottish mother, he had been commissioned as a

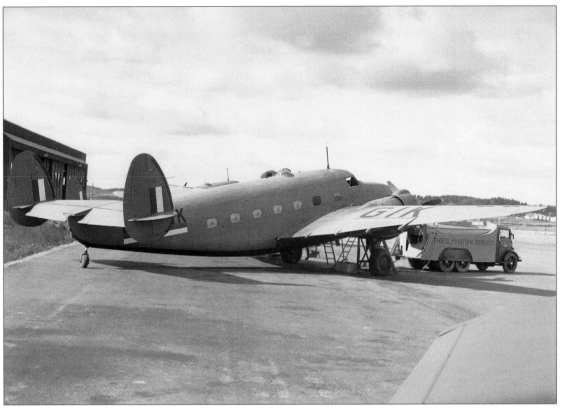

One of the Norwegian Lodestars loaned to BOAC and flown by NAS crews on the Leuchars to Stockholm route, at Bromma airport in Sweden. *(Bo Widfeldt)*

regular officer in 1930, and was languishing as an RAF flying instructor at the outbreak of war when he persuaded his superiors to post him to somewhere that was closer to the action. Too old to retrain as a fighter pilot, 'Whippy' Nesbitt-Dufort found himself at Sawbridgeworth, where for the next few weeks he practised getting a Lysander airborne from a muddy field in less than 40 yards. He had earned his nickname some years earlier after losing several trainee pilots on a cross-country exercise, when they had ended up making emergency landings in Whipsnade Zoo.

For his first operational mission Nesbitt-Dufort flew from Ford aerodrome on the south coast of Sussex, a few miles east of Tangmere. Here he picked up SOE agent Maj Gerard Morel, a former insurance broker who had been captured in early 1940 when serving as a French Army liaison officer attached to a British regiment. After he had suffered a serious illness the Germans released Morel from the prison camp, expecting him to die. However, by sheer will-power, he was able to make a tortuous journey back to England via Spain and Brazil almost a year later.

Having identified the designated landing field at La Champenoise, near Châteauroux, Nesbitt-Dufort circled for 15 long minutes waiting for the code letter to be flashed. When he eventually spotted the signal, it came from a different location some fields away. Not wishing to waste any more time, he headed straight for the dim flarepath, to find that not only was there barely enough room to land but taking off from the short, rutted field would be a bigger problem. After Morel had changed places with a fellow 'F' Section officer, Maj Jacques de Guélis, Nesbitt-Dufort selected full power. Although the Lysander avoided the trees at the edge of the field, it hit telephone wires and a high-tension cable, which snapped with a blinding flash that ruined the pilot's night vision. Almost as soon as he was safely airborne, Nesbitt-Dufort had to throw the Lysander into a steep diving turn to avoid prowling German night fighters, but eventually managed to land at Tangmere in the morning fog, trailing a length of French telephone wire from his undercarriage. During the return flight, his passenger told Nesbitt-Dufort that he had been delayed by a police checkpoint and when he heard the circling Lysander, while pedalling furiously on a borrowed bicycle, had chosen the nearest field, which turned out to be half the size of the intended landing ground.

Up until then dropping by parachute was the preferred method of inserting agents into occupied Europe, more so for the RAF than the agents. Jean Le Harivel, the 23-year-old son of an English father and a French mother, was a

The first RAF type dedicated to parachuting agents into occupied Europe was the AW Whitley V assigned to No. 1419 Flight, formed in March 1941. (ww2 images)

gunner with the Middlesex Regiment when he volunteered to be trained as an SOE wireless operator. Dropped over southern France for the first time in September 1941, he described the experience.

When we left the Nissen hut, walking from there to the aircraft, we were not very comfortable because the parachute was heavy and we felt rather tight in this stuff. Our emotions were a bit mixed, glad to get off at long last, but thinking, what the devil is going to happen to us once we get there? The plane was an old Whitley bomber stripped of everything inside. I remember feeling very cold, but the RAF escort officer was very kind and he had a Thermos of hot coffee which helped.

The flight was not very long. The Whitley was a slow, twin-engined bomber with a very wide wing that helped it slow down just before you jumped. This period is of course crucial. The pilot warned the dispatcher that we were coming near the dropping area, but unfortunately the people on the ground hadn't given a recognisable code. They had torches and had to signal two letters in Morse, but as we didn't receive the correct signal, the dispatcher was not satisfied and we went round, oh I think two or three times, before we were given the all-clear. This was a light which turned from red to green and when it was green you had to jump.

There was a hole in the floor and you jumped two at a time, one – two, very quickly. The curious thing about jumping is that the sensation as you leave the plane is fantastic; you're on a current of air, you don't drop suddenly, you drop gently for about three seconds and then the chute opens and you drop slowly. I can still remember the drop as if it were yesterday. It was a full moon, beautiful scenery, there was a large field and trees all around. The countryside was absolutely wonderful and I remember for a few seconds just admiring the view, not thinking about the actual jump.

After that, it was not so amusing because my chute decided to go slowly towards some trees. Luckily I remembered the sergeant at Ringway saying that if ever you have to jump into trees, keep your blooming legs together – actually he didn't say blooming – but luckily I remembered that and kept them together as I fell into a tree. I then had to get down to the ground, not too difficult but not that pleasant.

After managing to struggle to the ground and make contact with the reception committee, who took him to a safe house, Le Harivel was arrested within a week, but later escaped from a prison camp and eventually returned to England via Spain and Gibraltar.

With Bomber Command releasing the first of its war-weary Halifaxes to be converted for dropping agents, the days of the elderly Whitleys with No. 138 (SD) Squadron were numbered. Powered by four Rolls-Royce Merlin engines, the Halifax B Mk II heavy bomber had a maximum speed of 265mph and a range of more than 1,500 miles. With their service ceiling limited to 18,000ft, Bomber Command Halifaxes proved easy targets for German night fighters, but they were to prove ideal for the low-level SD operations. The aircraft's capacious fuselage added a comfort factor for those agents and dispatchers carried over long distances into enemy territory, and its large bomb bay could accommodate up to 5 tons of supplies and equipment. The first aircraft issued to the Squadron's 'A' Flight were hastily converted for Special Duties missions by the Airborne Forces Establishment at Ringway. These modifications included a para-dropping hatch cut into the bottom of the fuselage aft of the bomb bay, and having the tailwheel shrouded to avoid static lines from snagging.

SOE was anxious to expand its networks into eastern Europe, and Poland in particular, and the Halifax was seen as the ideal aircraft for such operations. Poland's government-in-exile, led by Gen Wladyslaw Sikorski, who was also Commander-in-Chief of the powerful Free Polish Forces from 1939, had negotiated a Soviet–Polish alliance following the German invasion of Russia in 1941. In return for releasing intelligence to the British government, Gen Sikorski pressed for a Polish flight to be formed as part of No. 138 Squadron.

As the first Polish pilots were transferred to the squadron from Bomber Command units, Whippy Nesbitt-Dufort was on another mission to France, to pick up a Polish Air Force officer codenamed Armand. Capt Roman Czerniawski – with the assistance of Lt Roger Mitchell, a Franco-Scottish gunnery officer codenamed Adam and one of his agents, a French Air Force officer – had selected an abandoned aerodrome near Compiègne for the pick-up. On the night of 1 October Nesbitt-Dufort had no problem finding the aerodrome in the bright moonlight and within minutes Armand had climbed aboard the Lysander and was in the air heading for Ford. While waiting in the officers' mess at Ford, the Polish agent almost gave away his point of embarkation to resident squadron aircrews by reading a copy of the previous day's *Paris Soir* newspaper. He was met by SIS agent Phillip Schneidau, who introduced himself as 'Flt Lt Phillipson', an RAF liaison officer who promptly whisked him away to London to meet British and Polish intelligence officers, before being decorated with the Order of Virtuti Militari by Gen Sikorski himself. Capt Czerniawski was parachuted back into occupied France from a No. 138 Squadron Whitley a week later.

One of No. 138 Squadron's new Halifaxes crash-landed at Tommelilla in Sweden on the night of 7 November. Operation 'Ruction' was the first SOE

Wg Cdr Roman Rudkowski's No. 138 Squadron Halifax crash-landed at Tommelilla in Sweden after running out of fuel during Operation Ruction on 8 November 1941. *(Bo Widfeldt)*

mission to be flown by a Polish crew and, following strong headwinds and severe icing, the Halifax ran low on fuel following a drop mission over Poland. Wg Cdr Rudkowski and his crew were unharmed, and set fire to the stricken aircraft before surrendering to the Swedish police. Roman Rudkowski was a former commanding officer of No. 301 (Pomorski) Squadron, one of two Polish Bomber Command squadrons flying Wellingtons, before being transferred to the Polish General Staff headquarters to organise air assistance to the Polish Underground Army. Three months after his unscheduled arrival in Sweden, he and his crew were flown back to Scotland in one of BOAC's Norwegian-crewed Lodestars.

Another RAF pilot was about to play a unique role in the Polish resistance movement. Sgt Keith Chisholm of No. 452 (RAAF) Squadron, based at Kirton-in-Lindsey in Lincolnshire, was an Australian fighter ace with six victories to his credit when he was shot down. He baled out of his Spitfire VB on 12 October off the coast of France and was picked up by a German air-sea rescue launch. After six months in a prison camp he escaped into Czechoslovakia, but was betrayed by a civilian who had offered him hospitality; he ended up in Stalag VIIIB at Lamsdorf near the German–Polish border, where his fellow prisoners included the legless RAF ace, Douglas Bader.

In August 1942 he escaped again with two others, one of whom was a Palestinian who spoke fluent Polish. The three of them crossed the Polish border and soon made contact with the local Resistance. Chisholm was to spend a year fighting with the Polish Underground Army, during which time both of his fellow escapees were captured and shot by the Germans. His covert battle ended with the Warsaw Uprising, after which he made his way across Europe to join the French Forces of the Interior (FFI) to fight with them against the Germans on the streets of Paris until the arrival of the Allied forces in August 1944. He was awarded the Military Cross for his exploits with the resistance forces.

Towards the end of 1941, SOE was reaching further afield to countries in occupied eastern Europe. On 7 November No. 138 Squadron made its first drop into Yugoslavia, which had capitulated in April after an uprising in Belgrade against a puppet government had been crushed by the Germans in an operation codenamed Punishment. This mission had been flown by Flg Off Austin using Whitley Z9158 on detachment at Luqa in Malta, its agents tasked with making contact with the Chetniks, a guerrilla force supported by Yugoslavia's ousted ruler King Peter and his London-based government. Earlier there had been an attempt to pick up an SOE agent from occupied Greece, which fell to the Germans only days after Yugoslavia, and fly him to Malta. Flt Lt T.F. 'Ginger' Neil, an ace with twelve confirmed victories, took off from Ta Kali on 17 August in a No. 249 Squadron Hurricane IIC with orders to meet a Blenheim flying from Greece with the SOE agent aboard. No contact was made, and there is no record of the aircraft or the agent having been heard of again.

During the December moon period No. 138 Squadron flew only a single pick-up mission, one that almost ended in disaster. Operation 'Stoat' began at 2210 hours on 8 December when Flt Lt A.M. Murphy, an athletic Irish extrovert known to all as 'Sticky', took off from Tangmere heading for a field near Neufchâteau in Belgium. Once over the Channel, Murphy flew low to avoid German radar. As the coast of France loomed up he climbed swiftly to 3,000 feet, a height good enough to pinpoint landmarks, too high for light flak and too low for the heavy stuff. Two hours later he brought the Lysander down to 1,000 feet to circle the snow-covered landing field looking for an identity letter to be flashed by the agent, Jean Cassart, a captain in the Belgian Air Force.

Murphy did see a light flashing in an adjacent field and, although it was not the correct letter, he got the impression that the agent was in danger and decided to land without a flarepath. He switched on the landing light and put the nose down. As he was about to touch down, he noticed what looked like a ditch in his path. Cursing the agent in charge of selecting the landing site, he overshot and went around again. On his next approach he tried the eastern side of the field but before landing he loosened his revolver. There was something suspicious about this operation. His landing was perfect but as the aircraft rolled to a standstill, Murphy was blinded by a searchlight. At the same instant a shot rang out, hitting the pilot in the neck. Sticky did several things at once. He dropped his revolver, held one of his wife's stockings – which he carried for good luck – to his bleeding neck and opened the throttle. The Lysander accelerated towards a row of trees at the end of the field. Murphy hauled gently back on the stick with his only free hand, missing the treetops by inches to arrive back safely at Tangmere with thirty bullet holes in the Lysander, but no passenger.

On the ground Cassart and his wireless operator Henri Verhaegen had run into a German patrol, guided to the field by information beaten out of a captured Resistance member. Jean was hit in the arm during the exchange of fire and Verhaegen was caught by one of the German soldiers, but managed to shake himself free and make his escape. A party of more than 20 Jagdkommandos had surrounded the field, some within 30 yards of the Murphy's Lysander, and more than 100 shots had been fired during the encounter. The wounded Cassart was captured a few days later and taken to Berlin by the Gestapo, but he too managed to escape and make his way back to England several months later.

Murphy's close encounter coincided with an event that would ultimately change the whole course of the Second World War: the Japanese attack on the US Navy base at Pearl Harbor on 7 December. Adm John Godfrey, Britain's Director of Naval Intelligence, and his assistant Cdr Ian Fleming, had flown to New York on the PanAm flying boat *Dixie Clipper* earlier in the year to meet the newly appointed head of a new American civilian agency.

William J. Donovan's Office of Coordinator of Information (COI) would collect, collate and disseminate all intelligence relating to US national security, and both parties were anxious to pave the way for a more open system of exchanging international intelligence between their two countries. This had now become a much higher priority. With America's declaration of war on Japan and the Axis members Germany and Italy, Churchill now had the one ally he had been hoping for, and the liberation of occupied Europe might become a reality. Resistance forces were to be encouraged and sustained by all means possible.

SOE was ordered to take a more aggressive role, with sabotage and assassination becoming part of its remit in addition to those of surveillance and gathering intelligence. One of No. 138 Squadron's last operations of the year was flown on the night of 28/29 December when two Czech SOE agents, Jan Kubic and Josef Gabcik, were dropped into Czechoslovakia from Ron Hockey's Halifax II. The object of Operation 'Anthropoid' was to assassinate the brutal Reich Protector of Bohemia-Moravia, Obergruppenführer Reinhard Heydrich. Dropped with the agents were two containers containing automatic pistols, a Sten gun, Mills bombs and plastic explosive.

After many false starts, the assassination attempt eventually took place on the outskirts of Prague on 27 May 1942. Heydrich was fatally wounded by splinters from a Mills bomb and died from his injuries five days later. The two SOE agents were cornered in the crypt of a Prague church and, having run out of ammunition after a prolonged gun battle, committed suicide. As part of a campaign of terrible reprisals, the Germans destroyed the nearby Czech villages of Lidice and Lezaky, shot all the male inhabitants, sent the women to concentration camps and the children to German institutions. Despite the appalling human cost, Operation Anthropoid was nevertheless hailed as one of the SOE's first successes.

By the end of 1941 No. 138 (SD) Squadron had moved its twelve Whitleys, three Halifaxes and three Lysanders back to Stradishall, having transported a total of thirty-seven agents to France and picked up five during the year. The number may seem small, but in the first full year of SOE operations it was a period of trial and error, which saw 55 per cent of its flights fail owing to bad weather or non-contact with reception committees. In May 1941 an Air Ministry staff officer had estimated that it would require some 2,000 sorties a year to support the 45,000 resistance fighters in western Europe alone. There was much to do.

CHAPTER 4

New Branches of 'The Firm'

While Britain's Special Operations Executive was building the foundations of an underground army that would set Europe ablaze, the Germans were also involved in a series of clandestine operations, one of which would set parts of Free French territory ablaze.

Although Operation 'Lena', the insertion of German agents into the British Isles, remained the responsibility of the Kommando Rowehl, some of its Staffeln were divided into small, self-contained units called Sonderkommandos and were named after the Hauptmann or Oberleutnant in charge. One of these operated in the deserts of northern Africa. A unit commanded by Hauptmann Theo Blaich had been conducting missions from remote airfields deep in the Libyan desert at Hun, some 400 miles south of Tripoli, and at Sebha, 250 miles south of Hun, against the sporadic attacks by 'L' Detachment, SAS Brigade, and the British Long Range Desert Groups (LRDG). These British commando units conducted surgical sabotage strikes against German targets such as ammunition dumps, fuel dumps, radio stations, airfields and other non-front-line units and facilities. One of the main bases for British LRDG operations was the Free French airfield at Fort Lamy on the banks of Lake Chad, which also formed part of the RAF's vital trans-African aircraft ferry route stretching from Lagos to Cairo.

On 21 January 1942, Sonderkommando Blaich's He 111H, flown by Leutnant Bohnsack, flew nearly 400 miles south from Hun to a desert landing strip at Bir Misciuro. The Heinkel was escorted by an Italian Savoia Marchetti SM-82 carrying fuel drums, and a three-seat Messerschmitt Bf 108B liaison aircraft with Hauptmann Blaich at the controls. At Bir Misciuro, codenamed Campo Uno, the He 111 was refuelled by hand with fuel brought by the SM-82 and, loaded with sixteen 50-kilogram bombs, took off at dawn the next morning heading south towards Fort Lamy.

Its navigator, Feldwebel Geisler, had to navigate by dead reckoning, as there were no radio stations that the bomber could use as a source for a direction-finding (D/F) check. Consequently, after flying for some hours, he discovered that they were more than 100 miles off course. However, it was still possible to

A Bf 108 Taifun four-seat communications aircraft was used by Sonderkommando Blaich for a clandestine raid on Fort Lamy on Lake Chad in January 1942. *(ww2 images)*

find Fort Lamy, located where the Schari and Lougone rivers merge at Lake Chad. The He 111 turned to the west and flew until it reached the Schari river, along which it flew to approach the fort for its bombing run. Soon after noon, the airfield and supply dump at Fort Lamy were spotted dead ahead from the Heinkel, which was flying at an altitude of 1,500 feet. Although their arrival attracted no anti-aircraft fire, there was time for only one low-level attack. Its bombs hit the fuel-dump at the edge of the field and the resulting explosions set fire to a number of Free French aircraft parked on the airfield, sending up a thick column of smoke.

As the He 111 headed north for the return flight, it was obvious that, owing to its long detour in reaching the target, it would not have enough fuel to reach Campo Uno. The crew calculated that they could reach only a point some 200 miles short of their destination. The flight engineer leaned the air–fuel mixture out as far as was possible and set the engines at 1,950 rpm. As predicted, radio contact with the Italians had been lost on the outward leg and it still could not be re-established. At about 1800 hours, as the sun set, Leutnant Bohnsack spotted a level, high plateau approximately 160 miles south of Campo Uno and carefully set the Heinkel down for a good landing on the firm sand. They had only about 20 litres of water left for the five-man crew, which included an Italian pre-war desert explorer, Maj Conte Vimercat-Sanvertono. The radio operator, Unteroffizier Wichmann, managed to set up on the plateau a 3-Watt Quartz-agenten radio antenna, which he extended with tent poles. Fortunately, because of its long range on 6197 KHZ, radio contact was established with a Fliegerführer Afrika radio operator in Benghazi, over 650 miles away. However, they were still unable to establish any radio contact with the nearby Italians. After three days Benghazi told them that it had contacted the Italians, who had launched a search flight.

When they had still not been found by day five, the German crew decided to transmit a D/F signal on the Heinkel's radio. It was fortunate that the pilot had landed the He 111 with some fuel left in the tanks, because an engine had to be run so that its generator could power the radio circuits. Sending the D/F signal worked almost immediately and an Italian Ca 309 landed at the site within an hour of making contact, bringing water and melons. At dawn the following day a Junkers Ju 52 arrived, bringing the stranded crew more water and fuel for their aircraft. Shortly afterwards the German bomber climbed into the air to complete its 1,500-mile mission. The He 111 flew to Campo Uno, where it was refuelled again before returning to Hun. Sonderkommando Blaich continued its LRDG search-and-destroy sorties with the He 111 until June 1942, when it crash-landed near Kufra oasis following an engine failure. This time the crew had to wait for only four days before being rescued, but they had to set fire to their trusty Heinkel before they left. The Sonderkommando was disbanded the same month.

Back in beleaguered Britain, a routine for No. 138 (SD) Squadron's Lysander operations to France had been established with a clear line of command and control by the beginning of 1942. When a Resistance group requested supplies or a pick-up, it also chose the landing ground and sent a detailed description and map references to London via the Bureau d'Opérations Aériennes (BOA). Once SOE or SIS approved these requests they were passed to A12(c), a branch of Air Intelligence within the Directorate of Intelligence (Operations) at the Air Ministry. A tasking order was then forwarded to the squadrons and coded messages broadcast to the Resistance group by the BBC's French-language news service. On the afternoon of a flight, agents accompanied by SIS or SOE escort officers – one of whom was Douglas Dodd-Parker, who had exchanged the Abyssinian heights for the corridors of Baker Street – would be driven down to Tangmere fighter station.

By one of the side gates to the airfield was a small country cottage that served as the operational base for 'B' Flight. Here the pilot was issued with the night's

Morse signals and aerial photographs of the landing field provided by the PRU, Sidney Cotton's former unit now based at RAF Benson. Using his 1:250,000 scale map and strips torn from a 1:500,000 scale map marked with prominent landmarks, obstructions and anti-aircraft defences, the pilot worked out his own route and timings. Before take-off, he would brief the agent on the mission, show him over the rear cockpit of the Lysander if it was his first trip, and make sure he knew how to open and securely close the canopy. He would also be instructed on how to wear the Mae West, clip on the parachute, and operate the intercom.

Most of the pilots wore a mixture of civilian clothes underneath their uniform, and carried spare shoes and often a hat, in the aircraft's escape-kit locker. The kit itself comprised forged identity papers, French money, a compass, a map printed on a silk scarf and emergency rations. During the first part of the flight across the Channel the pilot remained in radio contact with Tangmere using the callsign 'Snapper', borrowed from a local night-fighter squadron. He was also tracked by the appropriately named Blackgang radar station on the Isle of Wight and his progress was plotted at Headquarters Fighter Command at Bentley Priory on the outskirts of north London. On reaching the French coast, the Lysander was on its own.

Whippy Nesbitt-Dufort set off on what was to be No. 138 Squadron's last Lysander pick-up sortie in France. The object of Operation 'Beryl' was to carry one agent outbound, and pick up two – Roger Mitchell and Maurice Duclos, whose field name was St Jacques – from a field near Ségry on the night of 28 January. Apart from experiencing icing conditions over the Channel, it was a textbook mission. Nesbitt-Dufort had map-read his way to the landing ground just south of the River Loire, where he landed, off-loaded one 'Joe' and picked up the waiting two. As he climbed towards Fécamp and home, the weather worsened. Flying at a comfortable map-reading height of 1,000 feet, he was forced to fly through squalls at low level as ice formed over the windscreen. Hedge-hopping in blinding rain, he decided to turn back and try to climb above the approaching cold front. The Lysander headed south, deeper into France, and above the first loop in the River Seine Whippy turned again in the direction of the Channel. He was flying on instruments as the aircraft bumped its way up through the dark clouds. Once again a thin film of ice began to creep across the windscreen, but as the craft climbed higher the icing gave way to heavy rain at 7,000 feet. After that more icing, this time serious. With ice building on the leading edges, controls sluggish and the engine losing power, the Lysander wallowed along unable to maintain its height even at full power.

With the aircraft virtually uncontrollable and on the verge of spinning into the ground, Nesbitt-Dufort told his passengers that they would have to jump for it. There was no reply. In the turbulence, the intercom had become disconnected, so there was no option but to attempt a landing back in France and the pilot put the Lysander into a dive. Chunks of ice began cracking off the airframe as the airspeed wound up to 250mph before he pulled out of the dive at 2,500 feet. Cautiously losing more height, the pilot was relieved to see a break in the clouds at less than 1,000 feet. He turned the aircraft towards the west and flew along the edge of the front for nearly 50 miles, but there was no sign of a break in the front.

Five hours later and low on fuel, Nesbitt-Dufort reasoned that if he could find the River Loire again, he could land the two agents back where they started. Another hour had gone by before he picked up the river near Orléans and headed towards Issoudun, looking for any field large enough to land in. He almost made it. Despite his weariness, Whippy managed a good touch-down but struck a hidden ditch in doing so, breaking the undercarriage and tipping the Lysander on to its nose. The three occupants were shaken but not injured, and set about trying to set fire to the sodden aircraft without success.

Nesbitt-Dufort and the two agents managed to put a healthy distance between themselves and the aircraft in as short a time as possible. Dawn found the three men fast asleep in a small roadside hut. Later one of the agents went into the nearest town to make contact with the Resistance, and only a few hours later a car pulled up to the hut in broad daylight to drive the occupants to a nearby safe house. The agents both had forged papers, but Nesbitt-Dufort had nothing and had to stay hidden in the house for almost a month. In the meantime, he learned that members of the Resistance had managed to push the stricken Lysander across a railway line in front of an oncoming train, which comprehensively destroyed it.

Whippy was reported as missing in action, and Dr Hugh Dalton, the first chief of SOE – now commonly known as 'The Firm' – was replaced by Lord Selborne, who coordinated the activities of Military Intelligence (Research), the Department of Propaganda of the Foreign Office and Section 'D' of SIS. One of Selborne's first decisions was to expand the RAF Special Duties squadron, and on 14 February No. 161 (SD) Squadron began forming at Newmarket. Its nucleus came from No. 138 Squadron and from the King's Flight.

Formed in June 1936 at Hendon, with Wg Cdr Edward Fielden as its first captain, the King's Flight comprised an Airspeed Envoy and a Lockheed Hudson (Long Range), officially allocated to No. 24 (Communications) Squadron, at the outbreak of war. When No. 161 Squadron absorbed the King's

Flight, the Hudson was transferred to the new unit and Wg Cdr 'Mouse' Fielden became its first commanding officer. The new squadron's 'A' Flight, commanded by Sqn Ldr Murphy, was equipped with five Lysander IIIA (SD)s, while 'B' Flight had seven Whitley Vs and two Wellington IIs on strength. The Hudson served as the squadron hack.

Operation 'Crème' was its first covert mission, flown on 22 February when a Lysander carried two agents to a field near Villeneuve, north of Châteauroux. It also flew two missions of significance on the night of 1 March. The first was a Lysander pick-up flown by Flg Off W.G. Lockhart, formerly with No. 138 Squadron, and was a relatively straightforward operation to pick up two agents from a farm at Les Lagnys, south of Vatan. Jean Faillon, a member of the local Resistance network, had arranged with the farmer to have this field available throughout the year for clandestine parachute drops or pick-up operations; it would be used by the squadron during five moon periods in 1942 alone.

The second flight of the night was something of a breakthrough: the first pick-up from France using a twin-engined RAF aircraft. Following Whippy Nesbitt-Dufort's eventful landing at Ségry on 28 January, he had remained in hiding until the Resistance received a radio message informing them that an aircraft was scheduled to collect the pilot and the two agents who would have flown back with him in his Lysander. The aircraft chosen for Operation 'Beryl III' was Avro Anson T.1 R3316, a navigation trainer borrowed from a local Bomber Command Operational Training Unit (OTU) and painted black. Its pilot Sticky Murphy was accompanied by navigator Plt Off Henry 'Titch' Cossar. They took off from Tangmere at 2100 hours heading for the original landing field at Ségry, which was not reached until 0010 hours; they had been totally lost for more than an hour in thick cloud and driving rain. Whippy and the two agents, plus a fourth passenger, the Polish Gen Julius Kleeberg, codenamed Tudor, fell into the back of the aircraft as soon as it landed. A few minutes later the Anson, nicknamed 'Gormless Gertie' by its crew, splashed its way across the wet field at a steady trot before finally climbing slowly towards Dieppe on the French coast and a landing at Tangmere.

This proved to be Sqn Ldr John Nesbitt-Dufort's last flight with the squadron, as he was subsequently posted to HQ Fighter Command, on the same day that the squadron moved to RAF Graveley – but its stay there was to be a short one. Both SD squadrons were about to move to an airfield of their own. In July 1940 contractors John Laing and Balfour Beatty commenced construction of an RAF Class 'A' standard airfield on land known as Tempsford Flats, near Sandy in Bedfordshire. In January 1942 Wellington IIIs of No. 109 Squadron's HQ and Wireless Development Flight moved in to begin secret trials of Oboe radio direction-finding (RDF) equipment. Tempsford's clandestine career had begun.

No. 138 Squadron transferred its aircraft from Stradishall and Newmarket to RAF Tempsford for the first time on 11 March. As well as having its own operations and briefing rooms, maintenance hangars, motor transport, crew rooms and accommodation for squadron personnel, the new airfield was dedicated to covert operations. Secure communications had been established with SOE and SIS sections in Baker Street. A container-packing facility and agent-holding centre were set up at Gaynes Hall near St Neots, while staff and agents were accommodated at Hasells Hall, near the airfield on the road to Sandy. Buildings at Gibraltar Farm on the airfield's eastern perimeter were converted into high-security SOE stores, while the farmhouse served as an agent reception and pre-flight preparation centre.

Although Tempsford was off the beaten track, LNER's main-line railway to Scotland ran along its eastern perimeter, and the area was particularly liable to fog. However, by 18 March 138 Squadron was ready to mount its first operation from the airfield, a drop into northern France from a Whitley. Tempsford became totally devoted to Special Duties operations when No. 161 Squadron moved from Graveley on 10 April, while its Lysander detachment remained at Tangmere using the cottage as operations-cum-crew room for the pilots and agents in transit.

It was from here that Operation 'Baccarat II' was launched on 26 March. Guy Lockhart flew Col Renault-Roulier, codenamed Rémy, back to a field to the south of Saumur where two of his important Confrérie Notre-Dame network agents, Christian Pineau and François Faure, were to be picked up. Unfortunately Lockhart had overshot the flarepath and the Lysander became stuck in a ploughed field. It would take the reception committee and the three agents, plus the Lysander's Mercury engine at full power, almost 20 minutes to free the aircraft's wheels. Lockhart had a reputation at London bridge clubs of being a successful gambler, and he must have recognised that the odds he and the members of the Resistance faced, as he continued to rev his engine, were extremely poor. In the event, he got away without being discovered and returned safely to Tangmere.

Deliveries to No. 138 Squadron of the first Halifax IIs modified to carry metal supply containers had begun. Six-foot-long, C-type metal containers, divided into three compartments, were packed with weapons, ammunition, explosives and other heavy equipment requested by Resistance groups and were loaded into the aircraft's bomb bay. The Halifax could hold fifteen loaded containers weighing up to 250lb each, three more than the Whitley. By this time all the Halifax crews of 'C' Flight were Polish. As operations mounted –

An RAF Special Duties Halifax dropping six-foot-long C-type supply containers, fifteen of which could be carried in its bomb bay. *(Bruce Robertson)*

the SD Lysanders were now flying more sorties per month than they had flown in the whole of 1941 – so did losses. No. 138 Squadron lost another Halifax flown by its commanding Officer, Wg Cdr Farley, on 20 April. Making one of his infrequent operational flights, he and his Polish crew were carrying a group of Soviet NKVD agents to a drop zone in Austria when Halifax V9976 disappeared over Czechoslovakia in poor weather.

After the German invasion of the Soviet Union the previous June, an SOE mission had been established in Moscow and an agreement had been reached whereby agents of the Soviet People's Commissariat for Internal Affairs, the NKVD, could be dropped into occupied eastern Europe by RAF aircraft. The Soviets were desperately short of transport aircraft of any sort, even to support their own front-line troops. However, Lavrenty Beria, the feared head of the NKVD, was also responsible for partisan activities behind enemy lines and he virtually requisitioned the whole of the Soviet national airline, Aeroflot, to support the Soviet Army's covert operations.

Since July 1941 Polikarpov R-5, R-Z and Po-2 biplanes of the para-military GVF, a civil aviation organisation, had been integrated into operational detachments to liaise with partisans to carry or parachute agents and saboteurs behind enemy lines. The GVF units came to prominence during the desperate battles for Leningrad and its Lyuban pocket supply line in the summer of 1942.

The only way to reach the Soviet Second Assault Army, trapped behind German lines, was from the air using GVF biplanes and a detachment of 1 Transport Aviation Division (TAD) equipped with Soviet-built DC-3s, the PS-84. Maj Valentina Grizodubova, one of the most famous female Soviet pilots, commanded the detachment, part of the newly created Long Range Aviation (ADD). Daughter of Russian aviation pioneer Stepan Grizodubova, she was a pre-war flying school director and had been appointed a Hero of the Soviet Union after setting the world women's long-range air record in 1938. Valentina and two female crew members flew a giant, Tupolev-designed twin-engined ANT-37 named *Rodina* (Motherland) non-stop from Moscow to crash-land in a flooded valley at Amur in Siberia, a distance of 3,700 miles, in 26hr 29min.

Based at Khvoynaya airfield, the PS-84s of her detachment ran the gauntlet of experienced Luftwaffe night-fighter units, dropping their vital cargoes to the beleaguered troops from as low as 150 feet. More than ten were lost in the three-week operation, plus countless biplanes. PS-84s of the Moscow Aviation Group – Special Purposes of the Soviet Civil Air Fleet (MAGON GVF), later named the 10th Guards Transport Aviation Division – would remain virtually the only long-range aircraft to be used for covert NKVD operations.

It was now becoming obvious that Soviet forces would have to rely heavily on partisan groups operating behind the lines while the country re-equipped and gave new leadership to its demoralised regular forces. This decision led to the production of a military assault glider for landing partisans behind German lines, the A-7. Of wooden construction with fabric-covered wings and control surfaces, the spacious, streamlined glider could accommodate up to ten troops, with access through two sets of double doors. Towed by an SB-2 or DB-3 bomber, the A-7 featured a hand-cranked retractable undercarriage, and was the first design by Oleg Antonov, the Moscow Glider Factory's chief engineer before the war, to be put into quantity production.

It was during this period that Army Oberstleutnant Reinhard Gehlen was appointed head of the German OKH intelligence agency, responsible for gathering information on the Soviet Army. For this he built up an extensive network of anti-communist Russian agents and instigated the establishment of special detachments, known as Zeppelin Sonderkommandos, to undertake espionage and other clandestine operations in the east.

While the Halifaxes continued their long-range missions into eastern Europe, No. 161 Squadron lost its first Lysander, but not the pilot or his passenger. Flt Lt A.J. Mott made a routine landing in the field at Ségry in the early hours of 29 May with a Belgian MI9 agent on his way to join the Pat escape organization. Alex Nitelet was a former fighter pilot who had arrived in England at the end of 1940, was accepted for RAF pilot training and posted in August 1941 to de Grunne's old Squadron, No. 609, which had an all-Belgian flight.

On his first 'Circus' sortie, escorting bombers to France, Nitelet claimed a Bf 109 near Campagne, but almost immediately was shot down by another Messerschmitt flown by Oberstleutnant Otto Borris of 6/JG 26. Badly injured by a cannon-shell splinter, Nitelet managed to bale out and evade capture, although he had lost an eye. It was thanks to the 'Pat' line, run by fellow Belgian Albert Guérisse – known as 'Lt Cdr Pat O'Leary' – that Nitelet was able to escape to Lisbon via Spain. Here he was met in December 1941 by Donald Darling, codenamed Sunday, a staff officer with MI9 which was concerned with escape and evasion from enemy and neutral territories.

Both Nitelet and Mott now faced making their own escape when the Lysander became bogged down in mud after landing. Unlike Lockhart's similar incident earlier in the year, the combined efforts of the reception committee, agent and pilot, were to no avail. The plane could not be moved and after an unsuccessful attempt to set the Lysander on fire, it was abandoned to the Germans. Months later the black aircraft was the centrepiece of an exhibition at Nanterre, near Paris – as a war trophy.

As with Nitelet, evading capture in occupied France was not a new experience for Arnold John Mott. Four months earlier his Bomber Command Whitley had been shot down over France and he eventually made his way back to England via Spain and Gibraltar. This time he was not so lucky. Despite carrying papers belonging to one of the reception committee, who was himself subsequently arrested, Mott was apprehended by the Vichy police and held in Fort de la Rivère for some months, before escaping again while being transferred from an Italian prison to Germany.

Alex Nitelet also managed to escape unharmed and by July was working with 'Pat O'Leary' as his wireless operator. More than 600 Allied soldiers and airmen would pass along the Pat escape and evasion line that ran through central and eastern France, before Guérisse was arrested by the Gestapo in May 1943 and sent to Dachau concentration camp. He survived the war.

In the Mediterranean theatre, the tiny island of Malta was fighting for its life. Subjected to round-the-clock bombing by the Luftwaffe, the RAF's 'Z' Flight had little opportunity to fly its He 115 because of the risk of its being targeted by Malta's own anti-aircraft defences. However, at the height of the German air raids one of the island's few defending RAF fighters was used for a covert flight to support an SOE agent. Flt Lt Don Stores of No. 242 Squadron flew his Hurricane IIB of the Malta Night Fighter Unit (MNFU) from Hal Far to Sicily during the early hours of 3 February.

His mission was to drop two small containers, carried under the wings of his fighter in place of its 44-gallon auxiliary drop tanks, to an SOE agent dug into the snow on the slopes of Mount Etna in Sicily. This dangerous mission was made possible only by Stores' accurate pinpoint navigation, but without his underwing tanks he was at the extreme limit of his range and the operation was not repeated. Two days later, having flown a number of clandestine flights to North Africa during the winter, 'Z' Flight's He 115A BV187 was being readied for an air-sea rescue sortie when a pair of Bf 109s of 6/JG 53 strafed Kalafrana harbour, hitting the floatplane at its moorings. It capsized and was declared damaged beyond repair.

Viscount Lord Gort was, by coincidence, another visitor to Malta during the Island fortress's finest hour. He renewed his acquaintance with No. 10 Squadron RAAF, almost exactly two years after his clandestine flight to North Africa, when he boarded Sunderland W3993 at Gibraltar. At dusk on 1 May Flt Lt Tom Stokes began his approach to the dimly lit flarepath at Kalafrana as German bombers arrived overhead for another raid. Lord Gort was about to assume the governorship of Malta, and had brought with him the George Cross that His Majesty King George VI had awarded to the beleaguered island's people on 14 April.

Malta was obviously far too exposed to be a base for SD operations, but the requirement to transport agents into occupied countries around the Mediterranean remained a high priority. While the SD squadrons at Tempsford were wholly occupied with supporting resistance groups in northern and eastern Europe, No. 108 Squadron, based at Kabrit in Egypt, was selected for Special Duties. The squadron was the first RAF unit to operate the American Consolidated B-24 in the Middle East. Known in the RAF as the Liberator II, the four-engined heavy bomber's deep fuselage and long range would make it one of most popular SD aircraft of the war. The squadron flew its first SD mission on 23 May when Liberator II AL577/'N', on detachment to Fayid in Egypt, was flown by its commanding officer, Wg Cdr Wells, to Crete on a supply-drop mission.

British-based Special Duties units were now operating as far afield as the Middle East and the Arctic Circle. During January 1942, No. 138 Squadron had dropped the first two SOE agents into occupied Norway from Whitley T4166 during Operation 'Fasting'. Another new unit, formed at the same time as No. 161 Squadron, was No. 1477 (Norwegian) Flight, part of RAF Coastal Command and commanded by former NAS pilot Cdr Finn Lambrechts. Equipped with two Catalina IB flying boats and based at Woodhaven near Dundee, one of its roles was to transport agents and equipment to the burgeoning Norwegian resistance movements.

The rugged Consolidated PBY, first flown in 1935, became one of the most versatile aircraft ever built. It was one of the first American aircraft to be ordered by the RAF at the outbreak of war, with the first deliveries to No. 240 Squadron being made in early 1941. Christened the Catalina in British service, the all-metal flying boat was immensely strong. Its cockpit and front turret were totally enclosed, while bulkheads divided the hull into seven watertight compartments with bunks, a galley and toilet fitted for crew comfort on long flights.

Two reliable, 1,200hp Pratt and Whitney Twin Wasps were installed on the one-piece, 104ft span wing mounted high above the fuselage on the flight engineer's tower. Retractable drag-reducing floats folded into the wing tips. Although its top speed was only 170mph, it had a range of nearly 3,000 miles and an endurance of 18 hours, or more. It could cope equally well with heavy turbulence and high seas. Having no flaps meant that take-offs were a muscle-building experience for the pilot, but the 'Cat' would unstick in only 3,200 feet of clear water with a 6-knot wind. Even without flaps or slats, stalling speed was only 50mph.

No. 1477 Flight carried out its first clandestine operation on the night of 1 May when Lambrechts flew two SOE agents from Woodhaven to a fjord near Vikna Island aboard Catalina W8424, named *Vingtor*. However, it was another Catalina unit, No. 210 Squadron based at Sullom Voe in the Shetlands, that flew the RAF's most northerly clandestine flights in support of Operation 'Fritham'.

The operation was an Allied attempt to occupy the islands of Spitsbergen, which the Germans had claimed following their defeat of Norway. Only a small garrison was maintained on the islands, consisting mainly of mining and meteorological specialists who were supplied by aircraft from Wettererkundungsstaffel 5 based at Banak in northern Norway. In May 1942 a party of some 100 Norwegian mining engineers, accompanied by British and Norwegian officers, sailed from Iceland aboard an icebreaker and a sealer bound for Barentsburg, on the western side of Spitsbergen. Close to their destination, the two lightly armed ships were spotted by a Ju 88 from the Luftwaffe weather unit and on 13 May were attacked by four Fw 200 Kondors.

Both ships were lost in the attack, along with all the expedition's equipment, and thirteen men were killed, including the senior British and Norwegian officers. The survivors managed to cross the ice and take shelter in an abandoned mining settlement at Barentsburg which included an empty hospital, but were discovered by an He 111 operating from an ice field at Longyear City, 25 miles to the east. The Heinkel returned almost daily to bomb Barentsburg, but the unarmed British and Norwegians managed to avoid more casualties by taking refuge in a disused mineshaft.

As no word had been received from Operation Fritham for more than a week, a crew of No. 210 Squadron was ordered to fly to the islands on 25 May to find out what had happened to the expedition and to report on any enemy activity in the area. Flt Lt D.E. 'Tim' Healy and the crew of Catalina VA729, named *Polar*, arrived over Longyear City on Advent Bay exactly 12 hours after leaving Sullom Voe. The first thing they spotted was an He 111 which had made a forced landing nearby and had been abandoned by its crew. Suddenly men appeared from one of the nearby huts and began flashing a message that told the circling Catalina crew of the ships' fate, and that some of the wounded survivors required urgent medical attention. Low on fuel, *Polar* set course for Sullom Voe, which it reached after being airborne for more than 27 hours. Two days later, Healy and his crew were again airborne, loaded with winter clothing, blankets, food, medical supplies and a single Tommy gun. Low cloud en route meant that the Catalina had to fly into a strong headwind at less than 150 feet for most of the journey to Spitsbergen, which it reached after 12 hours of dead-reckoning navigation by its navigator, Flg Off Ernest Schofield. They circled the Norwegians for almost an hour, dropping the stores out of the blister gun turrets before returning to base.

The next operation would be the crew's most hazardous to date: an operation to pick up some of the wounded Norwegians. As they approached the island an He 111 appeared out of the clouds but did not spot the flying boat, which set down amongst the ice floes in the aptly named Ice fjord leading to Barentsburg. Healy and Sergeant 'Tommy' Thomas rowed ashore in the aircraft's dinghy where they were met by a party of survivors, while the rest of the crew kept a wary eye open for German aircraft. Six wounded were brought out by a skiff to the Catalina, which took off after less than an hour on the water.

The crew returned yet again on 14 June to pick up the senior British officer and Arctic explorer, Lt Cdr Alexander 'Sandy' Glen. As British warships prepared to sail to Spitsbergen from Iceland with a party of 100 British and Norwegian troops aboard on 26 June, Healy and Glen flew a photo-reconnaissance mission over Barentsburg before landing in Ice fjord to pick up captured German equipment that had been acquired during a raid by the Norwegians on the German settlement at Advent Bay.

After take-off, the Catalina was heading for Advent Bay when the crew saw a Ju 88 that had force-landed in a snow field near Longyear City. Healy decided to make sure it remained grounded and ordered his gunners to set about the task. Although the Germans returned the fire from the ground the Catalina was undamaged, while the Junkers was riddled with .303 bullets. Their mission now completed, the Catalina and the results of its ice reconnaissance headed for

Sullom Voe, low on fuel and in worsening weather. With fog shrouding the Shetlands, Healy decided to divert to Akureyri in Iceland, where visibility was only marginally better. After sighting Iceland the Catalina had to hug the coast at low level to reach its destination, from where the information and photographs were ferried out to the British warships by trawler.

The Allied force was successfully landed on Spitsbergen on 2 July without being spotted by German aircraft. Seven days later the last of the German garrison had been airlifted off the island by Wetterkundungsstaffel 5 and flown to Banak. Healy and his crew flew their last supply mission to Barentsburg on 29 July to deliver medical supplies. As Tim Healy neared the end of his tour with No. 210 Squadron, he flew his last convoy-protection sortie from the Russian seaplane base at Grasnaya, on the Kola inlet near Murmansk, on 21 September. Four days later he left Grasnaya for Spitsbergen, where he was to pick up Sandy Glen and fly him back to Sullom Voe. Some 200 miles off the North Cape the Catalina came under attack from a Ju 88. A long burst from the German fighter's ventral, rear-firing 7.92mm MG 15 machine gun raked the flying boat's cockpit, killing Flt Lt Healy instantly – the only casualty of the attack.

As the No. 210 Squadron Catalina set out for its first operation to Spitsbergen, one of the former NAS He 115A floatplanes that had been converted for clandestine operations, but stored at BOAC's flying-boat base at Hythe, was issued to No. 1477 Flight. Before moving to Scotland the aircraft, BV184, was flown to nearby Calshot by its Norwegian pilot, Lt Knut Skavhaugan, at the start of its clandestine career.

His navigator was a young Canadian serving with No. 240 Squadron who had volunteered for 'a very interesting few weeks of flying on special duties'. Flg Off John Iverach was briefed upon his arrival at Calshot in March by Wg Cdr Sofiano MBE, a charming, middle-aged officer from the SOE's Inter-Service Liaison Department (ISLD) and a familiar face at the Tangmere cottage. Iverach was also introduced for the first time to the 'black' Heinkel.

There followed a few nights of familiarisation flights with Skavhaugen and Lt Håkon Offerdahl, the former 'Z' Flight pilot, after which Skavhaugen and Iverach found themselves on their way to Malta with wireless operator/air gunner Plt Off Frank Gilbert. They remained at Kalafrana for six weeks, flying a number of operations to North Africa and Italy before returning to Calshot in early May, when 'Z' Flight was disbanded. Here their missions were mainly those of rendezvousing with French fishing boats off the coast in the Bay of Biscay to pick up agents or deliver arms and supplies for the Resistance; one such mission almost ended in disaster.

When returning in the early dawn, the Heinkel was always met by an RAF aircraft over the Channel to escort it safely back to base. On this occasion the escorting aircraft turned out to be an elderly, twin-engined Hampden bomber. Almost within sight of Calshot the Heinkel was raked with gunfire, setting the starboard engine on fire. Suddenly there was no sign of the escort, but Skavhaugen was shouting down the intercom, 'Dose are bloody Spitfires! Yonny, fire the recognition signal!' Unfortunately, the Very pistol was still loaded with German signals, but the pilot managed to land the floatplane on a calm sea and the crew set about extinguishing the fire. The Spitfires circled ominously overhead but held their fire. An hour later, after the fighters had departed, an RAF rescue launch from Calshot had them in tow. It transpired that patrolling Spitfires from a Polish squadron had not been informed of the covert mission and, seeing a Heinkel with what looked very much like a Dornier 217 – the twin-finned Hampden – had attacked. The Polish fighter pilots were later disciplined, not for attacking the German aircraft, but for failing to finish it off.

The He 115 was repaired and flown to RAF Stranraer at Wig Bay in Scotland for some gunnery practice at the West Freugh range, before being escorted to Woodhaven to join the Catalinas moored in the Firth of Tay. Wg Cdr Sofiano, known as 'Sofi' by the aircrews, was there to give the crew details of their next missions, the carriage of agents to and from Norway. At this stage of the war communication with the resistance networks was poor and pick-ups were largely hit-and-miss affairs. On the night of 14 July No. 333 (Norwegian) Squadron flew its longest mission to date. One of the Catalinas flew an agent and supplies

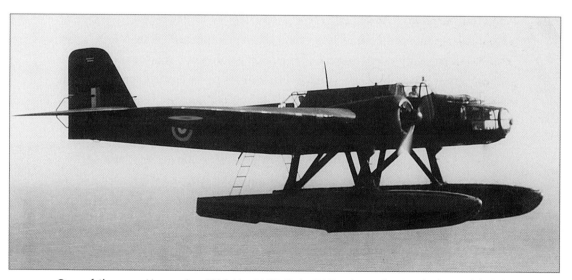

One of three ex-Norwegian NAS He 115B-1s in RAF colours, having been modified for clandestine operations from Scotland and Malta by Scottish Aviation. *(Bruce Robertson)*

from Woodhaven to the Lofoten Islands – off Narvik in Norway, 100 miles north of the Arctic Circle – and back in 17 hours 40 minutes.

John Iverach and radio operator Frank Dorr were aboard the He 115 in late summer as Knut Skavhaugen touched down in a small Norwegian fjord close to where members of the pilot's family lived. They had been briefed to pick up some agents – the number was vague – who were desperately trying to evade capture. Warned by Sofi that they 'should shoot first if in doubt', there was mounting tension as the pilot turned into the wind and shut down the engines to wait for a sign of any activity. The three crew strained their eyes towards the shoreline in the dark distance. Iverach was the first to see something. He later told the story:

> At first it was just a speck, with no perceptible movement. But, gradually, it transmuted to a shape, growing bigger, closer – a strange night creature crawling relentlessly across the water. And now its legs had become tiny oars, stroking their slow rhythm at the sides of the little boat, and its antennae became three human heads. 'They're coming, Knut!' I whispered hoarsely into the intercom. Knut's calm voice came back 'Okay, Yonny – Frank – be ready!' Quickly I shoved my small navigator's table forward on its runners, slid open the transparent hatch above my head, reached for my Tommy gun, and stood up. I peered tensely into the night, searching for the signal light that would distinguish friend from foe. Back in the cockpit, Frank stood likewise. I wondered if his palms, like mine, were slippery with the cold sweat of fear.
>
> For reassurance, I glanced at Knut, sitting calmly in the pilot's seat between Frank and me. He seemed devoid of any emotion. I though back to my previous trips and how, each time, I had felt an overwhelming regret at breaking the golden rule of longevity: 'Never volunteer!' Somehow I knew Knut was enjoying every minute of this. His trouble was that he didn't know when to quit. Here, he knew every living soul for miles around and every inch of the territory. How could Sofiano ever have doubted him, or thought that this might be too personal just because members of his family were involved nearby in the underground?
>
> Now the little boat was only about 200 feet away, closing fast, and still no signal. To Knut I said, 'Christ, they're getting too damned close! What'll we do?' The brief moment of silence seemed like an agonising hour. And then, came Knut's calm reply: 'Let 'em have it – and let's get outa here, fast!' The port propeller started to turn as I aimed at the dark forms, now close enough to see their faces. The sight was now full on, and I knew I couldn't miss. I daren't, for there would be no second chance. Tears blurred my eyes as I squeezed the trigger.

But nothing happened! I squeezed again – and again. And then I remembered. The safety catch! As I fumbled in a panic for the release, I wondered why Frank wasn't firing. He was still watching and waiting, as if part of another scene. By now both the BMWs were roaring and the Heinkel was starting to move. But the deafening noise couldn't cover the desperation in Knut's voice. 'Shoot! For Christ's sake, shoot!' But just as I found the trigger again, Knut let out another scream. 'Vait, Yonny – Frank! Yesus, hold your fire! Dere it is!' and he shut down the engines. It was only a pinprick of light but still enough to flash the code to tell us that these were indeed our passengers, not our executioners. 'Qvick, Frank, help them aboard. Ve're late already,' Knut shouted: but Frank didn't move or answer. His intercom had come unplugged when he stood up. Finally catching his attention, we scrambled down the steel ladder to the boat holding our priceless passengers.

In a matter of seconds we were thundering away over the water, our cargo lying breathlessly in the alleyway. One of them thanked us for waiting. He hadn't realised that his torch had failed, but was lucky to have a small pen-light in his pocket. As we banked sharply for home, I looked at the tiny boat bobbing in our wake. Its solitary skipper was waving goodbye, blissfully unaware of who the pilot was. It was the end of another routine operation.

Soon after the former Norwegian floatplane returned safely to Woodhaven, another He 115B departed from Santahamina in Finland to make a pick-up behind enemy lines. This one belonged to the Luftwaffe. On the night of 22 October the floatplane headed towards Lake Jungozero, carrying an Abwehr agent and tasked with retrieving a long-range patrol of Estonian volunteers, serving in the Finnish Army, from behind Soviet lines. However, the patrol had been captured by the NKVD and its radio operator was acting under Soviet control when the Heinkel touched down on the lake. All three crew members, as well as the agent, were killed by Soviet gunfire as the floatplane glided silently towards the shore with its engines switched off.

The seeds of an even more unsuccessful SOE operation to occupied northern Europe had been sown earlier in 1942, when Allied intelligence received reports that Germany had begun the production of deuterium oxide – known as 'heavy water' – at a plant in southern Norway. In early 1940 German refugee scientists working in Britain showed that an atomic bomb was possible, and that heavy water was a vital component in the production of deuterium gas which could be used in a fission device. Britain also held much of the world stock of heavy water, and it was clear that any German production facility would have to be destroyed by any means possible. This task fell to SOE.

In October 1942 four Norwegian agents were dropped over the remote Hardanger plateau by Ron Hockey to act as a reception committee for the attacking force. Operation 'Freshman' involved two No. 138 Squadron Halifaxes, each towing a glider carrying sixteen SAS commandos from Skipton-on-Swale to Norway on the night of 19 November. Their mission, which was the first combat operation involving the Airspeed Horsa Mk I glider, was to destroy the Norsk Hydro heavy-water plant at Vemork near the town of Rjukan. It was about to go disastrously wrong.

The commandos were trained at the SOE Field Training Base at Arisaig, near Fort William in Scotland, under the tightest security. Here they were introduced to agents from the Norwegian underground who were very familiar with the target and would meet them on the landing zone (LZ) and guide them to the target. They were also trained in silent killing by two SOE officers, former Shanghai policemen Sykes and Fairbairn.

The first glider was to be towed by a Halifax piloted by Sqn Ldr Wilkinson and carrying Gp Capt Cooper, who was in charge of the air side of the operation. The glider was to be piloted by Staff Sgt Strathdee and Sgt Doige. The second Halifax would be piloted by Flt Lt Parkinson and the glider by Plt Off Davies and Sgt Fraser. Final planning of the raid took place at SOE HQ. Three days before the scheduled take-off time, Skipton airfield had been put under tight security while the gliders and tug planes were fitted with secret new communications equipment known as Rebecca. The pilots of the two Halifaxes made a dummy run over the target before dropping pamphlets over Oslo, to make the Germans think that was their intended target.

The first aircraft took off at 1750 hours on 19 November, the second leaving 20 minutes later, and both headed off over the North Sea. At 2356 hours a signal was picked up from the radio operator of the first aircraft, 'Glider released in sea.' By intersections of bearings the position of the aircraft was found to be over the mountains of southern Norway, and at 0151 hours on 20 November, when the aircraft returned to base, this position was confirmed by a careful check of times and course. The glider had been released just over the coast but nowhere near the target.

On the outward flight the new Rebecca equipment had become unserviceable as the aircraft neared the Norwegian coast. This one fact was responsible for the failure of the raid. A landfall was made and the tug flew towards the target, but without success. On the second attempt the aircraft ran into thick cloud in an area about 40 miles north-west of Rjukan and was unable to climb out of it. By this time there was barely sufficient petrol to get the tug and glider home. Ice was forming on the aircraft and, worse still, on the towing rope. Both tug and glider lost height rapidly and eventually, in the area of the Norwegian coast, the rope broke. It was at this point that the wireless operator sent his signal. No further signal came from the second aircraft, and the tug-plane itself failed to return. From first light on 20 November Coastal Command aircraft and a Royal Navy destroyer searched the area from which the last message had been received, but nothing was found.

On 21 November an announcement was made over the German wireless: 'On the night of 19/20 November two British bombers, each towing a glider, flew into southern Norway. One bomber and both gliders were forced to land. The sabotage troops they were carrying were put to battle and wiped out to the last man.' Operation Freshman was over. The first Horsa had crashed into the side of a fjord while the second Halifax, with its glider still in tow, crashed into a mountain killing both crews and many of the commandos. The twenty-three survivors, many of them badly injured, were all captured and later executed by the Gestapo. This was in accordance with an order of the Führer which read, 'Caused by the growing number of cases where aircraft are used for the landing of saboteurs, and as through this, great damage has been done, I hereby order that crews of sabotage planes are to be shot at once by the troops isolating them.' The Norwegian reception committee was instructed to stay in the mountains and await further orders.

As the SOE spread its sphere of operations ever wider, the United States became firmly committed to the war in Europe. On 23 June President Roosevelt established the Office of Strategic Services (OSS). Modelled closely on Britain's SOE, the semi-military OSS combined the functions of several intelligence agencies including the COI. At its head was Gen Wild Bill Donovan, who made another trip to London in July, specifically to learn more about British methods of 'ungentlemanly warfare'. The OSS was empowered to plan and execute subversive activities, and to collect information through espionage. Collection of covert intelligence was assigned to the Secret Intelligence Branch (SIB) and Foreign Nationalities Branch (FNB), data from which were integrated by the Research and Analysis Branch (R&A).

On the operational side, the OSS Counter-intelligence Branch (X-2), which exposed and counteracted enemy espionage, and the Special Operations Branch (SOB), which provided teams to work behind enemy lines, were the most important. The US service effectively combined the functions of the four British security agencies MI5, MI9, SIS and SOE into one organisation. The first OSS field offices overseas were established in London, Madrid and Lisbon.

On the home front, Sticky Murphy was posted to HQ No. 3 Group and handed over command of No. 161 Squadron on 20 June to Guy Lockhart. This period coincided with a lull in SD flights from Tempsford, due to the fact that a large number of networks were under threat following the defection of Mathilde Carré, a French double agent known as 'The Cat'. AM Arthur Harris had been promoted to C-in-C Bomber Command earlier in the year, and wasted no time in repeating his reservations on diverting assets to SD units. He argued that as their operations were flown only during the moon periods, no more than 12 days a month, their aircraft were inactive for 50 per cent of the time. SD commanders countered this argument by pointing out that crew training and the maintenance required after the long flights, often carried out at low level, was not taken into account. It was thought politic, however, to release some of their aircraft during the lull in SD operations, and so for a few weeks, the Tempsford Whitleys and Halifaxes carried out conventional bombing raids on targets in France.

Low-key Lysander operations continued during this period, one of which was almost Guy Lockhart's last. On the evening of 31 August his Lysander took off from Tangmere on Operation 'Boreas II' with one 'Joe' aboard, bound for a pick-up near Arbigny. Unfortunately, the reception committee member responsible for selecting the landing site had been frequenting his local bar until the early hours and seems not to have noticed that he had laid out the flarepath across a ditch. At 0200 hours on 1 September Guy Lockhart touched down on the field, coming to an abrupt halt as the undercarriage was ripped off against the lip of the ditch. There was no alternative but to burn the wrecked Lysander and make his escape with his intended passengers, Christian Pineau and Jean Carvailles who, by luck, had contact with a Polish-crewed Royal Navy felucca from Gibraltar.

After making their way south they rendezvoused with the boat's crew on a remote beach near Narbonne, but as Lockhart, travelling under the name of 'Wg Cdr Henri', was being ferried to the felucca, French coastguards intercepted them. In the mêlée that followed, shots were fired, but no one was hit. Pineau and Carvailles took flight, only to be apprehended by local police as Lockhart's felucca was getting under way for Gibraltar. There he was debriefed by an MI9 officer, before returning to Tempsford on 13 September to discover he had been listed as missing in action. Two weeks later Sqn Ldr Lockhart was awarded an immediate DSO.

The first two female SOE agents were parachuted into France by No. 161 Squadron Whitleys on the night of 25 September 1942. Andrée Borrel and Lise de Baissac were both recruited from the First-Aid Nursing Yeomanry (FANY). Formed before the First World War, FANY was an all-women volunteer organisation working with the armed services. In 1940 the bulk of its members was made up of socially exclusive, intelligent, well-bred 'nice girls' recruited by SOE initially as secretaries, drivers and decoders. Many spoke fluent French and had lived or worked on the Continent, and the decision was soon made to train some of them as wireless operators on active operations.

Pat Martin, Sidney Cotton's former mistress, could have been a role model for these young women. At the outbreak of war she carried out a freelance espionage operation for Winterbotham in Italy which was then still neutral. Martin visited an old English schoolfriend living in Rome whose father was a diplomat. Speaking excellent French and some Italian, the charming young blonde Englishwoman was a popular guest at the many diplomatic receptions held during the spring of 1940, coming into contact with numerous high-ranking Italian officers, including Mussolini's son Carolino. Pat Martin was an excellent listener, and the cocktail party small talk she passed on to SIS confirmed Britain's fears that Italy would enter the war on Germany's side. In June 1940, it did.

Having made her way home via France, with a lift from Le Bourget to Manston in Kent in an RAF Blenheim bomber, Cotton asked her to join his RAF PDU at Heston as a flight lieutenant in the Women's Auxiliary Air Force (WAAF). But Pat Martin had an aversion to uniforms, and the pair agreed to part after seven years together. She volunteered to drive an ambulance in London, and in 1942 married an RAF pilot who would be killed in action only a year later.

At the time SOE made its decision to send female agents to occupied Europe, women were banned from carrying weapons in the British armed forces, and it took special authorisation from Winston Churchill himself to permit them to be armed. They were subjected to the same rigorous training regime as their male colleagues and soon proved adept at subterfuge and unarmed combat. More than 100 FANYs and WAAFs volunteered to work in the field; not all would make the grade.

Andrée Borrel and Lise de Baissac were two of those who did. Andrée, born to working-class parents in Paris in 1919, grew up with a love of the outdoors, spending her spare time hiking, climbing and bicycling. When war broke out she volunteered to work as a Red Cross nurse and joined an underground escape line guiding British servicemen to safety. When the line was discovered, Borrel travelled to England by way of Spain and Portugal, where she was enthusiastically recruited by SOE. Judged to be a tough and self-reliant agent, she was the first woman to be dropped into France to act as a courier to the chief of the vast Prosper network operating in the Paris area.

By contrast, 37-year-old Lise de Baissac, field-name Odile, was born to French settlers in the island of Mauritius and was thus a British subject; she had been working in Paris when France fell. With her brother Claude she escaped in

Borrel's footsteps via Spain and Portugal to England, where he joined SOE and Lise was recruited by FANY. Older than most of the female agents, de Baissac would become an expert at locating suitable parachute drop zones in France for agents and arms, while posing as an amateur archaeologist. Both she and Borrel were flown to France in the same Whitley on the evening of 24 September to a drop zone near Poitiers.

With more agents in the SOE pipeline, significant changes at RAF Tempsford were now taking place. Mouse Fielden was promoted to group captain on 1 October and appointed station commander, to be replaced as CO of No. 161 (SD) Squadron by one of the RAF's most charismatic pilots. Wg Cdr Percy Charles Pickard DSO, DFC, a tall blond Yorkshireman, had joined the RAF in 1936 and been posted to the newly created Bomber Command. In action over Norway, he was shot down in 1940 and survived 13 hours on the Arctic Sea before being rescued by a British warship. Appointed CO of No. 9 Squadron, Pickard took part in the Battle of France and the Dunkirk evacuation, before being replaced in August 1941 after completing a total of sixty-five night operations during his two operational tours.

Following a six-month ground tour, Pickard was given command of No. 51 Squadron and chosen to lead a covert raid to occupied France. On the night of 27 February 1942 twelve of the Squadron's Whitley V aircraft, carrying 119 British paratroops, took off from Thruxton in Hampshire. The drop zone (DZ) was Bruneval on the Normandy coast, north of Le Havre, the raiding force's target being a German Würzburg radar installation. When the force was later evacuated by ship the paratroops had succeeded, with very few casualties, in capturing vital parts of the radar. This comparatively small but significant raid was debriefed by the intelligence services when Pickard's efficient planning and execution of the air operation came to the attention of SOE. Within weeks he was seconded to No. 138 Squadron and flew on his first Whitley operation from Tempsford with Ron Hockey, the squadron's next commanding officer.

With Pickard's arrival the tempo of No. 161 Squadron's operations was raised considerably, and new equipment experimented with, including the Eureka/Rebecca communications system first used operationally in the Bruneval raid. Rebecca was a transmitter/receiver that could be carried by an aircraft approaching a DZ, while Eureka was designed for use on the ground by the reception team. When in range, a beacon was activated which transmitted a coded signal to enable the aircraft to home in to the DZ. Although failure of an early system had led to the disaster of Operation Freshman over Norway, Rebecca would prove popular with the RAF and military operators, but its bulk – it weighed over 100lb – made it less popular with civilian SOE agents.

Two twin-engined American Douglas Havoc Is, AW399 and BJ477, were also taken on charge to act as radio relays with agents in France on sorties flown from St Eval in Cornwall. The equipment used was the S-phone, developed by SOE scientists from a pre-war portable radio-telephone. It had a soundproofed headset and mouthpiece and, provided the agent's ground set was pointing in the direction of the aircraft's flight path, he could speak to the SOE operator on board. At a height of 10,000 feet the S-phone had a range of almost 40 miles, cut to 5 miles when the aircraft descended to 500 feet. Given good atmospheric conditions and relatively flat terrain, these flights, codenamed 'Ascension' operations, were to prove of great value to SOE, SIS and later the OSS.

New pilots continued to arrive at No. 161 Squadron, some of whom were poached from its sister squadron. Plt Off Frank Rymills, a former No. 58 Squadron Whitley pilot who had joined the RAFVR in June 1939, was posted to No. 138 Squadron in February 1942 to fly Whitleys and later Halifaxes. His introduction to his new boss was less than ideal. In the early hours of 28 October Pickard had just returned from his first Lysander operation, which he had had to abort, owing to low cloud over the landing field. To add insult to injury, he was shot at by a British convoy while over the Channel, and as he walked across the perimeter track after landing, he was nearly run down by a No. 138 Squadron Halifax returning from its operation. At its controls was 'Bunny' Rymills. Later, however, while relaxing over a drink and game of cards in the crew room, Pickard suggested that Rymills join his squadron to fly a real pilot's aircraft, the Lysander. Much to the dismay of his boss Ron Hockey, Rymills agreed and was soon moving his kit across the airfield.

As RAF Fighter Command had gone onto the offensive following the German invasion of the Soviet Union in June 1941, fighter raids across the Channel, known as 'sweeps', increased. Operating at the extremes of the ranges of its Spitfires and Hurricanes, Fighter Command paid a heavy price for these raids, losing more than 500 pilots between June and December 1941. Two of these lost pilots would be involved in the cloak and dagger world of covert operations.

Flt Sgt Jimmy McCairns of No. 616 Squadron, part of Douglas Bader's Tangmere Wing, was shot down over France in his Spitfire IIA in July. Flying at low level, he crash-landed near Dunkirk and had to be helped out of his aircraft by German soldiers after the canopy jammed. Within weeks of being sent to a prison camp in Germany, McCairns escaped and upon recapture spent time in solitary confinement at Stalag IX. During the severe winter weather of January 1942 he escaped again, with a Belgian colleague, and managed to make his way across the Rhine into Holland and Belgium in heavy blizzards. There he made contact with an SOE agent who had recently been parachuted into the country from a No. 1419 Flight Whitley. The agent revealed that he was trying to arrange for one of the flight's Lysanders to pick up McCairns when the weather improved. Unfortunately he was captured by the Gestapo, and with no access to a radio link with London McCairns was left with no alternative but to make the long and hazardous journey through France and Spain to Gibraltar. It was there in May 1942 that he met a Lt James Langley of MI9, who confirmed that an RAF unit dedicated to the transport of agents did in fact exist and was looking for recruits. On his return to England, McCairns volunteered.

Lewis Hodges, who had qualified as a pilot at RAF Cranwell in 1938, was another newcomer. Posted to No. 76 Squadron Bomber Command at RAF Finningley, he converted to the new Handley Page Hampden in time to go to war in 1939. Shot down by ground fire in September 1940, he spent the next ten months on the run or in prison camps before finally making it back to England. After a period of rest, 'Bob' Hodges was posted to Tempsford in November 1942 as a No. 161 Squadron flight commander, flying the Halifax.

On one of my Halifax operations I took off from Tempsford and flew south towards France. It was a clear night, with a moon, so we could be seen by the

No. 161 Special Duties Squadron Lysander III (SD) V9673 'J'-'Jiminy' Cricket, flown by Hugh Verity and Lewis Hodges from Tempsford and Tangmere; note the ladder to the rear cockpit. *(Lewis Hodges)*

enemy gunners and as we approached the coast and Le Havre my observer went down into the nose to get an accurate fix. The Halifax was bound for a prearranged dropping zone or DZ at a prearranged time.

I lowered the bomber down to 500 feet as soon as we crossed the coast and set course for the DZ. It was up to the navigator, using a map as we were at such a low altitude, to get the Halifax to the correct spot at the correct time. We kept the speed at 200mph and an eye open for any problems from the enemy. The countryside rushed past us at that speed and height, but in the moonlight I always thought it looked serene and peaceful. I had difficulty in imagining that this lovely country was under enemy occupation. As we approached the DZ, all of us looked for the winking lights which would guide us to the dropping area.

Members of the French Resistance risked their lives on a daily basis and knew that if they were caught out after curfew it meant certain death. On the ground the reception committee listened for the four engines, and when they could just make out the aircraft they sent a Morse signal by torch; this prearranged code signal was acknowledged by the aircraft and I gave the command, 'prepare to drop'.

Three torches on the ground formed a triangle to indicate the DZ. I flew overhead, turned and made my run-in towards the three lights. Bomb-bay doors open the aircraft sped in, red light on in the cabin and on the instrument panel, the dispatcher had already opened the hatch in the floor to drop a light load; the green light flashed on and he released his load and at the same time the bulky items in the bomb bay were also released. These operations were smoothly executed and brought weapons, ammunition and other materials sorely required by the Resistance in their war against the Nazis.

The whole of France was zoned into areas by SOE to build up a comprehensive network of agents in every area, capable of conducting sabotage operations and providing assistance to allied airmen who had been shot down and survived. The Resistance was also able to help them in the occupied territory.

No. 161 Squadron flew its first female agent into France during the October moon period. Mary Lindell, the Comtesse de Milleville, 47 years old and an MI9 agent working for Capt James Langley, had been trained in escape and evasion operations by staff officer Airey Neave, who was codenamed Saturday. She was flown from Tangmere to Thalamy by Flt Lt John Bridger on 26 October.

Two nights later a No. 138 Squadron Halifax B II, W7774/'T' flown by a Polish 'C' Flight crew led by Flg Off Krol, was over Warsaw – not to drop an agent, but to bomb the Gestapo headquarters. Having found the target Krol abandoned the attack owing to the close proximity of civilian buildings, and instead bombed Okecie airfield on the outskirts of the city. On its return over the North Sea the Halifax fought off an attack by Luftwaffe Bf 110 night fighters, but they had caused enough damage for the pilot, Warrant Officer Klowsowski, to ditch the Halifax in shallow water off the Norfolk coast. All the crew survived the 13-hour sortie and were quickly rescued by the Sheringham lifeboat.

As a consequence of Operation 'Torch', the Allied invasion of north-west Africa on 8 November, operations into France were seriously compromised three days later when the Germans moved into the former unoccupied zone, previously under Vichy control. Again Tempsford reacted to the new situation by increasing flights to France, despite worsening weather conditions. No. 161 Squadron attempted its first double Lysander operation on 18 November, when Guy Lockhart and Peter Vaughan-Fowler flew to Les Lagnys but were unable to locate the field because of bad weather. On his return flight Lockhard was caught by a searchlight and fired at by flak before being attacked by night fighters. After evading them by diving below clouds, he managed to land at Warmwell in Devon, short of fuel. A second mission by two aircraft to the same destination was successfully completed four days later.

Another new type introduced into the Tempsford fleet of covert transports was the Lockheed Hudson. Sticky Murphy's earlier rescue of John Nesbitt-Dufort in an Anson had shown that pick-ups using a twin-engined aircraft were possible, and on the night of 25 November Mouse Fielden flew Tempsford's hack Hudson to France for the first time. Lockheed Hudson N7263, ordered for the King's Flight in 1938, was one of the RAF's first Hudson Mk 1s. Officially known as the Hudson LR (Long Range), it had been extensively modified, with improved passenger comfort and extra fuel tankage to give it a range of 3,000 miles, but it retained its dorsal Boulton Paul turret with twin .303in Browning machine guns. Fielden did not particularly like the Hudson, pointing out that in its King's Flight fit it could carry only one passenger over its maximum range. However, with its VIP interior and long-range tanks removed it could carry up to eight passengers plus a three-man crew on the relatively short hops to occupied France.

By the end of November, five Halifaxes had been delivered to No. 161 Squadron's 'B' Flight to replace the veteran Whitleys, the Wellington being retained for parachute training. Some of these new aircraft were more extensively modified than the early B IIs. The Halifax B V Series I (Special) was stripped of all unnecessary equipment such as fin deicer boots, balloon-cable cutters, flare-chute fairings, navigation blisters and engine exhaust shields. Most of the weight savings came from the removal of the mid-upper and nose gun turrets, the latter being replaced with a streamlined metal fairing known as the Z-type nose.

Sqn Ldr Hodges, commander of 'B' Flight, was joined by another new recruit in command of the six 'A' Flight Lysander IIs. Hugh Verity had learned to fly with the Oxford University Air Squadron in 1938, while reading French and Spanish. A posting to Coastal Command on the outbreak of war, flying Ansons, was followed by a tour on Beaufighters with No. 252 Squadron, much of it based in Malta. On the return flight to England in May 1941, his Beaufighter ran out of fuel battling against strong headwinds and Verity was forced to make an emergency landing at Leopardstown race course in the Irish Republic. He and his crew were interned. An MI9 agent in Dublin organised a breakout from the internment camp, enabling Verity to board a train to Belfast and freedom. After a second Beaufighter tour he went to HQ Fighter Command at Bentley Priory as an intruder controller. It was there during the summer of 1942 that he watched plots of solitary RAF aircraft moving slowly across France. Referred to as Specials, they were in fact the 'moon' squadron's Lysanders, and through a colleague from Tangmere Verity was put in touch with the unit operating these 'Specials'. After being introduced to Pickard and Fielden, he was offered a posting to Tempsford, which he accepted with alacrity and was soon converting to the slow but highly manoeuvrable Lysander.

Sqn Ldr Ron Hockey's Halifax B II L9613 at Fayid, Egypt during a No. 138 (SD) Squadron detachment to the Middle East at the end of 1942. *(Andy Thomas)*

Several of Tempsford's Halifaxes were detached to Egypt and North Africa at the end of the year to support the newly established SOE mission in Algiers, Inter-Service Signals Unit 6, codenamed 'Massingham'. Based at a fashionable pre-war seaside resort for wealthy Algerians and colonial French – the Club des Pins, to the west of the city and close to the OSS Field Station – the mission was commanded by Col Douglas Dodds-Parker, who had earlier learned the craft of covert warfare with Wingate's Gideon Force in Abyssinia.

During 1942, the Tempsford squadrons had carried 155 agents and 23 tons of supplies to occupied France alone, and picked up 19 people during nearly 100 operations. Other SD flights were made to Norway, Poland, Holland, Belgium, Greece, Yugoslavia and North Africa, and to the Far East. These were set to multiply over the next 12 months.

CHAPTER 5

Ablaze and Betrayed

If SOE 'F' Section operations were beginning to bear fruit, the attempts by its 'N' Section to establish a viable resistance network in the Netherlands were an unmitigated disaster.

Before the fall of Holland in 1940 the Germans had already captured and 'turned' the two SIS agents Stevens and Best, and by March 1942 had arrested Dutch SOE wireless operators Thys Tacomis and Huburt Lauwers, codenamed Ebenezer, along with their radios and codes. They had been betrayed by George Ribberhof, alias 'Van Vliet', a double agent in the pay of both SIS and the Abwehr. Lauwers was interrogated by Maj Hermann Giskes, an experienced Abwehr intelligence officer, who persuaded him that he could avoid execution if he continued to transmit messages under German supervision.

In an attempt to alert London to his capture, Lauwers deliberately missed out the security checks on his first transmission under the watchful eye of Giskes. London simply acknowledged the message without picking up the omissions. Under Operation 'Englandspiel', British agents were captured as soon as they landed in Holland and their radios used to send more messages from Giskes. To make matters worse, by 1943 German listening services had tuned into Tempsford's wireless telephone and air traffic control frequencies; this, combined with the Abwehr's control of British espionage networks in Holland, caused losses to mount. During the winter months of 1942/3, 18 per cent of the squadron's sorties to Holland were shot down. In January 1943 a No. 161 Squadron Halifax crashed on take-off from Tempsford, injuring the crew and the Dutch NKVD agent Andres Kruyt, who was to be dropped into Holland. He was one of the lucky ones, because all ten SOE agents dropped into Holland by the Tempsford squadrons during the year would be captured as soon as they landed.

One of the few successful insertions into Holland had been the Dutch MI9 agent Dick Kragt, who managed to link up with a Jew named Joop Piller at Emst. Although Kragt had lost his equipment in the drop, including his radio, he built up a network to hide, protect and eventually smuggle downed Allied airmen out of Holland to either southern France or Switzerland. Another MI9 agent dropped into Holland by a No. 138 Squadron Halifax was less fortunate. Beatrix Terwindt, a former KLM air hostess and a colleague of Eric von Rosen's wife, was arrested in 1943 by her German reception committee. They assumed that she was another SOE agent, but knowing little of 'N' Section or its operations, Terwindt could reveal nothing of value to her interrogators. Realising that she was of little value to them, she was sent to Ravensbrück and later Mauthausen concentration camps; but against the odds she managed to survive.

Most of her captured colleagues were shot, although two SOE agents, Sgt Dourlein and Lt Ubbink – codenamed Cabbage and Chive – escaped from Haaren concentration camp in Holland and made their way to Switzerland with the help of Kragt's MI9 network. However, while they were travelling back to Britain via Spain and Gibraltar the Abwehr, using a captured SOE radio, denounced them as Gestapo agents and the pair were arrested on their arrival in England. Their revelations that SOE networks in Holland were being controlled by the Germans were disbelieved by the then director of 'N' Section, Maj E. Blizard, who had Dourlein and Ubbink thrown into prison. The pair were eventually released in January 1944 and were ultimately decorated by the British and Dutch authorities.

What seemed to be another Abwehr coup was the 'destruction' of the de Havilland aircraft factory at Hatfield in January 1943 by a British double agent. Eddie Chapman, born in London in 1908, was a petty thief as a teenager, and a master safecracker as an adult. At the outbreak of war he committed a series of audacious burglaries, stealing a considerable amount of cash and valuables. In the confusion of war he made his getaway to the Channel Islands, but was tracked down by Scotland Yard and given a lengthy jail sentence. The Germans occupied Jersey in June 1940, and when Chapman was discovered languishing in a cell he offered his professional services to the Abwehr in return for freedom and cash. Impressed by his criminal record, the Germans accepted his offer and he was immediately sent for training in sabotage techniques under the supervision of Kapitän Stefan Grunen.

Given the less-than-imaginative codename Fritz, Chapman was dropped over Cambridgeshire from a Kommando Rowehl He 111 bomber on 20 December 1940. He landed in a ploughed field near the village of Welbech, near Littleport, where he asked to be directed to the nearest police station. There he asked to be sent to MI5, where he volunteered to be a double agent if they promised to wipe his criminal record clean and drop any charges pending against him. They not only agreed but offered Chapman, now given the more appropriate SIS codename Zigzag, a considerable sum of money to go straight when the war ended. To convince his Abwehr handlers that he was more than an opportunist criminal,

MI5 agreed to destroy the aircraft factory for him and brought in an expert at subterfuge, Maj Jasper Maskelyne of the Royal Engineers' Camouflage Experimental Station. Large tarpaulins painted with burnt rafters and twisted machinery were draped over the factory's roofs, and wrecked workshops were mocked up alongside real ones. The result was completely convincing from the air.

On 28 January 1943 Chapman sent Grunen a radio message saying, 'Mission successfully accomplished.' Two days later a Luftwaffe reconnaissance aircraft flew over Hatfield, taking back pictures that would confirm the damage that had been inflicted. After several more transmissions, giving details of German raids and American troops arriving in England, Chapman sent a last message in February to the French collaborator who monitored him day and night on the Dauerempfang waveband, saying, 'Too dangerous to work. Am returning via Lisbon.' Chapman wanted to collect his cash from the Germans, and on his arrival in Paris a party was held for him at Maxim's. He was being sent on Abwehr missions to neutral Turkey and Portugal. A year later, Zigzag would be back in England to prepare for another operation in subterfuge and doublecross.

When compared, No. 161 Squadron's Lysander sorties to France fared much better than many of its sister units' operations to Holland, although for many of the agents they carried there was an ever-increasing risk of betrayal, arrest and execution. On the night of 14 January no fewer than three Lysanders departed from Tangmere. Hugh Verity picked up three agents from a field east of Lyons in an 8-hour sortie, while Vaughan-Fowler had to abort Operation 'Atala' near Mâcon because of heavy cloud. John Bridger delivered a Belgian agent to a deserted airfield near Thalamy to collect three 'Joes' including Commandant Léon Faye, a French Air Force major who headed the Alliance network's military operations. Led by Marie-Madeleine Fourcade, Alliance was the most effective intelligence network in France in 1943, but was used by de Gaulle's only rival, Gen Henri Giraud, as a power base and therefore was treated with some suspicion by 'F' Section.

On 25 January another FANY recruit, Jacqueline Nearne, was parachuted into France from a No. 161 Squadron Halifax to act as a wireless operator for the Stationer circuit. The Nearne family had been living in France, where their children were educated. Upon the fall of France the family made their way to Lisbon and flew back to London. In September 1942 Jacqueline and her younger sister, Eileen, joined SOE as 'F' Section wireless operators – known as 'pianists' – and both subsequently volunteered to train as agents.

By this time one of the Special Duties Unit's more colourful characters had arrived at Tempsford. Frenchman Philippe Level had served as an artillery colonel during the First World War, after which he became a successful and rich

A Westland Lysander in the colours of No. 161 (SD) Squadron. *(Cliff Knox)*

industrialist travelling frequently to the United States. At the outbreak of war, Level joined his old regiment guarding the Maginot Line until he was wounded in the knee early in 1940. Although reluctant to leave France when it was finally overrun, Level was determined to carry on the fight and to do so he had to reach England. Travelling first class by train to Lisbon and then by BOAC DC-3 on to Heston in April 1941 on false papers in the name of Philippe Livry, he was arrested as a suspected spy. Through good contacts in high places that included the British foreign secretary Anthony Eden, he was soon released, and despite being a father of five in his mid-forties, managed to join the RAF as a navigator. Following a tour with Coastal Command, during which he served in Trinidad for three months, he was posted to No. 161 Squadron with the rank of flight lieutenant in 1943.

As the only non-British or Commonwealth aircrew serving with the SD squadrons at the time, apart from members of the Polish flight, the 6ft 2in tall Parisian was obliged to assume the guise of an English gentleman. One of Livry's first flights was as part of a six-Halifax operation to drop parachutists into Norway on the night of 15 February. His aircraft carried six Norwegian SOE agents to the Hardanger plateau in an operation codenamed 'Gunnerside'. They landed in fair weather and managed to make contact with each other and take refuge in an isolated hunter's hut, but then were almost immediately caught in a heavy blizzard which trapped them inside for the next four days.

Their mission was to make contact with four of their fellow agents, dropped in the same area the previous October to act as a reception committee for Operation Freshman, the ill-fated commando raid to destroy a German heavy-water plant. Not only did the two teams manage to find each other between the blizzards, but on the night of 27 February they broke into the Norsk Hydro plant, set off charges between the storage tanks and succeeded in destroying 1,000 pounds of the vital heavy water. The six Gunnerside agents then skied their way to the Swedish border, from where they eventually made their way back to Scotland on a BOAC Lodestar from Stockholm.

Philippe Livry was not the only First World War veteran embarking on his first SOE operation. Forest Frederick Yeo-Thomas, who was born in London, fought with the French Army in 1918 before volunteering to fight for the Poles in the Polish–Russian war of 1919–20. Captured by the Soviets and put under threat of execution, he managed to escape, making his way back to Paris where his father ran a successful fashion house called Molyneaux. He worked there until the outbreak of the Second World War. In 1940 Yeo-Thomas joined the RAF in France as an interpreter, only to be evacuated from the Dunkirk beaches a few months later. Although too old for flying, he remained in the RAF as an intelligence officer and two years later was seconded to the SOE 'RF' Country Section as a liaison officer working with the BCRA, de Gaulle's Free French intelligence bureau.

On 26 January 1943 he was dropped by parachute from a Halifax into the outskirts of Rouen with Col André Derwarvin, codenamed Passy, the head of the BCRA, and Pierre Brossolette, a journalist and Gaullist Resistance leader. They were met by local pharmacist Roger Vinay from the Confrérie Notre-Dame network at Lyons-la-Fôret led by Gilbert Renault-Roulier, codenamed Rémy. Their mission was to try to integrate the aims and operations of the SOE and BCRA networks. Yeo-Thomas, using his field-name White Rabbit, would spend several months with Passy attempting to bring the arguing factions of the French underground into one unified force, acting under directions from London, and for the time being have them concentrate on intelligence gathering rather than ad hoc and uncoordinated acts of sabotage.

No. 161 Squadron completed its first successful Hudson operation on the night of 13 February, when 'Pick' Pickard took off from Tangmere bound for a field at St Yan, near Charolles, with five agents on board. The Hudson returned carrying only intelligence reports and mail, but the night turned out to be a busy one for the squadron. Operations 'Porpoise' and 'Prawn' were flown with the two Lysanders of Vaughan-Fowler and McCairns. Three 'Joes' were delivered to a field near Ruffey-sur-Seine and another four picked up, including the legendary Resistance leader Jean Moulin and Gen Charles Delestraint.

Moulin, a young prefect of Chartres when the Germans invaded, had formed his own Resistance circuit codenamed Combat. He managed to travel to London via Lisbon to meet de Gaulle in 1941, and had been parachuted back into France by No. 138 Squadron on 1 January 1942 as the general's delegate-general to the underground. By 1943 Moulin had succeeded in uniting most of the networks loyal to de Gaulle in the Conseil National de la Résistance (CNR), while the elderly General Delestraint was a so-called mothball soldier, brought out of retirement to be appointed a reluctant military commander-designate of France's secret army-to-be.

Another agent firmly committed to the de Gaulle cause was Col Paul Rivière, one of only three air operations organisers for the Resistance in Vichy France during 1942. After Operation 'Torch' and the German takeover of unoccupied France, Rivière, a 30-year-old schoolteacher from Lyons, became the Gaullist chief of air operations, overseeing both parachuting drops and aircraft landings over nearly a quarter of the country.

Held in equal esteem by the SOE and its pilots was a 33-year-old pre-war stunt pilot and French Air Force officer. Henri Déricourt, codenamed Gilbert, travelled to French-controlled Syria after the fall of France to take up his career as an airline pilot, and there he contacted British Intelligence officers in Aleppo. With the benefit of powerful contacts including Pierre Cot, a pre-war Minister for Air in the National Front government, and Maj Nicholas Bodington, 'F' Section's deputy director, in 1942 he made his way back to Paris and then along the Pat line to Gibraltar, where he offered his services to SOE. After training with 'F' Section in London and at Tempsford's Station 61, known as the 'Joe School' in the organisation of reception committees, he had been parachuted from a No. 161 Squadron Halifax into France, near Orléans, in January 1943. His task, under Major Francis Suttill, an Anglo-French barrister, was to prepare for air support of the Prosper network covering the south of Paris.

During the February moon period the Luftwaffe was dropping supplies to two of the Abwehr's most successful agents in the British Isles. In 1943 the Norwegian double agents Mutt and Jeff had been moved by their MI5 handlers to Scotland, where it was felt their operations could be conducted in greater security. For Tor Glad, however, the novelty of being a closely confined under-cover agent had worn off, and he would see out the rest of the war from an internment camp on Dartmoor. In the meantime, John Moe arranged for He 111s to drop money, explosives and equipment near Aberdeen in an operation codenamed 'Oatmeal'. As a cover for the supply drops the Luftwaffe mounted an air raid on nearby Fraserburgh, which killed a child and injured many others. Although Moe would continue to send spurious reports of his acts of sabotage for another year, he remained troubled by the air-raid casualties during Oatmeal and was released to join the Norwegian army-in-exile.

As the dust settled from the German air raid in Scotland, Hugh Verity came close to writing off his Lysander in the early hours of 25 February, and with it the head of Combat circuit. Operation 'Eclipse' had begun at Tangmere the previous evening, when Verity took off for a field near Issoudun with Resistance leader Jean Moulin in the rear cockpit. By the time the Lysander had crossed the French coast near Cherbourg, it was over a solid fog bank. There was nothing for it but to turn for home – only to find that the fog extended across the Channel to Tangmere. After an anxious descent to 300 feet the pilot caught sight of a 'Money' flare, an extra-bright flare used to augment the flarepath in such conditions, but at the last minute he lost sight of it, aborted the landing and went round again, and again. . . .

After his twelfth approach, running short of fuel and options, Verity was committed to landing and after sighting a brief glimpse of the 'Money' flares shining through the fog, he pulled back the stick and cut the throttle.

Unfortunately the Lysander was 30 feet off the ground when the aircraft ceased flying. In the subsequent arrival, the aircraft shed its undercarriage and propeller in quick succession, but Verity and his passenger were fortunate to climb out of the wreck unharmed. It would, however, be another month before John Bridger safely delivered Moulin back to France, a fateful journey for the Resistance leader and his fellow passengers, Gen Delestraint and Christian Pineau.

But before then Bunny Rymills and Peter Vaughan-Fowler flew a double Lysander operation to a field near Poitiers on the night of 17 March. Operation 'Trainer' was the insertion by Lysander of four agents including the second FANY recruit, Francine Agazarian, wife of SOE agent Flt Lt Jack Agazarian, the Prosper network's 'pianist'. Although they worked for the same network Francine and Jack did not work together. He worked alone, always changing locations to transmit messages two or three times a day, while his wife worked for the network chief Maj Suttill – codenamed François – passing and collecting information and delivering money, forged documents and weapons to members in the Paris area. In a textbook operation, the first of seventeen conducted by air movements officer Henri Déricourt, the pair of Lysanders picked up four agents, including FANY agent Lise de Baissac's brother Claude.

After the failure of the Dieppe raid in August 1942, the Soviets took every opportunity to remind their British allies that they had failed to open a second front in Europe. Although No. 138 Squadron's new commanding officer, Sqn Ldr Ken Batchelor, had dropped the first NKVD agent into Germany from Halifax II DT727 during Operation 'Tonic' on 25 February, it was another month before the squadron was permitted to fly operations to eastern Europe from Soviet air bases. However, the experiment was short-lived, although it was grudgingly given clearance to divert to Murmansk if an extreme emergency arose during long-range SD operations to northern Norway.

With the growing importance to SOE of the Balkans, which the Soviets already considered to be in their sphere of influence, and as the Allies prepared for Operation 'Husky', the invasion of Sicily, a new Special Duties squadron was formed. On 14 March the Special Liberator Flight and 'X' Flight of No. 108 Squadron were renumbered as No. 148 (SD) Squadron based at Gambut Main, Libya, equipped with Consolidated Liberator B IIIs, Halifax B IIs and Lysander III (SD)s.

Nevertheless France still remained the focus of SOE operations throughout the spring and early summer of 1943. One of 'F' Section's most flamboyant agents, codenamed Michel, was parachuted to Annecy for his third mission to France on the night of 14 April. Capt Peter Churchill was another larger-than-life character who was straight out of the pages of *Bulldog Drummond*:

One of two No. 148 (SD) Squadron 'Black' Venturas at Blida airfield in July 1943, where they were used for radio relays with SIS agents in the south of France. *(ww2 images)*

a Cambridge Blue who had played ice hockey for England, but whose forthright personality and flamboyant lifestyle had upset some of the French underground. To prevent any further conflict, 'F' Section had moved him from the Carte network on the Riviera – run by an equally strong-headed individual, the artist André Girard – to St Jorioz, near Annecy in the French Alps.

A member of the reception committee that night was his French-born courier. Odette Sansom had married the son of a British soldier who was billeted with her family when he was wounded during the First World War. She later settled in London with him and they had three daughters. When her husband joined the Army and was posted overseas in 1942, Odette answered a War Office advertisement for French translators, placed by 'F' Section of SOE. Because she was married and had children she was initially rejected for operational training, but her enthusiasm persuaded the recruiting officers to reconsider their decision. Having joined FANY and passed her training course, she was landed near Cannes on the Riviera by felucca in November 1942. Soon after the Germans had moved into unoccupied Vichy France she met Peter Churchill, who persuaded her to become his courier working between Cannes and Marseilles, until they narrowly evaded arrest when a Lysander landed at a disued airfield to fly Churchill back to London. On his return to Annecy in April 1943 the pair of them were unaware that one of Germany's most successful counter-intelligence officers was close on their heels.

Hugo Bleisher, a portly, balding 43-year-old with an eye for the ladies, spoke several languages and, with a background in business, had been recruited by the Abwehr in 1939. His lowly rank of sergeant belied his ability and power. Bleisher had personally arrested Polish network leader Col Roman Czerniawski, and had 'turned' his assistant Mathilde Carré, 'The Cat', into a destructive double agent, as well as his mistress. He took Czerniawski's Paris-based Interallié network apart piece by piece, before turning his attention to the large but lax Carte network in the south of France. Posing as 'Col Henri', a German intelligence officer who wanted to defect, Bleisher was able to penetrate the network with ease and extract information from indiscreet members that enabled him to close in on Churchill and Sansom.

They were staying at a hotel near St Jorioz as a married couple, confident of their safety. To many of their colleagues Churchill and Sansom had been over-confident about their abilities to stay one step ahead of the Germans, and according to an SOE report both had 'a complete unwillingness to admit that they could be wrong'. However, the patient Bleisher knew exactly where they were and arrived after dark with a squad of Italian troops to arrest them both, along with their wireless operator Adolfe Rabinovich. After a short time in Italian custody, when they tried to convince their captors that Peter Churchill was a distant relative of the British Prime Minister, Odette was transferred to the notorious Gestapo prison at Fresnes, to the south of Paris. Bleisher played no part in the brutal interrogations that followed. She divulged nothing. In June 1943 Sansom was condemned to death and sent first to Karlsruhe prison in Germany, where William Stephenson had been imprisoned during the First World War, and then to Ravensbrück concentration camp. After being subjected to many savage beatings without breaking, Churchill ended up in Sachsenhausen.

This period coincided with the largest number of sorties flown to date by No. 161 Squadron in a single month. In sixteen Lysander and Hudson missions flown during April, no fewer than forty-three agents plus an evading USAAF pilot were picked up; amongst them were Yeo-Thomas, Col Derwarvin and Pierre Brossolette in a double Lysander operation flown by Vaughan-Fowler and McCairns on the night of 15 April. John Bridger, one of the squadron's most experienced pilots, with over 4,000 flying hours, on the same night flew a long-range sortie to a high plateau to the south of Clermont-Ferrand to deliver two packages. The pilot was going to have to use all of his experience if he was going to make a success of Operation 'Pétunia'.

A long flight, much of which was in bad weather with cloud obscuring the ground, required all of Bridger's concentration and stamina, especially during the difficult approach to the landing field. To counteract the violent down-draughts caused by the wind rolling over the hilltops into the valleys, Bridger slammed open the throttle. Too much power saw him battling to get his aircraft onto the ground before it rolled off a cliff at the end of the short strip. Again he opened the throttle wide as the Lysander staggered over the edge of the valley, picking up speed as he put the nose down, just enough to climb above the crest of a hill at the other side. He cleared the crest by a few feet, but not the high-tension wire strung between two pylons on the hilltop. The searing flash as the wire broke ruined Bridger's night vision, but he was still airborne. There seemed to be no damage as he made a wide, high circuit of the landing ground. This time he judged his approach perfectly but the aircraft swung to port as it touched down; a tyre had been ripped open on the rocky ground.

With two 'Joes' aboard for the return flight, taking off with one tyre down would be a problem. The only way to solve it was to deflate the other tyre, but this proved more easily said than done. Stabbing with his commando knife and firing at it with his .38 service revolver failed to puncture it. It was the heavy-calibre .45 pistol borrowed from a local gendarme in the reception committee that finished off the job. The take-off on the hard, rocky strip went without a hitch, but Bridger was aware of some extra drag on the return flight, delaying him even more. On landing at Tangmere as dawn broke, the reason for his reduced cruising speed was clear for all to see. He had been trailing some 20 feet of copper wire behind him, plus another yard coiled around the propeller boss. Some wag observed that Bridger must have had 'an electrifying flight' home.

At the end of the month Bob Hodges took over No. 161 Squadron from Pickard, who flew his last Hudson operation to a deserted Florac aerodrome in south-eastern France on the night of 18 April to pick up eight passengers. Promoted to group captain, Pick was given command of No. 140 Wing of No. 2 Group, flying DH Mosquito VI fighter-bombers which would play a leading part in the rescue of a large number of Resistance members facing death.

The SD unit north of the border was also changing its identity, with No. 1477 Flight at Woodhaven becoming 'A' Flight of No. 333 (Norwegian) Squadron, Coastal Command on 5 May. It retained its Catalina IB flying boats for clandestine operations to Norway, the first of which took place on the night of 14 May when Catalina FP183/'D', named *Vingtor II* and captained by Lt Cdr Jorgensen, flew SOE agents Stefan Lines and Erling Moe to Molde fjord. There the flying boat was almost caught by a German patrol boat as it taxied towards the shore. On seeing the beam of the boat's searchlight reflected on the calm waters of the fjord, Jorgenson cut the engines and drifted silently behind a headland until the Germans had passed by. The two agents were then able to row safely ashore in their rubber dinghy.

A few days earlier a Luftwaffe night fighter had also landed in Norway to refuel at Kristiansand, prior to a mission over the Skagerrak to intercept and shoot down one of the BOAC Lodestars flying from Stockholm to Scotland. In fact by the end of the night it would be the Ju 88 and its crew that would be touching down at an airfield in Scotland. Based at Aalborg in Denmark with IV/NJG 3, the Ju 88A-1's crew of three, pilot Oberleutnant Heinrich Schmitt, flight engineer Oberfeldwebel Erich Kantwill and wireless operator/gunner Oberfeldwebel Paul Rosenberger were experienced night-fighter aircrew. Schmitt and Rosenberger had flown together since 1941, but had never shot down an Allied aircraft.

Their strange story began an hour after leaving Norway, when Rosenberger sent a message to the Luftwaffe Nightfighter Headquarters at Grove in Denmark saying that they had a starboard engine fire and were losing height. It was not true. There was no fire, but Schmitt had descended to sea level to get below German radar, dropped a life raft into the sea, and headed for Scotland. When Kantwill objected, he was held at gunpoint by Rosenberger. The Junkers was picked up by British radar east of Peterhead, to the north of Aberdeen, and two No. 165 Squadron Spitfires were scrambled from Dyce at 1750 hours to intercept the bogey, which was circling as though lost. As the fighters approached the Ju 88 dropped its undercarriage, fired Very lights and waggled its wings. One of the fighters moved into a position above and behind the German aircraft, while the other positioned itself 400 yards ahead. The three aircraft then headed for Dyce and when the airfield was in sight, the Ju 88 lowered its wheels, fired more red lights, did a short circuit and landed.

The Junkers was fitted with the latest FuG 202 Lichtenstein BC A1 radar, the first of its type to fall into British hands complete with the full operational documents. While Schmitt and Rosenberg both cooperated fully with British intelligence officers and scientists, Kantwill did not and soon found himself in a PoW camp. Heinrich Schmitt was in fact the son of the secretary to the former Weimar Republic's Minister of Foreign Affairs Gustav Streseman, and had visited England before the war. He had also landed in England on more than one occasion during 1941, while he and Rosenberger were serving with 2/NJG on clandestine intelligence missions. Soon after landing at Dyce on 9 May his safe arrival was signalled to his father in Germany, with the coded message 'May has come' broadcast by the British propaganda radio station Gustav Siegfried Eins, on which both Schmitt and Rosenberger would later make propaganda broadcasts. On 14 May the Junkers was flown by an RAF pilot from Dyce to

RAE Farnborough for a test programme; although Schmitt had volunteered to ferry the aircraft himself, this had been refused.

As one Luftwaffe aircraft made its unauthorised and clandestine flight to England, the Gruppe that was responsible for most of the authorised clandestine flights over the British Isles was being reorganised. The 1 Staffel of the Kommando Rowehl was to concentrate on the development of the Luftwaffe's high-altitude reconnaissance programmes, while 2 Staffel was to be entirely responsible for clandestine flights and was put under the command of Hauptmann Karl Gartenfeld.

The May moon period began, for the RAF's Special Duties Squadron, with Mouse Fielden leaving Tangmere at 2305 hours with his navigator Sqn Ldr Wagland and wireless operator/gunner Flg Off Cocker in a Hudson on Operation 'Tulip', another sortie to Florac aerodrome. After landing at 0225 hours its three passengers disembarked, to be replaced by six men, amongst them the former French Army chief-of-staff, Gen Joseph Georges, who held up their departure by arriving late at the field. As Fielden had also been delayed taking off from Tangmere and it was then 0255 hours, he decided to fly to North Africa to avoid possible interception by German fighters on dawn patrol over the English Channel. At 0555 hours they landed at Maison Blanche airfield on the outskirts of Algiers, having being shot at by Spanish anti-aircraft guns as they skirted the Balearic Islands. Gen Georges left the aircraft at Algiers and, much to SOE's dismay and embarrassment, reported immediately to de Gaulle's only rival, the American-backed High Commissioner for French North and West Africa, Gen Henri Giraud. Interned in Saxony after the fall of France, Giraud had escaped in April 1942 to Vichy France by way of Switzerland, to become a prominent member of the Alliance Resistance network before being smuggled out of the French Riviera to Gibraltar aboard a British submarine.

As Fielden headed for North Africa, the squadron's recently delivered second Hudson was flying Operation 'Blunderbuss' to a vast, flat meadow near Bletterans in eastern France, close to the Swiss border. Piloting his first Hudson pick-up was Hugh Verity, with navigator Philippe Livry and wireless operator/air gunner Sgt Eddie Shine. He was surprised by the length of the field, more than three times that of the standard 450ft flarepath normally used for Hudson operations. A single 'Joe' and twenty-four packages were delivered to the field, which was codenamed Orion, and eight French agents climbed aboard for the return flight to Tangmere.

By the end of May all No. 138 Squadron's Whitleys had been replaced by Halifaxes, twenty of which were on strength, with a similar number being

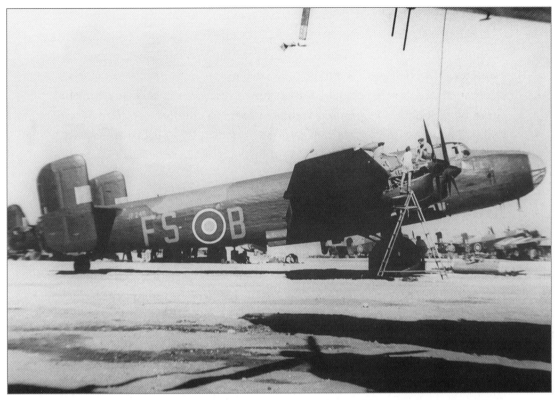

Fitters checking the Merlin XXs of No. 148 (SD) Squadron Halifax II Series IA JS246/'B' at Derna in Libya in September 1943; it was later written off at Brindisi after a clandestine operation in October 1944. *(ww2 images)*

assigned to No. 161; and on 28 May a third Halifax squadron was formed at Tempsford. No. 1575 Flight was renumbered No. 624 (SD) Squadron, and almost immediately its eighteen assigned Halifax IIs moved to Blida, some 20 miles south-west of Algiers, to support the SOE mission Massingham. A growing number of SD units were being assigned to the Algiers mission, including a detachment of No. 267 Squadron equipped with the new Douglas Dakota; they moved from Marble Arch, an airfield in eastern Libya, to Catania in Sicily. The first squadron to be placed under Massingham control was No. 148 (SD) Squadron based at Derna in Libya; it flew ninety sorties in its first month of operations, mainly to partisan groups in Italy and the Balkans.

While operations over France and the Mediterranean had been relatively free of losses by the SD units, the Tempsford squadrons were to suffer their worst losses of the war to date. On 1 June 1943 a No. 161 Squadron Halifax was shot down near Chaam in Holland, north of Antwerp, killing Flt Lt W.M. Hale RCAF and his crew of six as well as two SIS agents, C.M. Dekkers and J. Kuennen. Only two days later a Halifax B II, LL307 of No. 138 Squadron, was also lost over Holland with Flt Lt T.M. Thomas and his four crew and two SAS soldiers, Sgt L.G. Stroogants and Capt H.A.L. Filot. Two more Halifaxes failed to return that night, one of which was captained by Sqn Ldr L. Walker who had succeeded Bob Hodges as 'B' Flight commander.

What could easily have resulted in an even worse casualty rate for the month began when a No. 161 Squadron Halifax, piloted by Sqn Ldr Len Ratcliff with Philippe Livry navigating, took off from Tempsford at 2240 hours. It was carrying two agents and four containers to be dropped near Cluny, north of Lyons, but soon after crossing the French coast the aircraft was hit by flak, putting the outer starboard engine out of action. Flying at reduced speed, never more than 1,000 feet above the ground, Ratcliff continued towards the drop zone. With thickening clouds obscuring the ground he overshot the target, but the signal from the patient reception committee below was eventually spotted as the Halifax made a long slow circuit on three engines, and the agents were safely dispatched.

It was then too late to search for the second DZ and the containers had to be jettisoned into the River Sâone, south of Mâcon. As the sun began to rise in the east Len Ratcliff had already decided to continue flying south to North Africa, with Livry busy working out the shortest track to take them directly to Algiers. After flying at low altitude over the sea between the east coast of Spain and the Balearic islands, the crew were able to recognise Algiers at the base of the Atlas Mountains as the sun rose, and they called the American airfield at Maison Blanche for permission to land. There was no answer – it was closed for the night; but nevertheless Ratcliff landed safely on three engines with no further dramas. After a replacement Rolls-Royce Merlin engine, borrowed from No. 624 Squadron, had been fitted, the Halifax flew its crew back to Tempsford via a shopping trip to Gibraltar.

This period was not only one of mounting aircraft losses, but as the Resistance in France began to make a serious impact on the movement and deployment of German troops and equipment, counter-intelligence agencies, particularly the Gestapo, Sicherheitsdienst (SD) and SS, reacted with increased ferocity. By mid-1943 several circuits had collapsed and others had been infiltrated. The life expectancy for some 'F' Section agents in the field was now measured in weeks rather than months, and to remain one step ahead of the Germans and the French collaborators network wireless operators had to be constantly rotated or replaced. Even this was no guarantee of safety. Between 15 and 17 June a total of six Lysander operations were mounted to France by No. 161 Squadron, with McCairns and Rymills carrying three female SOE agents to a field near Angers during the night of 16 June under the direction of Henri Déricourt. All were WAAF recruits.

Noor Inayat Khan, a descendant of the last Mogul emperor of southern India was born in the Kremlin to an Indian father and American mother and brought up in England and France. Her privileged background saw her travelling widely during her youth, from India to almost every country in Europe, before settling in France where she and her sister trained as nurses. When the Germans marched into Paris the family was evacuated to England, where her brother joined the Fleet Air Arm as a pilot and Noor trained as a wireless operator with the WAAF. With her knowledge of French she was soon spotted by SOE, where recruiting officers were impressed by her quiet determination to become an agent in the field.

Early in 1943 Noor was posted to the Directorate of Air Intelligence, seconded to FANY and sent for training to Wanborough Manor, near Guildford. Here some of her instructors considered her to be too sensitive and lacking in confidence, while others praised her for her boundless energy and extreme conscientiousness. Nonetheless, 27-year-old Noor was accepted as a wireless operator in the field for the Cinema circuit, and given the field name Madelaine.

Cecily Lefort, codenamed Alice, was a 43-year-old Scottish international yachtswoman, married to a Frenchman who owned a large villa near the village of St Cast on the Brittany coast. After she returned to England in 1940 she volunteered and was accepted by the WAAF, despite being over the age limit. As with Noor, her knowledge of France and the French language marked her out as a potential recruit for SOE, which she joined at the end of 1942. She then placed her villa at the disposal of its 'RF' Section to become a vital link in the highly successful 'Var' escape line for Allied airmen. Her supreme fitness enabled Cecily to pass the SOE training with ease; her assigned mission in France was to be a courier with Francis Cammaert's Jockey circuit.

Diana Rowden, a mother of three, was another Scot who had spent much of her childhood on the French Riviera. Her education was split between France and England, ending at the Sorbonne in Paris, which Noor Khan had also attended. At the outbreak of war she volunteered for the ambulance corps of the British Expeditionary Force and remained in unoccupied France after the armistice. Eager to become involved in the war, Diana decided to make her way back to England, via Spain and Portugal, in the summer of 1941. She promptly enlisted in the WAAF and was soon promoted to section officer for intelligence duties before being recruited by SOE. Codenamed Paulette, Diana Rowden arrived back in France to work with the Acrobat circuit in the Jura mountain region.

Not one of these female agents who arrived in France on that night in June 1943 would survive the war. All three had been seen off from Tangmere by one of Col Buckmaster's most able civilian aides. Vera Atkins was a War Office intelligence officer who joined 'F' Section with Maurice Buckmaster at the end of 1941. As agents were sent to the field, she took it upon herself to see all of those who left for France, making arrangements for letters to be sent to relatives while they were out of touch, taking charge of the wills they drew up and of personal possessions left behind. Vera Atkins oversaw all aspects of their preparations for entering enemy territory, from the latest work and travel regulations to what they should wear, eat and carry at different times of the year and in different regions of the country. Although she played no part in their training, she would hold informal meetings with trainees, often at West End restaurants, which would act as a safety valve and enable them to confide their innermost hopes and fears to her. Sometimes Vera was asked to give her opinion when there was doubt about the trainee's suitability for working in the field; one such was Inyat Khan. After an informal lunch, Atkins was convinced that Noor's mood swings and erratic behaviour were caused by the fact that she was having difficulties taking leave of her close-knit family, a decision that Vera would later regret.

Despite the continuous influx of new agents, they hardly stemmed the damage to many of the networks following another series of disastrous arrests. These included that of Resistance chief Jean Moulin, whom many considered to be de Gaulle's only Free French rival. A natural leader, he succeeded in achieving a fusion of all the non-Communist networks in the former Vichy areas and chaired the first meeting of the Conseil National de la Résistance, all loyal to de Gaulle, on 23 May 1943. Three weeks later he was betrayed and arrested in Lyons, and within days was beaten to death by Gestapo interrogators.

On the night of 15 June No. 138 Squadron dropped two Canadians, Frank Pickersgill and his 'pianist' John Kenneth Macalister, to the south of Orléans to set up a circuit at Lorraine. It was the beginning of 'F' Section's own *Englandspiel*. Two days after making contact with their reception committee, one of whom offered to give them a lift to catch a train to Paris, they were stopped at a routine road block. When the car was searched, Macalister's radio and the transmitting codes were found. Following the usual brutal interrogation the two agents were sent to Fresnes prison, near Orly, and their radio to a Sicherheitsdienst wireless expert in Paris, Dr Josef Gotz. He was able to set up a 'ghost' circuit at Lorraine codenamed 'Archdeacon' that the Germans operated for almost a year, luring many agents into their trap. Whenever 'F' section asked questions they could not answer, they brought Pickersgill back to answer them, from the concentration camp in Germany where he was being held. It was during one of these visits to Paris that the Canadian managed to kill two of his guards with a broken bottle, before being shot by another. He was dragged back to the camp and executed.

Only a week after the Canadians were caught, leading members of the Prosper network were arrested in a café in Paris; they were its leader Major Suttill and his courier Andrée Borrel, the first FANY agent to be dropped into France. In the following weeks the largest network in the Paris area was systematically destroyed and most of its operatives arrested and later executed. Worse was to follow.

While the action temporarily shifted from France to Italy as Operation Husky, the Allied invasion of Sicily, was launched on 9 July, Tempsford managed to mount another fifteen pick-up sorties, and dropped forty agents and nearly 100 tons of supplies to the French mainland during the July moonlight period. Bunny Rymills flew high-priority Operation 'Howitzer' on the night of 15/16 July, flying out empty to a small, very rough field to the south-west of Auxerre to pick up two French agents. The less-than-adequate landing field had been chosen at very short notice, as the agents were carrying detailed maps of German defences along the coast of Morbiham in Brittany.

The next night Mouse Fielden flew Jean-Pierre Levy, a founding member of Moulin's National Council of the Resistance, and Baron d'Astier de la Vigerie, another of de Gaulle's close aides, to St Vulbas, near Lyons, in Hudson 'O'-Oboe. As no contact was made with a reception committee, Fielden decided to make his second visit to North Africa within three months. After landing again at the deserted American airfield at Maison Blanche before dawn, he made the short flight to the British airfield at Blida 30 miles south-east of Algiers, where the crew grabbed a well-earned breakfast. Unfortunately, a Blenheim on final approach to the airfield shed a propeller and, although the pilot managed to crash-land the bomber with only minor injuries to his crew, parts of his aircraft damaged the wing of the former King's Flight Hudson in the process. Luckily the airfield was busy with visiting aircraft involved in the Sicily landings, and so the crew and the agents managed to hitch a lift back to England in an RAF Lancaster.

Within days the Baron and Dr Levy were airborne again for the long flight to St Vulbus in Hudson 'P'-Peter, flown by Hugh Verity, Livry and Shine. This time Rivière's reception committee was ready and waiting with eight passengers for the flight back to England. The reason that no signal was seen during the previous sortie was that Paul Rivière had been some distance away. He had just been dropped from a Halifax after a period of air organisation training with the RAF in England, and had left his reception committee in other, less competent hands. However, when it became time to leave the field Verity had other

problems. During the take-off run, one of the engines of the heavily loaded aircraft developed a misfire, inducing a swing to port that caused him to clear the
boundary hedge by a whisker before a slow climb to the south. He followed
Fielden's tracks back to Tangmere, flying via Blida and a shopping trip in
Gibraltar.

Algeria had by this time become the most important centre of covert
operations outside London. Since the OSS had established a mission at Algiers
its director of SIB, French-born Henry Hyde, had been campaigning to insert
his own agents into France to establish OSS networks. Although he had excellent relations with the head of SOE's Massingham operation, Douglas Dodds-
Parker and his 'F' Section head, Maj de Guélis – who had been the first agent to
be picked up by a No. 138 Squadron Lysander in September 1941 – Hyde was
determined to deploy his own agents in southern France.

A cause for some concern between the British and American agencies, how-
ever, was the OSS's backing of General Giraud, who represented the old tradi-
tion of the French military hierarchy and not that of de Gaulle. Working with
the SR, French Army Intelligence and Giraud's head of cabinet, Col André
Poniatowski, Hyde was able to recruit several Frenchmen, including Jean
Alziary de Roquefort and Mario Marret, for his organisation codenamed Penny
Farthing. They were sent to the OSS parachute training camp at the Algiers
Club de Pins, where British, American and French agents trained together, and
the training school in Chrea. By June 1943 they were ready to be inserted into
France. But Hyde's Penny Farthing operation had no transport assets of its own,
so he had no alternative but to turn to his London contacts for help. Although
SIS had an agreement with the OSS station in London to conduct joint missions,
its head, Sir Stewart Menzies, was reluctant to support independent OSS
operations. SOE, however, proved to be more flexible and agreed that the two
agents should fly to England.

In fact a No. 161 Squadron Lysander had already flown Lt Marcel Clech, a
Breton taxi-driver, and an OSS wireless operator codenamed Bastien from
Tangmere to Tours in May 1943. On the night of 13 July de Roquefort and
Marret, who were codenamed Jacques and Toto, took off from Tempsford aboard
a No. 138 Squadron Halifax, but the operation had to be aborted at the last
minute when their SOE reception committee was overrun by the Germans. The
two OSS agents finally arrived in France when they made a blind drop near
Lyons on the night of 16/17 August.

In the air at the same time for the second consecutive night was Hugh Verity,
on his way to a field near Tours. Two hours out from Tangmere he was suddenly
aware of aerial activity in his 'Twelve o'clock', with tracer lighting up the sky. It

was not aimed at him, but he had a grandstand view of an RAF bomber being shot down by night fighters less than a mile ahead. A relieved but subdued Verity picked up 'F' Section's Maj Bodington with Claude and Lise de Baissac, who had formed the Scientist circuit in 1942. Two days later Bob Hodges was assigned to Operation 'Dyer', an urgent pick-up of ten agents whose networks had been compromised and who were in imminent danger of capture.

Those anxiously waiting at a field full of cattle near Angers for the sound of the Hudson included Tony Brooks, who was 'F' Section's youngest agent when he made a blind drop into France in July 1942. He had earlier been arrested and released, under the very noses of the Gestapo, by a gendarme who was a member of the Resistance. Also in the party were Victor Gerson, a Jewish businessman who set up the 'Vic' escape line; the threatened Spruce circuit leader Maj Boiteux-Burdett; and his courier, FANY recruit Marie-Thérèse le Chêne.

Robert Boiteux-Burdett, a small, dark, London-born Frenchman who had been stranded in England at the fall of France, was an early SOE recruit and a dab hand with explosives. The 35-year-old former hairdresser, gold prospector and prize fighter was dropped near Lyons from a Polish-crewed Halifax in May 1942. During the six months he spent as a member of the Heckler network he had had a narrow escape when plain-clothes French police arrived late one night to search his flat in the suburbs of Lyons. Hidden in the log cabinet was a large amount of explosives, while his transmitter was at the bottom of a deep drawer. Neither was found, the police leaving with a warning that he might face prosecution for breaking blackout regulations. It was time to move on.

One of his fellow passengers on the flight back to Tangmere that night was an agent whose taste for danger and ability to survive had made him a living legend. Robert Benoist was a First World War fighter pilot who later became France's most successful racing driver, winning five Grands Prix in the 1920s driving Delages and Bugattis. Amongst his fellow Bugatti drivers of the period was former chauffeur William Charles Frederick Grover-Williams, who had been born to a French mother and an English father. Driving under the pseudonym Williams he won the 1929 Monaco Grand Prix in a Bugatti Type 35B, beating the mighty German Mercedes team.

In 1937 Grover-Williams was part of the all-conquering Bugatti team that won the gruelling 24-hour classic at Le Mans, the winning drivers being Robert Benoist and his young co-driver Jean-Pierre Wimille. A month later Wimille was in Long Island, New York, to compete in the Vanderbilt Cup road race in his Type 59 Bugatti, when he met Sidney Cotton for the first time. A fellow Bugatti driver, the Honourable Brian Lewis, had damaged his car in practice and took over Cotton's ERA in the race, which was won by the all-conquering

German Auto Unions. Wimille, however, was to win the 1939 Le Mans, again in a Type 59, only weeks before the outbreak of war.

When Germany invaded France Grover-Williams left for England and a year later found his way to 'F' Section. He parachuted into France on 30 May 1942 – a blind drop from a Whitley, appropriately near Le Mans – charged with setting up the Chestnut circuit in the Paris area with wireless operator Lt Roland Dowlen. Having made his way to the city, he recruited his old Bugatti team-mates Benoist and Wimille, plus Robert's brother Maurice, a successful black-marketeer and Ettore Bugatti's secretary. Arms and explosives were stored at Benoist's estate on the outskirts of Paris, and for almost a year their Chestnut circuit operated with spectacular success.

It came to an end when the ever more capable German radio-hunters, the Funkhorchdienst, homed in on Dowlen's radio transmissions. Although for security reasons he was not living in Benoist's house, his arrest on 31 July had fatal results for the close-knit Chestnut network. Next to be targeted were Maurice and his elderly parents. All were arrested in Paris and had information about Robert's house and its arms cache beaten out of them. Under interrogation Maurice agreed to guide the Germans to the house to save his parents from further punishment by the Gestapo thugs. On the morning of 2 August Sicherheitsdienst troops raided Benoist's house, capturing Grover-Williams but missing Robert and Wimille, who managed to escape. Two days after the raid Benoist was arrested by the Germans while trying to contact his parents in hospital but again escaped, this time by jumping from a moving police car. By 19 August he had made his way to the field at Angers, by way of several safe houses and high-speed chases, to be flown to safety aboard Hodge's Hudson.

During the month of August, the Tempsford SD Squadrons had dropped 66 'Joes' and 194 containers in 18 sorties. Forty-three agents had been plucked from France in thirteen Lysander and three Hudson flights.

No. 138 Squadron was also heavily involved in operations to Poland. Sqn Ldr Krol's crew, with WO Klosowski at the controls, dropped three agents, including the first female agent, Elyzbieta Zawacka, and stores on the night of 9/10 September. Although they were attacked by German night fighters on the return route, they landed safely at Tempsford. Subsequent operations to Poland were not so lucky. Only a week later no fewer than four of the squadron's Halifaxes were lost in one night, 14/15 September. Two were shot down on the outward-bound leg of the sortie, another was bought down by flak over Poland and the fourth over the Baltic Sea, inbound to its forward base at Kinloss in Scotland.

No. 161 Squadron carried out a successful double Lysander operation to Angoulême, near Limoges, on the night of 18 September, carrying among others

No. 161 Sqn Hudson with crew; left to right: Wg Cdr Lewis Hodges, Sqn Ldr Wagland, Flt Lt Reed, Flt Lt Corner at Tempsford, 1943. *(Lewis Hodges)*

Tommy Yeo-Thomas and his good friend Pierre Brossolette, who was making his last visit to France. A week later, in the early hours of 23 September, one of SOE's most capable female agents was parachuted into the Auvergne region of France from a No. 138 Squadron Halifax piloted by Flight Sergeant Cole. Pearl Witherington had been born in Paris in June 1916, living in the city until 1940. She was then working for the British air attaché in Paris, but as a local had to remain in France when the embassy staff was evacuated to England. It would take her and her family almost a year to travel via Spain to Portugal, where Pearl was able to find work again for the British air attaché in Lisbon before they eventually returned to England in July 1941. In London the three Witherington sisters all enlisted as WAAFs, but Pearl was determined to be more than a paper-pusher at the Air Ministry and volunteered to join SOE. During training she proved to be an excellent shot, to be strong-willed and to have remarkable stamina – all attributes which would be tested to the limit in the coming months.

Two Armstrong-Whitworth Albemarle Is, P1378 and P1390, joined No. 161 Squadron's detachment at St Eval as possible replacements for the two Havocs on Ascension operations. Designed as a medium bomber, the twin-engined Albemarle was soon adopted as a glider tug and for supply drops to the French Resistance. As it proved unsuitable for Ascension operations, however, it was decided that the versatile Hudson should take on this additional role. The first Hudson sorties, flown by Plt Off Johnnie Scragg in 'N'-Nan patrolling off the French and Belgian coasts at high altitude, made regular contact with two SIS agents codenamed Bullet and Player.

In August three Liberators had been delivered to No. 138 Squadron's Polish Flight; the first of them was lost on an operation to Poland. The crew of Flt Lt Malinowski, with WO Hulas at the controls, had successfully dropped stores to the Polish underground, but headwinds had delayed their outward flight and it was clear that they did not have enough fuel to get back to their forward base at Kinloss. By the time the Liberator was over the Baltic Sea it was daylight, and the decision was made to abandon the aircraft. The crew successfully baled out over Sweden and, after a lengthy internment, they were finally returned to Scotland in a BOAC Lodestar.

Hudson III T9465 *Spirit of Lockheed Vega Employees* was issued to No. 161 (SD) Squadron in 1943 after serving with RAF Coastal Command. *(ww2 images)*

On the night of 16 October the squadron flew no fewer than six pick-up sorties, one of which, Operation 'Shield', was flown by Hugh Verity and Philippe Vitry to a field at Manziat, near Mâcon. Among the eight people who boarded the Hudson for the return leg was one of France's most distinguished military commanders, Gen Jean de Lattre de Tassigny. After his army's defeat in 1940 and his vocal opposition to the German occupation the Vichy government sent him to Tunisia, where obvious Allied sympathies led to his arrest in 1942 and a 10-year jail sentence. With the assistance of many sympathetic officials, de Lattre was able to escape from Riom prison a year later and was passed to the Resistance, who arranged for his pick-up at Manziat. He would later command de Gaulle's 1st French Army in North Africa.

Two nights later the first double Hudson operation was flown to the Bletterans field. Bob Hodges and Plt Off Affleck flew Operation 'Helm', on the latter's first pick-up. Scotsman John Affleck had completed a tour with Bomber Command before joining No. 161 Squadron as a sergeant pilot to learn his trade flying Halifaxes to Norway, transferring then to the Hudson Flight. Of the four 'Joes' flown out that evening, two were OSS agents on an SOE mission.

American-born Elizabeth Reynolds, who had had a privileged education at an English public school and a French finishing school – which gave her excellent contacts with members of Europe's aristocracy – was to be a courier for the Marksman circuit. She was accompanied by a fellow American, Capt Denis Johnson; he was the 'pianist' for the circuit made up of bands of guerrilla fighters in south-western France known as the *maquis* and headed by Lt Col Richard Heslop, who was also on the Hudson that night. One of the eighteen agents picked up from the field was Baron d'Astier de la Vigerie, who had flown from England three months earlier, while his fellow passenger, Vincent Auriol, was a future president of France.

Across the Mediterranean at the OSS station in Algiers, Henry Hyde was still concerned about the lack of air transport available to support his embryo networks in southern France. After informing his boss of the problem, Wild Bill Donovan took up the cause and persuaded his old friend and former vice-president of Eastman Kodak, Gen Curtis of the Army Air Force staff in Tunis, to release a handful of his B-17 Fortress bombers. A few weeks later the USAAF 885th Bombardment Squadron (Heavy), formerly the 122nd BS (H), was moved into Blida with its B-17s, alongside a detachment of No. 267 Squadron Dakotas that were flying SD sorties to Greece as part of Operation 'Feather'.

Initially the USAAF Twelfth Air Force had been as reluctant as RAF Bomber Command to support SD operations, having its hands full with the invasion of North Africa and later Sicily. One of its bomb groups, the 97th, was deployed to

Algeria to attack targets in Tunisia as a prelude to the invasion of Sicily. While based at the new desert airfield at Biskra Oasis to the south of Constantine, it had not only to contend with sand, sun, wind and rain, and with all maintenance work having to be undertaken in the open, but with saboteurs too. The Luftwaffe emulated 'Z' Flight in Malta by dropping Arab agents provocateurs at night to disable the American B-17s by placing hand grenades into wheel wells, so that as soon as the undercarriage was retracted the pins would be pulled and they would explode. At least one of the bombers from the base was lost before Free French Foreign Legionnaires were brought in to guard the bombers.

The OSS mission in Algiers was not the only one to receive its own, dedicated American transport unit. The London Station had been advised that a new USAAF SD unit, equipped with B-24 Liberators, was being formed in the United States for deployment in England in the new year. The 22nd Anti-Submarine (AS) Squadron had recently joined the 4th AS Squadron at Dunkeswell in Devon after working up at Langley Field, North Carolina, when their commanders were told that all maritime operations were to be handed over to the US Navy and the two squadrons were to join a day-bombing group in East Anglia.

Lt Col Clifford J. Heflin, 22nd AS Squadron's commanding officer, was summoned to a classified briefing at Bovingdon, Hertfordshire, on 24 October attended by Gp Capt Fielden and Maj Brooks of OSS London Station. He was told that his squadron was to become part of Operation 'Carpetbagger', tasked with flying agents and supplies to occupied Europe. A week later twenty-five personnel of the USAAF 801st (Provisional) Bomb Group arrived at Tempsford for training and air experience flights with the RAF's SD squadrons.

On the night of 3 November USAAF Capt J. Estes flew his first SD mission, an SOE supply drop on board No. 138 Squadron Halifax B II DT726, which crashed at Marcels-les-Eaux in the Ardèche. The aircraft hit high ground while evading searchlights, killing the pilot, Plt Off H.F. Hodges, five of his crew and Estes. Rear gunner Flt Lt John Brough survived the crash with only minor injuries, to be picked by a No. 161 Squadron Hudson early in the new year. Another American was killed on an SD sortie over France on the night of 9/10 November during a Penny Farthing operation with No. 161 Squadron. Halifax V EB129 crashed near Chartres, killing OSS agent Lt B.W. Gross USAAF and the six RAF crew.

Earlier that day, there had been an outward and visible sign for the aircrews and their commanders that the importance of Tempsford had been officially recognised at last, when the airfield was honoured by a royal visit from HM

HM King George VI and Queen Elizabeth meeting members of No. 161 Squadron during a visit to Tempsford in 1943, with a Lysander and a Hudson in the background. *(Lewis Hodges)*

King George VI and Queen Elizabeth, who were introduced to personnel from both Nos 138 and 161 Squadrons, as well as the visiting US airmen.

The following night the Halifax of Flt Lt Bartler was one of two No. 138 Squadron aircraft sent to deliver agents and stores to DZs in Denmark. As the agent was about to jump, the Halifax was attacked by a Ju 88 night fighter, which destroyed the intercom system with its first pass and set the wing on fire with its second. Being at low speed and altitude for the drop, Bartler was able to make a skilful forced landing in a nearby field, with no injuries to the crew or the agent who was still on board. As the Junkers followed the doomed aircraft down to the ground, the Halifax's rear gunner continued firing and a lucky burst caught the night fighter, which crashed only a mile away, killing its crew of three. As the fire consumed the wrecked Halifax, five of the crew were captured but three others, and the agent, managed to evade capture with the aid of the local Resistance. They were later smuggled across the Swedish border and flown home in January 1944 by a BOAC Lodestar.

The two USAAF anti-submarine units were deactivated on 22 November and new squadrons formed: the 406th commanded by Col Heflin, and the 36th

Ammunition, radios and other supplies being loaded into the rear fuselage of a Carpetbagger B-24 at Harrington, to be dropped over France from the 'Joe' hole. *(Harrington Museum)*

under the command of Maj Robert Fish. Its B-24Ds moved into RAF Alconbury, an Eighth Air Force base close to Tempsford. Its assigned aircraft began to be modified for their new role, the ventral ball turret being removed and a 'Joe' hole fitted in its place to provide an exit for agents and supplies.

Strong points for parachute static lines, a handrail fixed to the right side of the hole and a plywood floor were fitted in the interior above the bomb bay. In the bomb bay, American bomb shackles were replaced by RAF-pattern release units for dropping British-style cylindrical containers. As an aid to the pinpoint navigation required for SD missions, a Mark V drift-sight was fitted in the navigator's position in the nose section. Modifications to the B-24s, all of which were painted in an overall gloss-black scheme, were carried out at Burtonwood.

Although the American SD units began operations over France, they were now ready to supply partisan groups further afield, including Italy where new OSS units were established. Despite the fact that an armistice had been signed by a new Italian government, which ousted Mussolini from power after the success of Operation Husky on 5 September, the Allies were not able to exploit the situation. The large German force in Italy, under the command of the Luftwaffe's FM Kesselring, and Italian troops loyal to the deposed *Duce* were able to prevent the Allies from overrunning the peninsula for the foreseeable future.

In November 1943 No. 334 Wing, commanded by Fighter Command ace Wg Cdr James Rankin, was established at Brindisi to improve and coordinate supply dropping to the Resistance in Italy and the Balkans. Within the Wing was an Inter-Service Liaison Dept (ISLD) known as Force 266 for combined SOE and OSS operations in Yugoslavia, codenamed Surbiton, and Albania, codenamed Barking, which initially had at its disposal Liberators and Halifaxes of Nos 148 and 624 (SD) Squadrons. By the end of the year USAAF 8th Troop Carrier Squadron (TCS) of the 62nd Troop Carrier Group (TCG) based at Gioia del Colle had become part of the wing, as had the recently formed Polish No. 1586 (SD) Flight with its two Halifaxes and a Liberator. No. 1586 Flight was commanded by the former No. 138 Squadron 'C' Flight commander, Sqn Ldr Krol.

A much faster mode of transport was about to be put into service by BOAC on its dangerous North Sea route from Scotland to Sweden. The RAF's 400mph, twin-engined DH Mosquito fighter-bomber had been adapted to carry a passenger as well as diplomatic mail, propaganda newspapers and the all-important cargo of ball bearings. Three disarmed Mosquito FB VIs were modified to carry a single passenger, who was strapped into the specially padded bomb bay that was fitted with lights, an intercom and an oxygen supply.

This passenger version of the fast plywood bomber replaced some of the Lodestars that took more than twice the time – almost five hours compared with the Mosquito's two – to fly the route, and was certified on 17 November. This

Civilianised Mosquito bombers flew the 'Ball-Bearing' run from Scotland to Sweden; G-AGFV crashed at Bromma in July 1944. *(Richard Riding)*

enabled a Ministry of Supply executive to fly to Stockholm to forestall a German attempt to obtain exclusive rights to the Swedish SKF's ball-bearing output, following the costly USAAF daylight raids on the Schweinfurt ball-bearing factories.

Even before it was certified, the Mosquito was used to snatch one of Europe's most important scientists from under the Germans' noses. Danish physicist Niels Bohr, who had identified uranium-235 as being the vital component of a weapon which derives its explosive force from nuclear fission – an atomic bomb, was smuggled out of Denmark to Sweden on a fishing boat. Following the SOE raid on the German heavy-water plant in Norway earlier in the year, it was imperative that Bohr should be in Allied hands as soon as possible. On the evening of 6 October Bohr was secured in the bomb bay of the BOAC Mosquito on the first stage of his successful flight to the United States, which was completed a few days later in considerably more comfort on board a PanAm transatlantic Boeing Clipper.

It was not only the weather that the night-flying Mosquitoes had to contend with; it was also German night fighters, which had been alerted by the Deutsche Lufthansa airline staff at Bromma Airport, whose offices were next to those of BOAC. Whenever one of the British aircraft was about to depart, coded radio signals were transmitted to Luftwaffe units based in southern Norway. Aircraft operated by Sweden's own airline, ABA, flying the dangerous 'Ball Bearing' route to Scotland were just as vulnerable as the BOAC aircraft.

In August its chief pilot, Capt K.G. Lindner, his crew and three passengers died when his DC-3 *Gladan* was shot down by a German fighter. While Berlin tried to convince Sweden that it respected its neutrality, disaster struck again only weeks later. On the fifth flight after the *Gladan* tragedy, its sister plane *Gripen* suffered the same fate. Only one member of the crew and one passenger survived the crash on 22 October 1943. At least two of the nine Mosquitoes eventually used on the route would fall victim to German fighters.

In the meantime, the RAF's equally hazardous clandestine flights to France continued unabated. Over a two-day period in November no fewer than eleven pick-up operations were flown by No. 161 Squadron, with mixed success. Three Lysander flights were thwarted by bad weather, while another on 17 December ended with the aircraft having to be burned after sinking in mud. This had been Flt Lt Hooper's second attempt to reach a landing ground near Niort on consecutive nights. On the previous night's Operation 'Conjuror' a Hudson pick-up from a field near Angers, flown by Bob Hodges and his navigator Sqn Ldr Wagstaff, seemed to have ended in success. Among the ten waiting passengers were five downed Allied aircrew, circuit leader Francis Cammearts, whose courier Cecily Lefort had recently been arrested at Montélimar, and a 'Capt Moreland', the codename for François Mitterrand, another future French president. However, although the return flight to England was uneventful, the operation had been watched by Paris SD chief Joseph Keiffer, who arrested three of the agents soon after they landed, casting further doubts on the loyalties of the air operation's organiser Henri Déricourt.

However, as the Allied bombing offensive gathered pace during 1943 Sir Arthur Harris, C-in-C of RAF Bomber Command, still a reluctant supporter of SOE operations, had been considering the possibility of establishing another special unit to take responsibility for operations against German fighters, but again without compromising Bomber Command's primary role. There was extensive correspondence between Harris and various departments of the Air Ministry on the subject, and as the idea was discussed the favoured choice of aircraft to carry the necessary equipment clearly fell on the B-17 Flying Fortress. By this time the Air Ministry had authorised the formation of No. 100 Group, but had not given it priority. Harris used his connections and was able to have the new group established on 1 December 1943.

Chosen to command the group was Wg Cdr E.B. Addison, the former head of No. 80 Group, which had been instrumental in foxing the homing beams that the Luftwaffe used to guide their bombers. Addison had the experience in the world of radio counter-measures that Harris required to fool enemy defences against Bomber Command operations.

Before the specially modified Fortress would be available, and as Lancasters could not be spared from Bomber Command Main Force squadrons, a Halifax unit, No. 192 Squadron, was moved to Foulsham and equipped with Mandrel for jamming German early-warning radar. The highly classified equipment used in jamming and deception operations by the electrical counter-measures (ECM) Halifaxes, developed by the Wireless Intelligence Development Unit, made the No. 100 Group squadron one of the most highly classified units in Bomber Command.

Meanwhile, the Tempsford Squadron's loss rate continued to climb as the year came to its end. Soon after midnight on 11 December one of a double Lysander sortie, flown by New Zealander Flg Off Jimmy Bathgate on his ninth pick-up operation, was caught by German night fighters between Laon and Rheims. Flg Off McBride, in the other Lysander, had abandoned Operation 'Sten' owing to worsening weather, but by that time Bathgate had already been shot down and killed along with the two agents he was carrying.

In the early hours of 17 December three Lysanders were returning from pick-ups; two were from the field near Châteauroux, each with two agents on board.

A 'Black' Fortress B III HB796/'G', seen after conversion for its counter-measures role with No. 100 Group by Scottish Aviation, prior to delivery to No. 214 Squadron at Oulton. *(Bruce Robertson)*

The third, flown by Bob Hodges, had picked up Robin Hooper, who had been hidden by members of the Resistance since his last unsuccessful operation to France in November, and had flown him back to Tangmere in worsening weather. With fog obscuring the airfield, Hodges was talked down by the controller using the 'ZZ' approach and landing. This was a basic instrument-approach procedure for airfields and aircraft not equipped with the more capable standard-beam approach (SBA) system. It involved the pilot being talked down to a good heading and when he was over the end of the runway, being given the code 'ZZ' to land straight ahead.

When the first Lysander from Châteauroux arrived, the fog had worsened and its pilot Jim McBride elected for a 'ZZ' approach, the first of which was aborted. On the second approach the Lysander crashed short of the runway and caught fire. Rescuers, including Hodges, arrived to find the two agents walking around in a daze but otherwise unharmed. McBride was trapped in the cockpit and died in the fire. The other Lysander, flown by Stephen Hankey, was diverted to nearby Ford airfield but the pilot became disorientated in the thickening fog and lost control of his aircraft, which crashed into a hillside killing Hankey and his two passengers.

These were not the SD Squadron's only losses of the night. With fog closing in all over southern England, several Halifaxes came to grief. Flt Sgt Caldwell and his No. 161 Squadron crew were forced to bale out after running short of fuel. Two of Flt Lt Gray's crew were killed when his aircraft crashed attempting to land at Bomber Command's emergency runway at RAF Woodbridge in Suffolk, which was equipped with FIDO – Fog Investigation and Dispersal Operation equipment – lines of large burners used to disperse fog. At the same time Flg Off D.R. Harborrow was forced to ditch his No. 161 Halifax V, LK899/'T', on Operation 'Wheelwright 37', one of his crew being drowned.

No. 138 Squadron lost another three aircraft returning from operations over France. Flt Sgt Thomas ordered his crew to abandon Halifax LW280 over the sea near Harwich in Essex, and four of them drowned. LL119 was also abandoned over the coast of Sussex, but all of Flg Off Johnson's crew survived. In addition Flt Sgt Watson and three of his crew became further victims of the fog when he crashed on approach to Woodbridge.

The bad weather in December also claimed one of the BOAC Lodestars on a flight from Bromma to Scotland when G-AGDE, named *Loch Lesja*, crashed into the sea off Leuchars after losing an engine, killing the Norwegian pilot Martin Hambre.

By the end of the year Hugh Verity had been posted away from No. 161 Squadron to the Air Liaison (Operations) section at SOE headquarters, and navigators Philippe Livry and Alan Broadley joined their old boss, Charles Pickard, at No. 140 Wing at Sculthorpe, flying Mosquito fighter-bombers. During 1943 the RAF SD Squadrons had flown 625 sorties from Tempsford, taking 102 passengers into France and picking up 223, as well as dropping 589 tons of stores to the networks: but their losses continued to mount.

CHAPTER 6

Build-up to Invasion

At the beginning of the new year, No. 161 Squadron had an establishment of five Halifax B Vs, two Wellington B IIs, five Hudsons and ten Lysanders. On 1 January 1944 Sqn Ldr Robin Hooper was appointed to command the Lysander Flight at Tempsford, but owing to exceptionally bad weather no pick-up operations were flown during the month.

The Halifaxes were restricted to only a handful of sorties, on one of which two agents, including 20-year-old WAAF Anne-Marie Walters, were parachuted into Gascony in south-western France on 4 January. Anne-Marie was to be a courier to the Wheelwright circuit leader, George Starr, a former Belgian mining expert. Walters' father was British, her mother French; she was raised in France, but was at school in England when war was declared. Working alongside the circuit's 'pianist' Yvonne Cormeau in one of the underground's most efficient units, Anne-Marie would take many risks to carry information between Starr and his Resistance fighters. She was stopped and searched by Vichy police and the Gestapo on several occasions, before being identified by an informer in July 1944 and narrowly escaping capture to make a hazardous escape over the Pyrenees into Spain, and eventually on to England.

On the same night Col Clifford J. Heflin flew the 801st Bomb Group's first Carpetbagger operation from Tempsford to France in a B-24D co-piloted by Lieutenant Stapel. During the January moon period a total of six missions were flown to France by the 36th Squadron and nine by the 406th. The American Liberators were equipped with 'Gee' – a medium-range radar aid employing ground transmitters and an airborne receiver which was prone to jamming over enemy territory – plus Eureka/Rebecca and the 'Sugar-phone', as the Americans called the two-way S-phone, for close range communication.

The OSS was spreading its operations throughout occupied Europe, as well as neutral Sweden, Switzerland and Spain. At the beginning of the year Wild Bill Donovan had flown to Moscow to attempt a meaningful relationship with Stalin's intelligence apparatus. He was not entirely successful, but did manage to establish an OSS mission in the Russian capital.

In January OSS agent Aline Griffith flew from Long Island Sound, the only woman among thirty-two passengers on a Pan American Boeing clipper to Lisbon, and later on to Madrid's Barajas airport on a small aircraft which parked alongside a Deutsche Lufthansa (DLH) Ju 52. Griffith, a young business graduate, had trained at an OSS camp known as 'The Farm' on an estate 20 miles outside Washington. For the next year she worked at the 'American Oil Mission' in Madrid – a front for the OSS mission – with a triple agent recruiting female communist agents to work as secretaries or cleaners in the German and Japanese embassies located in the Spanish capital. The mission also circulated misinformation about the expected Allied invasions of the north and south of France, counter-intelligence on German covert operations in Spain, and it monitored the Axis escape line through the country to safe havens in South America.

With marginal improvements in the weather over north-west Europe, three Lysander – including one double – and two Hudson operations were mounted on the night of 4/5 February. Two were prevented from landing by low cloud while Operation 'Knacker', flown by Sqn Ldr Len Ratcliff, managed to land safely near Soucelles to pick up nine people. Among them was the former racing driver Robert Benoist, who had been on the run since his house was raided six months earlier and who was making his first visit to wartime England.

Two nights later a No. 138 Squadron Halifax was about to make a one-way flight to France with navigator Flt Lt Lewis as part of the crew. Reginald Lewis had joined the RAF in 1941, when he was 18 years of age. He was sent to No. 33 Air Navigation School at Mount Hope in Canada to train as an air observer. On his return he flew a tour with Bomber Command, before being posted to No. 138 (SD) Squadron at RAF Tempsford. Here he joined aircrew from all over Europe and the British Commonwealth flying Halifaxes; their mission was to support agents in countries under German control.

Special Duties flying required a high degree of flying skills and above all, accurate navigation from its aircrew. Missions were flown at low level – the modified Halifax bombers carried no oxygen – often below 1,000 feet on moonlit nights. Navigation was by map reading and dead reckoning, later augmented by 'Gee'. Drop zones were identified by a series of four or five lights from torches in an 'X' to show wind direction, placed by the reception parties on the ground. If conditions were right, the Eureka/Rebecca and S-phone could be used to talk to the reception party. Drops were typically made from 750 feet although 'blind' drops, with no reception party, would be made from higher.

Flt Lt Reginald Lewis, the navigator of No. 138 (SD) Squadron Halifax II LW275/'O', which was shot down near Valence on 8 February 1944 while flying Lt-Col Francis Cammaerts to the south of France. *(Reg Lewis)*

My flights involved long sorties of up to 15 hours to the south of France, Norway, Poland, Czechoslovakia, and later Germany. One flight via Algiers, Brindisi and Yugoslavia to Poland took over nine hours each way.

Our contacts with agents, or 'Joes', was limited although there was a training ground for them at Tempsford House close to the airfield. We did meet some of them socially at leaving parties and one of the most experienced and brave agents, Sqn Ldr Yeo-Thomas, a dynamic character, gave a talk to the squadron before he returned to France in a Lysander from Tempsford.

I flew a mission to Poland during December, a month in which the squadron lost five Halifaxes. The weather at the time was appalling and it continued into the new year. Our crew flew only once in January 1944, and that was a 30-minute air test.

Early in February we attempted to fly some 'Joes' to the south of France, one of whom was Lt Col Francis Cammaerts. The son of the Belgian poet

Emile Cammaerts, Francis was a former school teacher and conscientious objector who had joined SOE in 1942 after his brother in the RAF had been killed. He had already built up a very successful *maquis* network in south-eastern France under the codename Roger, and was flown back to Tempsford from a field near Angers on 15 November 1943 by a No. 161 Squadron Lysander for an urgent conference with the SOE head of 'F' Section, Col Buckmaster.

However, on this occasion in February, we were beaten by the weather and had to return to Tempsford with our passengers. We made another attempt, Operation 'Jockey 5', on 7/8 February, again in bad weather. Our Halifax, LW275/'O', iced up near Lyons and two engines caught fire. The captain, Sqn Ldr T.C. Cooke DFC, 'A' Flight Commander, ordered Cammaerts and the crew to bale out over Hauterives.

All baled out successfully and I landed safely near an isolated farm north-east of Valence. In the farmhouse were a mother and young daughter whose husband had been taken away to work in Germany. After 48 hours word of my whereabouts had circulated through the local grapevine and I was taken to meet three of my crew in a village pharmacy owned by Jean Chancel. We walked for approximately 24 hours before meeting an American OSS agent openly wearing the uniform of a US Marine captain. Peter Ortiz, a former Foreign Legionnaire who spoke excellent French, had built up an enthusiastic band of Resistance fighters in the mountains of Vercors.

A few days later we were taken to a *maquis* camp in the mountains above Chabeuil, where we stayed for nearly three weeks. While we were there a member of the *maquis* was executed for talking about us in a nearby village. We were then driven 30 miles south by Peter Ortiz to Montelimar, where we stayed with Dr and Madame Sambuc and their two nieces, who were *maquis* couriers.

One of our crew, Flg Off Len Gornall, a 19-year-old flight engineer from Cheshire, along with Sqn Ldr Cooke and Flg Off Withecombe, met up with Francis Cammaerts and his Resistance fighters soon after we baled out. After spending some weeks with the *maquis*, Gornall volunteered to stay with them before the skipper ordered him to leave France in a joint attempt to reach Gibraltar. He later trained as a fighter pilot, but was shot down and killed over Holland in 1945.

After spending three weeks with the Sambuc family, Peter Ortiz accompanied myself and three members of the crew on an overnight train from Valance to Carcassonne. I was with Stan Reed, the wireless operator, Ernest Bell and Bob Beattie, a Canadian who was the only one who could speak any French. At Béziers about 100 German soldiers boarded the train, but no contact was made before they got off at Narbonne.

On leaving the train, we were met by Frenchmen who escorted us towards the Pyrenees which took us a week to cross, accompanied by about 40 other evaders from all over Europe, including a number of US airmen. Our guides put us onto a lorry, covered us with a tarpaulin and after a three-hour drive, the four RAF aircrew were told to get out. We found ourselves outside the British Consulate in Barcelona.

After a couple of days we were driven by car to the British Embassy in Madrid, where we were issued with false papers and put on an overnight train to La Linea, on the border with Gibraltar. We crossed over at 7 o'clock in the morning with a group of Spanish dockyard workers and made our way to the RAF station on the Rock. We all returned to Britain in May in an RAF Liberator. The four of us were in the cargo bay while some high-ranking German PoWs travelled in comfort in the passenger cabin.

Following a debrief by SIS at Dorset Square I was given a few weeks' leave, my first after nearly two years of constant operations. I was eventually posted to HQ South East Asia Command where I remained until the summer of 1946, by which time Germany and Japan had made their unconditional surrenders.

My final journey for the RAF was aboard the liner *Mauretania* from Singapore to Liverpool. Much safer and more comfortable than a Halifax!!

The appalling weather would continue to play a part in the Tempsford operations during the month. On the night of 8 February Hudson pilot Flg Off John Affleck was battling his way across France towards Dijon on Operation 'Bludgeon' with seven passengers, for a routine pick-up. Having spotted four dim lights in the field near Bletterans, Affleck made a good landing on what seemed to be smooth ground. So far, so good: but when he attempted to backtrack he realised that there was a problem. The Hudson had come to a halt and despite opening the throttles, she would not move. The aircraft's wheels were slowly sinking in thick mud. When it was obvious that the Hudson would not move under her own power, Affleck switched off the engines and jumped down from the cockpit to assess the situation. He was met by a crowd of French men and women, members of the reception committee, and his anxious passengers. These included a Resistance leader who had escaped from the death cell of the local prison with the help of his family, who were with him: his pregnant wife, mother, father and baby son. Also hoping for a lift home was an RAF evader, Flt Lt John Brough, the only survivor of a No. 138 Squadron Halifax crash three months earlier.

Every minute on the ground spelt danger for all those in the field. With a German garrison only 3 miles away, all hands were mustered to manhandle the aircraft onto firm ground. Local villagers, woken by the noise of the revving engines, offered their help, a team of horses and an ox. While the men, women and animals strained to free the trapped Hudson, the drone of an approaching aircraft was heard. With no time to camouflage the stricken Hudson, everyone sank into the shadows and waited. The sound began to fade, the immediate danger was over, but by then, the Hudson had sunk even lower into the mud. It was very cold and beginning to snow.

Affleck seemed to have little alternative but to set fire to the aircraft and try to make his escape overland, but he decided on one last bid to extricate it from the quagmire. He asked some of the Frenchman to dig around the main wheels, while others dug trenches in front of them. After what seemed an age, he climbed back into the cockpit and started the engines. With more pushing and pulling, the Hudson finally slithered and staggered out of the clinging mud. The problem then was that only two-thirds of the take-off run was on firm ground, and with a full load the plane might not clear the trees at the edge of the field.

He decided that only the French escapee Raymond Aubrac, his wife and son, and the RAF gunner could be taken on board; but there was no guarantee that they would get off the ground. In the event, the Hudson wallowed into the air at little more than 50mph and cleared the trees. After two and a half hours on the ground, the tired crew set a course for home. As they approached the coast, the radio operator could not transmit the arrival codes; the aerials had been ripped off during the struggle to free the Hudson and there was a real possibility of its being greeted by English anti-aircraft fire. Again luck was on their side and they touched down safely at Tempsford as dawn broke. The next day Madame Aubrac gave birth to a baby girl in a London hospital.

That same night Flt Lt L. Whittaker flew two agents in his Lysander to a field near Tours on Operation 'Grower'. Leslie Whittaker, a former Photo-Reconnaissance Unit (PRU) pilot, had been interned in Sweden after he force-landed his Spitfire in 1943, and had to be spirited out of the country in a Norwegian-crewed BOAC Lodestar. One of the two people waiting to be picked up was the very person who had arranged this flight and many others: Henri Déricourt. The other was his wife.

Déricourt had been summoned to England by Col Buckmaster following growing suspicions that he was acting as a double agent, although there was no hard evidence to substantiate these allegations. In fact he had overseen seventeen operations between March 1943 and February 1944 involving twenty-two aircraft – seventeen Lysanders and five Hudsons – during which forty-three passengers were landed and sixty-seven, including himself twice, picked up. Very few of these had failed through unsuitable landing grounds or lack of reception committees, although a number of the best French agents had been arrested soon after landing at one of Déricourt's fields, most of which were in the Angers region 150 miles south-west of Paris. The fact that members of Keiba's Sicherheitsdienst were watching as Whittaker's Lysander took off for an uneventful flight to Tangmere rather confirmed Hugo Bleacher's assertion that Gilbert, Déricourt's codename, was a double agent, but not working for the Abwehr.

Déricourt had many supporters, including SOE staff officer Maj Nicholas Bodington and several circuit leaders, who pointed out that had he been working for the Germans many more agents would have been arrested from the flights that he had organised; also, more importantly, he would not have returned to England voluntarily if he knew he was under suspicion. Some maintained that he was being paid by SOE to deliver misinformation to his German contacts, but none of this was proven and he remained in England for the rest of the war, where he was neither arrested nor charged.

By 1944, the relationship between the Abwehr and the Sicherheitsdienst had become similar to that which the SOE and SIS had had in 1941. One military and the other political, the two agencies had been competing with each other in the occupied territories of Europe, which were shrinking by the month; but that was about to change.

On 20 February a new, clandestine Luftwaffe unit, Kampfgeschwader 200 commanded by Oberst Heinrich Heigl, was formed at Berlin-Gatow. Its task was the covert transport and supply of German agents on behalf of the RHSA (Central Security Department of the Reich) headed by Heydrich's successor, Ernst Kaltenbrunner, to behind enemy lines on all fronts. Formed by the Luftwaffe High Command (OKL), the first units came from an amalgamation of Experimental Units of the Abwehr 5th Branch responsible for testing captured aircraft, and from Versuchsverband Ob.d.L, which used various German and captured transport aircraft for overt and covert missions to support German forces.

Maj Karl Gartenfeldt, commanding officer of 1 Gruppe, KG 200, had almost 100 experienced aircrew at its disposal and was equipped with some sixty aircraft of more than twenty different types, ranging from Bücker Bü 181 Bestmann trainers and DFS 230 gliders to more exotic captured aircraft, including French LeO 246 flying boats and a Russian SB-2. The mainstay of the fleet was still the He 111. Gartenfeldt was one of KG 200's most charismatic and experienced commanders. As a Hauptmann he had flown most of the agents dropped into England and Northern Ireland during the early years of the war, flying both Ju 88s and He 111s from Chartres in France. His immediate superior then was Maj Nicholaus Ritter of the Abwehr. Gruppe Gartenfeldt, which became KG 200's 1 Gruppe, had inserted more than 400 agents into France, Italy and Greece during a six-week period at the end of 1943.

Unusually for an elite German military unit, not all of KG 200s pilots were Germans or even Austrians. Some came from German-speaking regions of Poland and Czechoslovakia, while others were natives of Alsace or the Flemish region of Belgium. An unlikely member of the elite unit was Willem Eduard De Graaf, the son of a Dutch father and an Indonesian mother. After learning to fly with the Netherlands Air Force in 1933 De Graaf had joined KLM, flying European and, later, Asian routes. After the German invasion he joined the right-wing NSB party and in 1942 applied to join the Luftwaffe and was eagerly accepted, despite his mixed-race background. After training at Salzwedel, De Graaf was posted to a ferry unit flying new production aircraft to Berlin-Rangsdorf airfield. There he came into contact with the Versuchsverband Ob.d.L to which he was posted in 1943. In November he received a serious leg injury when his B-71, a Czech-built Tupolev SB-2 built under licence by Letov at Letnany-Prague, crashed in the northern Crimea. However, he had recovered sufficiently to transfer to KG 200 in February 1944 and would fly several different types of aircraft on numerous clandestine missions in eastern Europe for nearly a year.

As the Luftwaffe had learned to its cost at Demyansk in the winter of 1942, and at Stalingrad exactly a year later, the development of transport aircraft had received a very low priority from the German High Command and KG 200, like its British and American counterparts, had to rely on converted bombers for the bulk of its fleet. Some of its senior commanders would have preferred to use the American Douglas DC-3 airliner, several of which had been impressed when Poland and the Netherlands were overrun, but by 1944 spares were scarce and they were seldom used for covert operations.

A type used with some success during the Stalingrad airlift was the four-engined Junkers Ju 290A-1 transport, originally designed for Deutsche Lufthansa (DLH). Several were converted to long-range maritime reconnaissance bombers and this variant was produced by the Letov factory in Czechoslovakia as the A-5. Ironically, three of these maritime aircraft were reconverted for transport duties and flown by both Luftwaffe and DLH personnel, and it was this variant that was extensively used by the KG 200's long-range Staffel. Capable of carrying up to 40 troops more than a range of more than 3,000 miles

The workhorse of KG 200's long-range fleet was the transport variant, the four-engined Junkers Ju 290A maritime-reconnaissance bomber, here showing its rear ramp. *(MAP)*

at a cruising speed of 224mph, the Ju 290A-5 was fitted with a unique, hydraulically powered, ventral loading ramp, the Trapoklappe. This could be used for loading and unloading heavy cargo, or be lowered in flight for paradrops.

As the Luftwaffe's new Geschwader evolved into a cohesive unit, February would prove to be another bad month for the Tempsford SD crews. On the night of 10/11 February, a double Lysander operation was flown in poor visibility by Flg Off D.S. Bell and J.D. McDonald, an Australian, to a field near Bourges. 'Dinger' Bell landed first and was on the ground when McDonald made two unsuccessful approaches; on his third he overshot the flarepath, stalled and the Lysander burst into flames. McDonald was killed while his two passengers managed to climb out of the wreck, one of them badly burned.

Exactly a week later one of the RAF's most celebrated wartime pilots and former commanding officer of No. 161 Squadron Group, Capt P.C. Pickard DSO, DFC, and his faithful navigator Flt Lt J.A. Broadley DSO, DFM, DFC, were killed. Soon after Pickard had been chosen to lead No. 140 Wing, comprising three Mosquito VI squadrons – No. 21, No. 487 (RNZAF) and No. 464 (RAAF), based at Hunsdon near North Weald – the Air Ministry's Intelligence Service received an urgent request from the veteran Resistance leader Dominique Pochardier to mount a raid on Amiens prison, where dozens of political prisoners were awaiting death or deportation. Leading Operation 'Jericho', Pickard relished the opportunity of rescuing some of his old friends, serving in the Resistance, whom he had flown into France in Hudsons and Lysanders. During the low-level daylight attack by eighteen Mosquitoes on 23 January the walls of the prison where breached by delayed-action bombs, releasing some 250 of the prison's population of 700. When Pickard saw that one of the New Zealand squadron's Mosquitoes had been hit by flak and was going down, he circled overhead to see if any of the crew had survived the crash. While his attention was focused on the burning wreck below, a pair of Fw 190s dropped on them from above, shooting down the Mosquito and killing 28-year-old Pickard and his 22-year-old navigator, Bill Broadley.

This was also a disastrous period for many of the agents and their networks. On 24 February Wg Cdr Yeo-Thomas was dropped near Clermont-Ferrand on a mission to rescue his Resistance companion Pierre Brossolette, who had been arrested and was being held in Rennes prison. Having travelled to Paris by train on 21 March, Yeo-Thomas was arrested at Passy Metro while waiting for a courier. He was subjected to horrific tortures before being transferred to Buchenwald concentration camp, by which time Brossolette had committed suicide by jumping through a fifth-floor window at Gestapo headquarters in Avenue Foch.

Dinger Bell flew another operation to France on the night of 2/3 March, with Robert Benoist and his wireless operator Denise Bloch aboard the Lysander. Benoist had been trained by SOE during the winter and, after landing near Chartres, the pair met up with Benoist's former Bugatti co-driver Jean-Pierre Wimille to prepare to set up a new circuit in preparation for the planned invasion. Operation 'Gitane', flown on the same night by Flt Lt 'Andy' Murray Anderson, a Scottish former PRU pilot, carried Paris barrister Maitre Jean Savy, head of the Wizard circuit, and his 'pianist' Eileen Nearne to a field near Orléans. Known as 'Didi', Eileen was the younger sister of two SOE agents, Jacqueline and her brother Francis. All the agents flown to France that week, with the exception of Savy, would face capture and concentration camps.

On the night of 3 March Plt Off Johnnie Scragg flew Robert Boiteux, the Bond Street hairdresser, his Spruce wireless operator Gaston Cohen and 21-year-old Roger Aptaker to a DZ near Marseilles. However, the Hudson was almost shot down by flak near Bordeaux, and a prolonged series of evasion manoeuvres led Scragg to be late over the DZ. Seeing no lights, he was forced to return to Tempsford with his passengers. The following night they were dropped by the 801st/492nd BG in one of its first Douglas C-47 Carpetbagger operations.

At the end of the month an American detachment from Harrington arrived at Leuchars for Operation 'Sonnie'. This involved disguising its B-24s as civil aircraft, with their crews wearing airline uniforms, to fly to Stockholm's Bromma airport. Their mission was to bring back several hundred American engineers working with Swedish industry, including the SAAB aero works, and Norwegian aircrew trainees who had made their way to neutral Sweden. The Liberators joined the BOAC Lodestars and Mosquitos running the gauntlet of Luftwaffe fighters based in Norway to fly this dangerous route in daylight, without loss.

The diplomatic negotiations between Sweden and the United States that brought about the clearances for Operation Sonnie also paved the way for Operation 'Felix', the replacement of ABA Swedish Airlines DC-3s on the 'Ball-Bearing' run with American B-17 bombers. Carl Florman, the chief executive of ABA, held a luncheon for high-ranking British and US military personnel at which he presented his plan to convert B-17s that had made emergency landings in neutral Sweden, for high-speed courier operations. It was not until Col Felix M. Hardison took over the position as US air attaché in Stockholm in early 1944 that Florman's proposition began to be taken seriously.

A new Swedish airline, Swedish Intercontinental Airlines (SILA), had been founded in 1943 by private investors in close cooperation with the state-owned ABA to take over the long-range overseas routes from ABA, which would concentrate on its short-range routes in continental Europe. A deal whereby interned USAAF aircrew would be released, in exchange for seven B-17s free of charge, became known as Operation Felix.

Two B-17Fs and five B-17Gs were transferred to SAAB Aerospace for conversion into civil aircraft at its Linköping facility. Two additional interned B-17Fs were cannibalised for spare parts. Before they entered ABA/SILA service, SAAB engineers removed all military equipment. The front gunner's turret was extended to accommodate the navigator's cabin and a Honeywell autopilot was installed in the cockpit. Bomb bays were transformed into cargo and baggage compartments and an internal elevator was installed to lift payloads from the ground. The rear fuselage contained two passenger cabins with limited space for the accommodation of a maximum of fourteen passengers. Although no parachutes were available for passengers, large life rafts were carried on board for a possible ditching in the North Sea.

Compared to the DC-3, the civil B-17 could fly much further and higher. Its maximum range of over 2,000 miles allowed a northern routing to Scotland, around the dangerous Skagerrak region, to be taken. The Felix flights crossed occupied Norwegian territory north of the city of Trondheim in relatively unguarded airspace. As a precaution the rear gunner's position was retained as a lookout for enemy aircraft, although the twin .50 machine guns were not. The first converted B-17, SE-BAH named *Sam*, left Stockholm-Bromma airport on 9 October 1944 bound for Scotland's Prestwick airport near Glasgow.

The changes were being rung at RAF Tempsford on 1 April, with Wg Cdr Alan Boxer, No. 138 Squadron's 'A' Flight commander, being promoted to replace Bob Hodges as CO of No. 161 Squadron. Lewis Hodges left to take up a position at the RAF Staff College; Sqn Ldr G. Sells took over 'A' Flight from Robin Hooper, who moved to A12(c); and 'B' Flight commander, Len Ratcliff, was given the newly established Hudson flight tasked with parachuting and Ascension operations.

Lt Per Hysing-Dahl, Royal Norwegian Air Force, who had finished a tour with No. 138 Squadron Halifaxes, moved across the airfield to join No. 161 Squadron's Lysander flight to fly his first sortie on the night of 3/4 March, part of a double operation to Issoudun with Dinger Bell. Having picked up two agents, Bell had crossed the French coast when his engine began to misfire. Rather than risk ditching in the dark, he turned back and crash-landed north of Caen, injuring his leg in the process. His passenger suffered only minor injuries, but the wrecked aircraft had to be abandoned. This was the only recorded Lysander operation to France that was aborted due to mechanical failure, a testament to the Tempsford groundcrew's high standard of maintenance. Hysing-Dahl's return was uneventful, while Bell and his passengers were successfully picked up by Andy Murray Anderson from a field near Angers ten days later.

Yet more female agents were flown to France during the month of April. All were circuit wireless operators or couriers, pressed into action as the SOE and SIS's appetite for human intelligence on German troop positions and movements reached fever pitch during the build-up to an Allied invasion. On the night of 5/6 April WAAF recruit Lilian Rolfe and Anglo-French FANY recruit Violette Szabo were landed near Tours in a double Lysander operation from Tempsford.

Violette Bushell was born in Paris in June 1921 to a British father and a French mother and spent much of her early life in France until the family moved to London shortly before the outbreak of war. After the fall of France Violette met and married a Free French legionnaire, Etienne Szabo, who was killed at El Alamein in October 1942. A widow with a baby daughter, Violette Szabo was determined to fight to avenge her dead husband and less than a year later was recruited by SOE. Although her initial assessments were less than promising, Szabo was finally selected for operations in France. Her mission was to assess the state of local Resistance networks after large-scale arrests in the Paris district.

Her pilot had been Flt Lt Bill 'Willie' Taylor, a former night-fighter pilot, on his first Lysander sortie to France. His second was one of particular significance. In Operation 'Chauffeur', flown on the night of 9/10 April to the field near Châteauroux, he carried Maj Philippe de Vomécourt and Lise de Baissac. De Vomécourt, who had persuaded double agent Mathilde Carré, 'The Cat', to return in February 1942 to England, where she was detained in Holloway prison, was to head a circuit in the Loire Valley. Lise de Baissac had been working in Paris when France fell to the Germans, and on her return to England joined the SOE with her brother Claude. Both were parachuted into the Bordeaux area in 1942 to establish the Scientist circuit and Lise was returning for her second mission in France, as her brother's second-in-command.

Of the three people to be picked up that night by Willie Taylor, two were female agents. One was Jacqueline Nearne, who been in the field for almost a year, during which time her sister Didi had been flown to France as Maitre Jean Savy's wireless operator. Savy himself was also on the flight, bringing with him vital intelligence about V-1 rocket sites in France. The third passenger was Josette Southgate, wife of Jacqueline Nearne's chief, Hector circuit leader Sqn Ldr Maurice Southgate.

In the Mediterranean theatre, OSS SIB Chief Henry Hyde was getting more dedicated air support with the formation of the 122nd Liaison Squadron, formed at Blida in Algeria and initially equipped with ten assorted aircraft, including seven B-25 Mitchell twin-engined medium bombers. Further to the east No. 462 (RAAF) Squadron, equipped with Halifax IIs and based at El Adem in Libya, had been flying a series of operations to drop bundles of propaganda leaflets known as 'nickels' to occupied territories, mainly on mainland Greece and the islands of Crete, Rhodes, Leros and Samos. The squadron would carry out other 'black' operations the following year, but in another theatre.

In April No. 161 Squadron lost its first Hudson, although not to enemy action. It happened during a navigation training sortie, when Hudson T9439/'R' flown by a new crew became lost over the North Sea and found itself over neutral Sweden. It was intercepted by Swedish Air Force J 22 fighters and forced to land at Gothenburg, where the Hudson and the crew were interned. A few weeks later the red-faced crew was repatriated to Scotland by BOAC Lodestar. The Hudson Flight, however, suffered its first operational loss when on 31 May Flt Lt 'Sugar' Hale, a former Lysander pilot, and his three crew were shot down and killed over Tilburg in Holland.

Only a few weeks after the loss of Pickard and Broadley came the news that another of the 'moon' squadron's best pilots, Wg Cdr Guy Lockhart, had been killed during a bombing raid over Bavaria on the night of 27/28 April. During

No. 161 (SD) Squadron Hudson T9439/'R' was interned in Sweden in April 1944 after becoming lost during a navigation exercise, its crew returning by BOAC Lodestar. *(Bo Widfeldt)*

this lead-up period to the planned invasion, operations from Tempsford continued apace, despite Harris's preoccupation with No. 100 Group and the Allied strategic bombing campaign.

On the evening of 30 April Operation 'Organist', involving two Lysanders flown by Flt Lt Bob Large and Flg Off J.P. Alcock, picked up three agents from Issoudun, including Violette Szabo who was returning to England with her circuit chief, Philippe Liewer, after his cover had been broken. On the homeward leg Large's Lysander was hit by flak near Châteaudun, without suffering any apparent damage. However the flak had peppered one of the main-wheel tyres, which exploded on touching down at Tempsford, causing the Lysander to ground loop. His passenger Violette Szabo was shaken more by the fact that her intercom had become unplugged and she was afraid that they had crashed in occupied France, than by any physical damage.

Less fortunate was Les Whittaker, on his way to pick up three men from a field near Chartres on Operation 'Forsythia'. In the early hours of 4 May Whittaker stumbled into an RAF raid on Châteaudin that had not been mentioned in his briefing. As he sought to avoid the German searchlights and night fighters attracted to the area like moths to a candle, he inadvertently flew low over Etampes-Mondésir airfield, a Luftwaffe Me 110 base. The Lysander was hit by flak and crashed nearby, killing Whittaker and scattering on to the airfield thousands of French banknotes that he was carrying.

Watching the raid from the edge of a field a few miles from Châteaudin were two SIS agents and an evading USAAF pilot. They had seen Whittaker circling the field bathed in strong moonlight, so strong that the pilot was unable to see a torchlight flashing the recognition letter. After a few minutes the Lysander was seen heading north in the direction of the German airfield. The following day the two French agents were able to attend Whittaker's funeral; he was buried at a local cemetery with two other RAF airmen shot down during the raid. Having slipped quietly away from the graveyard, the agents met up with the American airman and the three of them made a hazardous overnight journey, avoiding German roadblocks and patrols near Boisseaux to reach another landing field to the north of Orléans by dawn the next day. The American evader was Maj Walker 'Bud' Mahurin, a fighter ace with the 56th Fighter Group, known as the 'Wolfpack', flying P-47 Thunderbolts from Halesworth in England. He had been credited with nineteen victories when shot down a month earlier. The three men, and several half-emptied bottles of wine, were successfully picked up by Flg Off Alex Alexander and landed at Tempsford on the morning of 7 May.

In response to the growing threat that the Resistance posed to the German occupying forces in France, the Luftwaffe deployed an Aviazione della RSI unit tasked with the destruction of partisans and their bases in north-western and south-eastern France. Equipped with Italian Reggiane Re.2002 Ariete fighter-bombers, sixty of which had been delivered to the Luftwaffe in early 1944, the hastily formed Schlachtgeschwader of twenty-five aircraft was based initially at Etampes-Mondésir, where at least two of the fighter-bombers were destroyed on the ground in May – by members of the Resistance. The following month a Staffel of eight Re.2002s was detached to the Limoges area to be used against the *maquis*.

During the spring of 1944 the Luftwaffe's new KG 200 was undergoing a period of intensive training for its clandestine role, which was becoming ever more urgent with the increasing Allied gains on all fronts. Initially it had to rely on the veteran He 111, first used in the Spanish Civil War and the type used to drop most of the German agents into England since 1940; but that was about to change. Within three months of its formation, the first of several captured US heavy bombers was delivered to 2 Staffel of I/KG 200 at Finow.

On 12 December 1942 USAAF 8th Air Force B-17F 41-24585 *Wulfe-Hound* of the 303rd Bomb Group had made a wheels-up landing in a field near Melun in France, 60 miles south-east of Paris. The Germans moved the Fortress to Leeuwarden airfield in the Netherlands, where it was found to have suffered minimal damage apart from a crushed ball turret, and the decision was made to put it back into airworthy condition. It was first flown by the Germans on 17 March 1943 when it was ferried to the Luftwaffe Test and Evaluation Centre at Rechlin; there it was used for interceptor training with Zerstoerer Schule 1 at

Wulfe-Hound, a former 303rd Bomb Group B-17F 41-24585, was captured in January 1942 and later served with KG 200's Gruppe Gartenfeld. *(303rd BGA)*

Neubiberg, and Orly near Paris, which became a B-17 spares centre for the Luftwaffe. It was delivered to Versuchsverband KGzbV at Berlin-Rangsdorf in German markings during September 1943, transferred to KG 200 on its formation and took part in training for its first clandestine operations later in the year.

One of KG 200's first B-17 operations was planned to take place in May with its Kommando Tosca based at Kalamaki in Greece. Oberleutnant Korn was tasked with dropping a group of agents in North Africa, but having spent little time on the American bomber he chose the more familiar Ju 290 for the mission. The delayed Operation 'Anti-Atlas' eventually took place on the night of 25 July, when the Junkers slipped through a gap in the Allies' radar cover to drop the agents successfully into Libya south of the Gulf of Sirte.

KG 200's most audacious operation yet, aptly codenamed 'Etappen-Hase' (Hopping Hare), was to establish a series of landing strips behind Allied lines along the Algerian–Tunisian border and had been launched the previous November. Drawing on the North African success of Sonderkommando Blaich two years earlier, the aircraft chosen for the mission by Kommando Tosca were the reliable He 111 and a rugged, single-engined Messerschmitt Bf 108 communications aircraft borrowed from 3 Staffel. The four-seat Taifun, flown by Oberleutnant Horst Dümcke, was fitted with extra fuel tanks, as its normal maximum range was only 600 miles; it was towed into the air from Athens Kalamaki airfield in Greece by the He 111 piloted by Oberleutnant Paul Karger, so as to save fuel before being released over the Bay of Sirte. The destination was an abandoned former Italian emergency landing strip at Wadi Tamet in Libya, where the Bf 108 landed safely and set up a W/T station codenamed Traviata. Supplied with water, food and fuel by the He 111 and an Italian tri-motor SM.75 transport, the Taifun flew towards Tunisia over a six-week period, selecting three main landing sites en route. Arab agents, who had been trained in Berlin, were then carried to the sites to set up fuel dumps and man radio links by the captured B-17 *Wulfe-Hound*, wearing the German code letters DL+XC and flown from Marseilles on one of its first clandestine missions. By the spring of 1944, the network was operational. However, while the Bf 108 was away on a reconnaissance mission on 14 March, the SM.75 landed at Traviata to be met by a large Long Range Desert Group force. The aircraft was set on fire and its crew captured. When Dümcke returned to the airfield accompanied by the He 111 the LRDG had withdrawn, leaving the Germans to escape back to Greece in the Heinkel after leaving a disabled Taifun behind.

It took Oberleutnant Dümcke almost two months to convince his KG 200 superiors that it was safe to attempt to reactivate the Traviata network, and on 16 May he took off from Kalamaki in a B-17 bound for Wadi Tamet. Seeing no obvious sign of the enemy, he landed but kept the engines running. He was greeted by small-arms fire, which hit the aircraft and wounded him in the hip. Nevertheless, Dümcke managed to take off and head out across the Mediterranean at low level towards Athens, but the B-17 was losing fuel. It made it as far as the Bay of Kalamata, where the injured pilot successfully ditched the bomber in shallow water without any loss to his crew.

While the Luftwaffe was getting to grips with its captured American bombers, the USAAF's 801st Provisional Bomb Group (H) officially took over Station 179, Harrington aerodrome in Northampton, an airfield dedicated to its Carpetbagger operations. Here secure communications had been established with OSS London Station and the Group's OSS Liaison Officer, Lt Robert D.

'Black' B-24D Liberator 42-40992 *Red Bull Express* of the US 8th Air Force 801st/492nd Carpetbagger Group based at Station 179, Harrington. *(Harrington Museum)*

Sullivan. Two more squadrons moved into the airfield, the 788th and the 850th, the latter flying its first B-24 supply drop mission to France on the night of 11 May with its commanding officer, Maj Jack M. Dickerson, acting as second pilot on the mission.

Arms and equipment containers for the American SD units were loaded at a supply depot at nearby Holme and driven to Harrington in British Army Ordnance Corps lorries, while the 'Joes' were driven up to the airfield from London by their OSS escorts in large American limousines with closed curtains. The agents were received by the armament officer and taken to 'dressing huts' where they were helped into padded jump suits and rubber helmets unlike those carried by the RAF. They were also given a meal before being accompanied to the waiting aircraft, where they were handed over to the dispatcher.

Following operating procedures evolved by the RAF SD Halifax crews, Carpetbagger operations were flown to the DZ at between 2,000 and 5,000 feet, where radar and sound-detecting devices had less time to focus on the low-flying aircraft. At the DZ, Carpetbagger pilots descended to within 600 feet above ground level (AGL), the ideal height for dropping agents, while containers and packages could be dropped from as low as 300 feet at a speed of 130mph. After the Liberator's rear gunner reported on the accuracy of the drop, 'nickels' were dropped some 50 miles from the DZ on the way home.

Two other USAAF units, the 36th and 406th Bomb Squadrons equipped with 'Black' B-24s and B-17s and based at nearby Station 113, RAF Cheddington, were also carrying out 'nickel raids', as well as dropping fake German newspapers and dead homing pigeons – with false messages attached to their legs: but not agents.

In the next few weeks the first specially trained, three-man Special Operations (SO) teams arrived at Harrington for parachute training prior to being dropped into France, Belgium or Holland. Known as 'Jedburghs' and named after a twelfth-century band of fighters from the Jedburgh area of Scotland who conducted guerilla warfare against English invaders, each consisted of one SOE or OSS officer, one officer native to the country to which the team was sent, and a wireless operator. Assembled in London by the newly formed SOE/OSS combined Special Force Headquarters (SFHQ) and sent to a field training base at Milton Hall, they would bring professional expertise in sabotage techniques to the *maquis* and other Resistance groups. More than 100 Jedburgh teams would be dropped into France, Belgium and Holland.

Also headed for Harrington were larger teams called Operation Group (OG) units, which were an OSS commando force of twenty to thirty men, two of whom were commissioned officers recruited from the US Army. Trained at Fort

A USAAF 8th Air Force B-24H of the 86th BS based at Station 113, Cheddington, which flew 'nickel' raids over occupied Europe in 1944–5. *(Richard Riding)*

Benning, Georgia and the Congressional Country Club near Washington DC, the first of fourteen OG units had been deployed to Algiers in March 1944. These OG units, along with thirteen Jedburgh teams, were to be dropped into Italy and France by the 122nd Liaison Squadron based at Blida. On 1 April this unit was redesignated the 122nd Bombardment Squadron (BS), commanded by Col Monro MacCloskey, and its complement was increased to seven B-17s and eight B-24s. The Liberators had been modified for SD operations, to the same specifications as those of the 801st Bomb Group in England, at a secret USAAF Depot at El Aourina, Tunisia. Initially considered a second-line unit, many of its flight personnel who had been rejected by regular front-line bombing squadrons were to prove first-class SD aircrew.

Following the Italian surrender at the end of 1943, the Allies began to look more closely at the Balkans, and Yugoslavia in particular. British Member of Parliament and former member of 'L' Detachment, SAS Brigade, Brig Fitzroy Maclean had been parachuted into Yugoslavia on a clandestine visit to Josip

Tito's partisan headquarters as Churchill's personal envoy, to assess his ability to fight the Germans. Maclean recommended that the Allies should throw their weight behind Tito and his 250,000-strong communist resistance fighters. In May 1944 the Yugoslav government-in-exile dismissed the Chetnik leader Mihajlovic and began negotiating with Tito through Maclean, who had returned to Yugoslavia to take an active part in the partisans' battles. One of Maclean's closest aides was John Henniker-Major, with whom he had served in the Foreign Office before the war. The son of a First World War RFC pilot, Henniker-Major had spent a year's convalescence in South Africa after suffering serious wounds while serving with the Desert Rats in 1942. He was recruited to the SOE by Maclean, who wanted him to join his mission in Yugoslavia, and was parachuted into Bosnia in September 1943 as Maclean's second-in-command.

In order to support the partisan war, the Balkan Air Terminal Service (BATS) and the Casualty Air Evacuation Unit were formed in May to control and select airstrips in Yugoslavia suitable for partisan supply and evacuation flights, with Tito's air representative, Col Parc, liaising with its commanders. At the same time No. 1 Squadiglia of the Italian Co-Belligerent Air Force, with Cant

122nd LG C-47s and B-17s, based at Blida airfield in Algeria, were the first aircraft assigned to support the US Office of Strategic Services (OSS) in 1943. *(ww2 images)*

Z.1007s and SM.-82s, came under the control of No. 334 Wing. So also did the Dakota-equipped No. 267 Squadron which had moved to Bari in February, along with a pair of Soviet PS-84s. These Russian-built Douglas DC-3s, the civil predecessor of the C-47 Dakota, served the Soviet Mission which was attached to Tito's headquarters, and they would become the first element of the only Russian unit to be placed under Western command during the Second World War.

Pinpointing drop zones or well-camouflaged, improvised airstrips in remote areas of Yugoslavia had proved to be extremely difficult at the beginning of the Balkans campaign. Although Eureka beacons had been dropped to the partisans, few of the RAF SD Halifaxes and Dakotas carried the Rebecca receivers. In contrast the USAAF 60th TCG was fitted with AN/PPN-1 beacon responders and were thus able to reach their DZs with greater accuracy. For dropping agents and supplies to remote DZs in the mountains where enemy ground defences were non-existent, No. 148 Squadron's Liberator pilots would lower wheels and flaps to fly as low and slowly as possible.

A new air headquarters for Balkan operations, known as 'G' Force, was established on 22 May. Within hours the Germans launched Operation 'Wolf', a

A Soviet PS-84, a licence-built DC-3 that served with the GVF to support Russian partisans operating behind German lines and Yugoslav partisans under the command of No. 334 Wing in Italy. *(MAP)*

glider-borne and parachute landing against Yugoslav partisan strongholds, culminating in Operation 'Roesselsprung', an attack on Tito's headquarters at Drvar on 25 May. The Soviet PS-84s had flown their first SD mission to Yugoslavia on the night on 16/17 March, and on 3 June one of them rescued Tito and his staff from an airstrip in the Kupresko Valley of the Prekaja Mountains as the Germans tightened the noose around his headquarters.

On 1 June 'G' Force became the Balkan Air Force under the command of AVM William Elliot; parts of it were No. 334 Wing and the Parachute Training Centre at Gioia. Within the Balkan Air Force was Force 399 based at Bari, part of SOE's Special Operations Mediterranean set up to coordinate operations in Poland and Czechoslovakia. The first supply drops to Polish partisans were made by No. 148 Squadron and No. 1586 Flight Halifax IIs based at Brindisi, and began in April.

A Lysander flight had been added to No. 148 (SD) Squadron in February, based at Calvi in northern Corsica and commanded by former No. 161 Squadron veteran, Peter Vaughan-Fowler. Formed at Maison Blanche near Algiers, the flight's three pilots, Flg Offs Manning, Franklin and Attenborrow, trained at a grass airfield at Leverano, near Brindisi. The flight's first official operation was a navigation exercise to Greece on the night of 2/3 March flown by Flg Off Neil Attenborrow, followed by the real thing in May when Vaughan-Fowler accompanied the same pilot to land three agents and pick up seven, a record number for two Lysanders.

The pair flew another Lysander double on the night of 4/5 June, making the squadron's first operation to France. On Operation 'Thicket' that night, four agents were landed at the field at St Vulbas near Lyons, and six were picked up. After a difficult flight through the Alps the overloaded Lysanders reached Calvi safely, 24 hours before RAF Halifaxes of No. 100 Group carried out spoof raids, while dozens more were to take off from airfields in England towing gliders. The invasion of France was about to begin.

CHAPTER 7

Liberation and Retribution

In the early hours of 6 June 1944, as Operation 'Overlord', the Allied invasion of France, was launched, seven Halifaxes of No. 138 Squadron and four from No. 161 Squadron dropped dummy parachutists some distance away from the Normandy beaches in an effort to confuse the German defenders. As they hit the ground, powerful firecrackers attached to the dummies exploded to simulate gunfire. On the same operation, Flt Lt Harry Johnson dropped a team of six live Special Air Service (SAS) soldiers in the area.

During D-Day itself all supply and pick-up missions from Tempsford were suspended, although No. 161 Squadron's five Hudsons flew a total of twenty-two Ascension operations on D plus 1. Demand for these missions was such that the squadron borrowed Anson III NK720 to supplement the hard-pressed Hudsons.

Most of No. 138 Squadron's serviceable Halifaxes – the squadron had lost five aircraft and crews during the week preceding the invasion – joined No. 100 Group's aircraft to fly a counter-measures mission dropping 'window', strips of one-foot-long metallised paper that blinded German radar screens with false echoes. Typically, some twenty-four aircraft in two formations of twelve would fly line abreast, the first formation 30 miles ahead of the second and with the aircraft two and a quarter miles apart. Every aircraft would release bundles of window at the rate of thirty a minute. What appeared on the German radar screens was a formation of over 500 aircraft.

Other clandestine missions were still being mounted from Tempsford while Allied forces were establishing their bridgehead in Normandy. SOE agents and Jedburgh teams had gathered together at Hasells Hall on 5 June, all spending their last day in England before being parachuted into France. Amongst them were Violette Szabo and several SAS officers. During the night of 6/7 June 1944 Szabo, Philippe Liewer, his assistant Bob Maloubier and an OSS wireless operator were dropped near Limoges from a Carpetbagger B-24 flown by Lt Fenster during Operation 'Stationer'. Liewer's mission was to take charge of the Resistance circuits in the area, one of which was being run by Pearl

Witherington. Three days later, Szabo had set out to make contact with a large network in Dordogne in a car driven by local Resistance leader, Jaques Dufour, when they ran into an SS roadblock. They fled on foot into a wood, armed with Sten guns. After a gunfight, during which Dufour escaped, Szabo was finally arrested after running out of ammunition, and was sent to SD headquarters at Avenue Foch in Paris for two months of violent interrogation.

On the same night as the Limoges drop a No. 161 Squadron Hudson dropped five SAS officers over Rouvray, near Avallon, while a No. 138 Squadron Halifax flown by Plt Off Bill Strathern RNZAF dropped more SAS commandos behind German lines in Normandy from a height of 700 feet, and then packets of supplies to a secondary DZ. At the beginning of July Strathern and his crew dropped a French Corps Auxiliaire Féminin (CAF) agent, Josiane Gros, south of Paris with SIS agent Felix, Flt Lt Phillip Schneidau, making yet another jump into his homeland. During this period Strathern's 'G'-George was one of the few No. 138 Squadron Halifaxes that wore three Swastikas on its nose, victims of accurate shooting by its rear gunner Sgt Gordon 'Snowy' Dunning.

'A' Flight of No. 138 Squadron had received its first Stirling IVs, which would replace the war-weary Halifaxes by the end of the year. The type, which had been withdrawn from Bomber Command's main force and relegated to glider-towing and transport duties, did not meet with universal approval from the squadron's aircrews. Considered overweight and underpowered, the slab-

Many No. 138 Squadron Stirlings were lost over France during supply drops to the Resistance in the lead-up to the Allied invasion of Normandy in June 1944. This one, LJ932/'N', made it back to a crash-landing in Lincolnshire. *(Mrs Nora Curtis via Andy Thomas)*

sided Stirling was prone to accident-inducing swings on take-off which were difficult to counter with its small rudder surface. In its defence, the Stirling had excellent low- and medium-level performance, was extremely manoeuvrable for an aircraft of its size, had a range of 3,000 miles and could carry twenty containers in its bomb bay. In the days following the Normandy invasion, two No. 138 Squadron Stirlings were used to drop SAS commandos and an SOE agent near Fetigny; and on 21 June five planes dropped containers to them at isolated DZs at Vieux Dun and La Valottes on the Côte d'Or.

The squadron suffered another loss on the night of 18/19 June when Halifax LL364, flown by Flt Lt John Kidd, whose twin brother also served on the squadron and was flying the same night, was involved in a mid-air collision with a Carpetbagger B-24 over a DZ in France. There were no survivors.

The 122nd Bomb Squadron had begun dropping agents into the south of France again and on 29 June Operation Groups (OG) 'Justine' and 'Eucalyptus', two British missions with an OSS wireless operator, Lt André Pecquet, were dropped into the Vercors, a vast, high plateau south-west of Grenoble. Their mission was to support a large group of *maquis* who were planning a campaign of open resistance against the Germans in response to a directive from de Gaulle's Direction Générale de Services Spéciaux (DGSS). Two other OGs were later dropped into the Ardèche, west of the Rhône, where they worked with the Forces Françaises de l'Intérieur (FFI), the successor to Moulin's CNR.

RAF SD flights from Tempsford had resumed, with the first pick-ups being conducted on the night of 2/3 July when Lysanders flew to fields near Issoudun

B-17F Fortress 42-29644 of the 885th Bombardment Squadron takes off from Blida on an OSS support mission over the south of France in 1943. *(ww2 images)*

and Orléans. Two days later the first post-invasion Hudson sortie was flown by Flt Lt Peter Affleck, who carried eight agents including Marie-Madeleine Meric and picked up the same number from Egligny. That night one of the squadron's Hudsons was shot down over Holland, killing Flt Lt Menzies, his three crew and four agents.

One of the more exotic WAAF recruits to SOE was dropped into France on the night of 6 July, for the last of many visits she made to occupied Europe. Christine Granville – born Krystyna Skarbek near Warsaw on 1 May 1915, the daughter of Count Jerzy Skarbek and his Jewish wife Stephanie – was in Kenya with her husband, a Ukrainian adventurer named Jerzy Gizycki, when war broke out. She immediately travelled to London, joined the WAAF and through diplomatic contacts became one of the first women to be recruited by the Australian SOE recruiting officer, George Taylor; she was given the codename Granville, which she later adopted as her surname.

The petite, olive-skinned woman with jet-black hair was strong-willed, quick-tempered and an excellent athlete. After several journeys to Hungary and her native Poland, some of which involved skiing across the Tatra mountains, she teamed up with a fellow Pole, Andrew Kowerski, who had built a number of escape lines used by Polish and Czechoslovakian volunteers for service abroad. Having evaded capture on more than one occasion, once by bribing a Slovak border guard and the second time by convincing a Hungarian doctor working for the Gestapo that she had tuberculosis, Granville and Kowerski – who was by then one of her many lovers – reached Cairo by way of Yugoslavia and Turkey.

From there SOE sent the pair into Syria during the campaign against the Vichy French, but on their return to Egypt they languished in Cairo for nearly a year while the local SOE mission tried to make up its mind what to do next with its flamboyant Polish agents. In the event, Kowerski, now known as Kennedy, was sent to Italy at the beginning of 1944 as an instructor at a Polish parachute school, while Christine was trained as a wireless operator prior to being dropped blind into Hungary. At the last minute it was decided that she should be sent to France, and in May 1944 she arrived at the Club des Pins in Algiers to begin an intensive training period with the Massingham mission. Granville was to be a courier for Cammaert's Jockey circuit.

Within days of being parachuted into the Vercors, Granville was climbing Alpine passes into Italy, despite a badly bruised hip gained during her heavy landing at the DZ. Her mission was to make contact with Polish alpine troops fighting for the Germans and persuade them to desert, while Cammaerts was making desperate efforts to organise supply drops of arms and equipment for local *maquis*, who had now declared the Vercors plateau liberated.

In the immediate aftermath of the D-Day landings several RAF fighter pilots came into close personal contact with the Resistance; two of the most unlikely ones were natives of Austria and of the United States. Sqn Ldr Count Manfred Beckett Czernin, son of an Austro-Hungarian diplomat born in Berlin, had studied in England and joined the RAF's Auxiliary Air Force in 1935 to train as a bomber pilot. At the outbreak of war he retrained as a fighter pilot and shot down ten German aircraft during the Battle of Britain, flying Hurricanes of Nos 85 and 17 Squadrons. For his second tour with Fighter Command Czernin was posted to No. 146 Squadron at Dum Dum, in north-east India, equipped with obsolete Curtiss Mohawks and Brewster Buffalo fighters. He took command of the squadron when it re-equipped with Hurricane IIBs in May 1941. After shooting down another three enemy aircraft, Czernin returned to England; declining the proffered desk job, he joined SOE and was dropped into occupied Italy by No. 148 Squadron on 13 June 1944 to act as a liaison officer working with the Osoppo brigade in the Udine region. He would become a regular passenger on No. 148 Squadron Lysanders along with an SOE staff officer, the multilingual Christopher Lee. Educated at Wellington College, Lee was the cousin of Ian Fleming, assistant to the Director of Naval Intelligence. He volunteered to fight for the Finnish forces during the Winter War against the Soviet Union in 1939, then served in the Royal Air Force before joining SOE. Christopher Lee would later become an international film star.

In July Czermin recruited the young sister of one of the Osoppo leaders, Renato Din, who had been killed during an attack on a German garrison in the walled town of Tormezzo three months earlier. Her two other brothers were already in prison as suspected partisans, but Paola del Din was determined to uphold the family honour on the battlefield. She eventually completed the 500-mile journey to Florence, staying at convents and thumbing a lift on a German ambulance while carrying a pouch of secret documents, just as part of the city was liberated by partisans on 8 August. A month later Paola was sent to the parachute training school at Brindisi and trained as a wireless operator.

Californian Flt Lt Arthur 'Arty' Ross was another Fighter Command pilot to come into close contact with the Resistance that summer. Having volunteered to join the RAF, he underwent flying training in Canada before being posted in 1943 to No. 609 Squadron, flying Hawker Typhoon fighter-bombers at Manston, Kent. At the beginning of July 1944 the squadron was one of the first to operate from temporary airstrips in Normandy within sight of the beachhead, many of them selected by members of the Resistance. Within days of his arrival in France Ross was shot down behind enemy lines while attacking a column of German tanks, and was picked up by local *maquis* who guided him back to B7 airstrip at Martragny. So impressed was he with their courage and the strength of the organisation that he decided to throw in his lot with the band of *maquis*, rather than take the leave that was due to him. It was not until the squadron was preparing to move into Belgium three months later that Ross took his leave of the Resistance fighters and rejoined his unit.

The night of 6/7 July was of special significance for the 492nd Bomb Group: its first operation to occupied France. A Harrington C-47, crewed by Col Heflin, Capt W. Stael and Maj Edward Tresemer, the group's navigation officer, flew Operation 'Mixer I' to a landing strip near Izernore in the Ain, between Mâcon and Geneva, with eleven agents on board including an SOE demolitions expert.

Lt Gordon Nornable had been recruited from the 6th Battalion Gordon Highlanders in 1943 by SOE's chief recruiter, the thriller writer Selwyn Jepson, who had previously spotted Lise de Baissac, Noor Inayat Khan and Violette Szabo. An accomplished athlete with a good knowledge of French, Nornable also proved adept with small arms and explosives. His mission in the Ain was to train a 5,000-strong *maquis* group assembled by Richard Heslop, head of the Marksman circuit, in the use of small arms and demolitions.

While Nornable and his colleagues melted into the woods and valleys of the Ain, the C-47 was camouflaged and concealed at the field while a surgeon codenamed Parsifal who had flown out from Harrington visited wounded Resistance fighters, some of whom would be flown back to England. The C-47 eventually took off on the evening of 9 July, arriving at Harrington in the early hours of the following day with ten passengers on board, including four badly wounded SAS soldiers and Lt Col Heslop. Twenty other SAS troops had been

A Carpetbagger C-47 takes off from Harrington on D-Day, with a B-24 being loaded with containers. *(Harrington Museum)*

Carpetbagger C-47 *Gooney Bird* 43-47981 of the 801st Bomb Group (H) Provisional on a pick-up operation from a field near Biarritz. *(Harrington Museum)*

taken out in a double No. 161 Squadron Hudson operation from the same field three days earlier.

After D-Day, a new task was assigned to No. 161 Squadron's Lysander flight, although not a new one for the RAF: that of Mail Pick-Up (MPU). It was first carried out on the North-West Frontier in the 1930s by Army Cooperation Wapiti and Atlas biplanes equipped with a message pick-up hook. On the ground a wire loop was stretched between two poles, the end of the loop being attached to a mail sack lying on the ground. The aircraft would then fly low and slowly between the masts, with its hook lowered, to snag the loop and the attached bag without landing. The Lysander, however, was not equipped with an integral hook and had to rely on a long bamboo pole, resembling a fishing rod, being lowered from the rear cockpit by one of the air gunners borrowed from the Hudson flight. On the night of 7/8 July Flt Lt Bill Taylor and air gunner Flt Sgt Tommy Thomas – who had a French mother – flew Operation 'Toupet', a Mail Pick-Up sortie to north-west France. Another Lysander fell prey to trigger-happy anti-aircraft gunners in the Normandy sector during the same night.

Having successfully completed his eighth pick-up, part of a double Lysander Sussex operation flown for the French security organisation Réseau Écarlate from an area near Tours on the night of 7/8 July, Per Hysing-Dahl headed for the cleared air corridor across the Normandy coast at Trouville and into bad weather. Suddenly he was off track and under fire. American anti-aircraft guns found their target, damaging the Lysander's wing and the engine, which seized 20 miles from the coast. There was no alternative but to ditch in the Channel. On hitting the water at 70mph, the Lysander's heavy fixed undercarriage dug into the waves, causing it to cartwheel and throwing one of its three passengers out through the open cockpit. The plane sank almost immediately, before the pilot and the other two agents could scramble clear. Hysing-Dahl had been injured in the hand by shrapnel but, despite a torn and useless Mae West, he managed to extricate himself and reach the surface where he made contact with the agent. Weakened by fatigue and loss of blood, the pilot dived down to the aircraft and was able to pull one of the other agents to the surface. The third drowned in the aircraft. Having managed to inflate and board the aircraft's dinghy, a second agent died of exposure before they were rescued by an American MTB after spending four hours on the water.

When it was clear that the Allies had a firm foothold on continental Europe, German wrath was directed towards anyone connected to the Resistance. The uprising by the Vercors *maquis* had been brutally crushed by two German divisions which included SS troops and special units of KG 200, nine-man glider assault sections recruited from Luftwaffe personnel convicted of military offences. They were landed in DFS 230 gliders at an airfield at Vassieux built by *maquis* for SOE aircraft. Two of the German gliders were shot down, but more than 200 SS troops landed at the airfield to carry out summary executions of captured Resistance fighters, and many more reprisal killings of civilians caught up in the battle. Many of the containers dropped to *maquis* by dozens of USAAF B-17s in daylight missions during Operation 'Cadillac' on 14 July fell straight into German hands, while Francis Cammaerts and his courier Christine Granville were among the few SOE agents who managed to escape from the region and make their way south. Further to the west two of the Schlacht-gruppen Re.2002 fighter-bombers were shot down by *maquis* in the Limoges area.

Elsewhere, wholesale arrests resulted in the torture and execution of countless Resistance fighters, circuit members, and many SOE agents. Among those who had passed through Tempsford for the last time were two female agents, Andrée Borrel and Diana Rowden, who were murdered at Natzweiler concentration camp within a month of the Allied landings. Eileen Nearne had been arrested and sent to Markleburg, while Odette Sansom was incarcerated at Ravensbrück. French agent Marie-Madeleine Meric, the moving force behind the Alliance

circuit, had also been arrested after her flight from England on 6 July, but
would escape to fight another day. The cost of setting Europe alight was proving
to be a heavy one.

The invasion of France had also been the catalyst for an attempt on Hilter's
life on 20 July. Led by dissident generals and covertly supported by many senior
members of the Abwehr, the plot failed when Hitler escaped with only minor
injuries from the blast of a bomb planted by Count von Stauffenburg at
Rastenburg. Both the SOE and OSS had been aware that a putsch was being
planned, but had no direct contact with those involved. However, in the
aftermath the head of the Abwehr, Adm Wilhelm Canaris, was arrested for anti-
Nazi sympathies and his intelligence organisation was absorbed into the RHSA
under SS Gen Walther Schellenberg.

It was also a time when the Luftwaffe's KG 200 expanded its covert operations. The bulk of the long-range fleet, including the Fw 200C, the Ju 290A,
Ju 252A and Ju 52, belonged to the 1 Staffel based mainly at Berlin-Finow.
Medium-range transport types such as the Ju 88, Do 217 and Ju 188, plus fifty
gliders, were assigned to 2 Staffel headquartered at Finow and responsible for
operations in combat zones, and were deployed to six main operational detachments. These comprised Kommando Olga at Stuttgart-Echerdingen, covering
operations in western Europe; Carmen at Bergamo in Italy, covering southern
Europe and North Africa; Sud at Wiener Neustadt in Austria, covering the
Balkans and Middle East and Tosca at Kalamaki, covering North Africa, Maria
in Minsk covering the Soviet Union and Klara at Bug am Rugen covering
northern Europe. A third Staffel for training and support had been established
in May 1944, also based at Finow and equipped with twenty-five assorted types
of plane such as the Fw 44 and Klemm Kl 35.

Recruiting agents posed no problem, as Nazi sympathisers were to be found
in abundance in most countries in occupied Europe. Those fit for service were
accepted into the Waffen-SS, while many of those rejected by the military volunteered for training to return to their native countries as agents. Those destined to
be dropped into the Soviet Union were trained at the SS-Jagdkommando G
(Raiding Detachment G) at Schwarzenberg in the Riesengebirge mountains.

Radio operators, known as V-Männer, were issued with standard Luftwaffe
VHS transceivers enabling them to speak directly to the aircraft. Arab agents,
many of them of Egyptian origin, were trained at Berlin-Rangsdorf. The only
nationals suitable for training as agents who were in short supply were the
British. By D-Day MI5 had either 'turned' or isolated almost all of the 120
agents operating in the British Isles. There would be few to take their place in
the coming months.

Typical of KG 200's missions in mid-1944 were operations to insert agents into the Soviet Union and support them. Between 23 May and 29 June KG 200 lost three Junkers Ju 290As, and a Ju 252 which flew behind enemy lines in the Ukraine from Zilistea in Romania. One of the Ju 290s was shot down by Soviet Hawker Hurricanes, while the other three aircraft were lost when attempting to land groups of Kalmuks near Elista, the former capital of the Soviet Republic of Kalmutskaya. Soviet forces had overrun the landing site in the Kalach steppes.

Within a four-week period following D-Day, aircraft of KG 200 dropped more than 250 agents behind Allied lines including some from the B-17s, which also carried other agents to Col T.E. Lawrence's old stamping ground – Trans-Jordan. On 26 June Leutnant Wolfgang Pohl flew a second Operation 'Anti-Atlas' from Istres in the south of France carrying several SS agents dressed in Arab robes, this time in a B-17G. While flying south off the eastern coast of Spain, the B-17 developed a fuel leak and was forced to make an emergency landing at a Spanish Air Force base at Valencia. After its 'passengers' had been spirited away by their Abwehr escort, the German Air Attaché in Madrid had to negotiate the release of the crew, while the B-17 was impounded by the Spanish authorities.

Over the same period RAF Lysanders of No. 148 Squadron flew one single and four double aircraft operations from a forward base at Borgo airfield, south

A Junkers Ju 252, one of the many long-range transports used by I Staffel of the Luftwaffe's Kampfgeschwader 200, being refuelled with its integral ramp down. *(Bruce Robertson)*

of Bastia in Corsica, into southern France. On Operation 'Thicket 2' to the field at St Vulbas on the night of 11/12 July the engine of the Lysander flown by one of two new French pilots on the squadron, Lt Georges Libert, could not be restarted and the aircraft had to be burned.

Further to the east, the intelligence services were making tentative plans to work with the Soviet Army as it fought its way towards the Balkans. SOE Cairo had not had the spectacular successes of London and Algiers, and was seen by some to be dragging its heels concerning the offering of any assistance to its Soviet allies, including Churchill's personal representative in the region, Fitzroy Maclean. It was left to the Naval Intelligence Division (NID) to mount a covert mine-laying operation in the lower Danube with Tito's partisans prior to the arrival of Soviet forces on the river. The officer selected to become British Liaison Officer Middle Danube was Lt Cdr A.R. Glen DSC RNVR, who had played a leading part in Operation 'Fritham', the Allied attempt to occupy Spitsbergen in 1942. Although SOE Cairo opposed the operation, SOE HQ London agreed to support Sandy Glen not only by providing him with an experienced wireless operator, a Sgt Turner, but also by instructing SOE Bari to arrange for them to be dropped into Yugoslavia some 30 miles north-east of Nis. On 28 June Sandy Glen prepared to leave Italy.

A flight of No. 267 (SD) Squadron Dakotas based at Bari in 1944 – also under the command of No. 334 Wing of Balkan Air Force – seen over the Adriatic. *(ww2 images)*

Sgt Turner and I dined well in the Navy mess and reported in good time at Brindisi. We were thrilled to learn that one of the great Polish Halifax squadrons was to take us. We knew that no hitch or setback would stop *them*. Their welcome was, as always, warm and friendly, yet we both sensed something – a restraint, not quite Polish. It was only much later that we realised their fears were for those in Warsaw under immediate attack by the Germans, heightened by the doubt as to any help being likely from the advancing Red Army.

This had no impact, however, on the competence and kindness of our aircrew, who dropped us precisely on target and on time. As their aircraft flew on, the prospect that it, together with the entire Polish squadron, was to perish in the final heroic but impossible attempt to bring aid to Warsaw, was unthinkable.

'Dwi minuty!' The Polish pilot's voice crackled into the earphones and the dispatcher tapped first Sgt Turner and then myself on the shoulder. The warning light flashed red, two fingers indicating it was only a couple of minutes to the drop zone. I went first, a bit slowly, crouching with the weight of parachute and accoutrements under limited headroom, then arranging myself comfortably on the edge of the hatch, legs dangling. Red to green and, with a hefty Polish push from the dispatcher, out into the slipstream, with that exhilarating silence – and the comforting view of Sgt Turner, not far above.

As Glen and Turner, now part of the SOE 'Twilfit' Mission, made contact with Tito's 23rd Partisan Brigade, No. 334 Wing's Balkan SD operations were beginning to take their toll, especially on No. 267 Squadron. On 16 July Dakota KG472 stalled on overshooting a landing ground at Ticevo in Yugoslavia, killing the pilot, Flt Lt Gardiner, and injuring a number of passengers including Winston Churchill's SOE agent son, Randolph, and the author Evelyn Waugh, who were on their way to join John Henniker-Major's partisan mission in Serbia. A second Dakota, KG752, went missing on a supply drop over northern Italy on 21 August. While on a Yugoslav supply operation on the night of 21/22 July, USAAF 10th TCS C-47 41-18388, flown by Lt Horser, was shot down by a German night fighter and crashed near Nocim airstrip, killing the pilot. Its co-pilot, 2/Lt Largent, baled out and was rescued by the partisans who were awaiting the supplies the doomed aircraft was carrying.

However, it was on the evening of 25 July that No. 276 Squadron began its most demanding clandestine operation yet attempted. Earlier in the year, the squadron had successfully carried out two hazardous, long-distance operations

Flt Lt George Culliford DSO with a Polish major in front of his No. 267 Squadron Dakota III, KG523, which took part in Operation Wildhorn III, a clandestine flight to Poland in July 1944. (ww2 images)

into enemy-occupied Poland; the first, codenamed 'Wildhorn I', carried two SOE agents and had picked up a general of the Polish Home Army on 14/15 April. 'Wildhorn II' was flown by Dakota III KG477 fitted with four long-range tanks; it had a crew of four: pilot Flt Lt Mike O'Donovan, navigator Plt Off Jack Strain, wireless operator Plt Off D. Thomas and, acting as co-pilot and interpreter, Plt Off Btochi from No. 1586 (Polish) Flight.

The Dakota took off from Brindisi with two Polish officers and 1,000lb of ammunition on board at 1735 hours on 29 May with an escort of two No. 1586 Flight Liberators, which turned back as they entered Hungarian airspace. Two hours later radio communications were successfully established with the Polish underground reception committee, after which the torchlight flarepath was spotted by the crew. Unfortunately, as the Dakota had arrived ahead of schedule, the hastily prepared flarepath was some 200 yards short of the briefed 1,000 yards! Nevertheless, O'Donovan made a perfect landing and after less than ten minutes on the ground took off with two Polish Air Force officers and a diplomat aboard. They touched down safely at Brindisi some four hours later.

Operation 'Wildhorn III' was not so straightforward. It entailed flying more than 700 miles from Bari to a remote airstrip in Poland to collect vital components of Hitler's latest revenge weapon, the V-2 rocket. Carrying four Polish Army agents – a major, a captain and two lieutenants – and their equipment,

Dakota III KG523 headed north over Yugoslavia, escorted by a No. 1586 (Polish) Flight Liberator. The Dakota's captain, New Zealander Flt Lt George Culliford, had with him a co-pilot from No. 1586 Flight, Flt Lt Kazimir Szrajar, the experienced navigator Flg Off John Williams who had been on Wildhorn I, and wireless operator Flt Sgt Appleby. The moonless flight crossed Romania, Hungary, Czechoslovakia and the Carpathian mountains before descending towards Zaborow near Tarnow – only 65 miles from Berlin.

As German troops had been reported in the area the previous day, and with heavy rain softening the landing ground, Culliford made his approach with some apprehension. However, a safe landing was made after an overshoot, but as the four agents disembarked and others began loading the valuable cargo, the wheels of the Dakota sank slowly into the mud. At one time it seemed that the aircraft would have to be abandoned and plans were made for its destruction, but after much digging and revving of engines, which threatened to wake any Germans in the area, the wheels came free. Culliford managed to avoid the soft parts of the field and other hazards in the darkness to pull the Dakota off, after spending more than an hour longer on the ground than he had planned.

As the darkness gave way to light, the main concern was enemy fighters beginning their dawn patrols. Although Ju 88s were seen they kept their distance and the Dakota crossed the Dalmatian coast four hours after leaving Zaborow, only to be greeted with the news that strong cross winds were blowing across Brindisi's main runway. In the event Culliford managed to land into the wind on a half-completed second runway, without brakes: the hydraulic lines had been accidentally severed while trying to free the aircraft in Poland. The five agents and their vital V-2 parts were transferred to another Dakota to be flown the short distance to Bari, and two days later they all arrived safely at RAF Hendon on board a third No. 276 Squadron Dakota. On 8 September the first V-2 rocket fell on London, killing thirty-six.

In order to keep up the momentum created by the Allied advances into France, and to replace captured agents, the August moon period was to be a busy one for the Tempsford squadrons. Five Lysander sorties were flown on 4/5 August, one single and two double operations. During one of the doubles to a field near Tours, Flg Off Alex Alexander damaged his tail-wheel, elevator and R/T aerial when landing among bundles of hay. Having picked up his two passengers, Robert Bloc-Richard and his courier Marguerite Gianelli, who had hurt her hip, he managed to take off again using maximum power and had an anxious flight back without radio, to find England covered in thick fog. He was very lucky to overfly RAF St Eval in Cornwall which was using its FIDO equipment, large paraffin burners, to burn off the fog.

Although Alexander landed his two passengers safely, he incurred the station commander's wrath: first by his unannounced arrival – unknown to him he had landed in the opposite direction to a flight of Liberators taking off at the time – and then when he blocked the active runway with the Lysander owing to its broken tailwheel. To make matters worse, when Alexander returned to his aircraft in the Station Commander's car to collect the agents, who had remained in the cabin while he made the long walk around the perimeter track to the control tower, the couple were found in an amorous embrace on the cabin floor. They later married.

One of the Lysanders flying the other double mission of the night was not so lucky. While en route to a farm near Vatan in central France, Peter Arkell, a former Army Cooperation squadron Mustang pilot on his first pick-up operation, witnessed the experienced Flg Off J.P. Alcock, the second pilot on the Vatan sortie, being shot down by flak near Messac in Brittany. The Lysander crashed in flames, killing the pilot and the Réseau Ecarlate agent it was carrying.

Bad weather dogged the remaining single operation of the evening, and when Flg Off Lamberton's Lysander arrived over the field near Bourges, no signal could be seen and he returned to England without landing. This was one of several No. 161 Squadron flights that were launched from an advanced base at Winkleigh in Devon, both to cut the flight time to France and to release Tangmere and Ford for units of the 2nd Tactical Air Force supporting the invasion. Two more pick-ups were flown the following night from Winkleigh, one of which would prove to be the last by a No. 161 Squadron Lysander when Les Ratcliff flew a seven-hour sortie to pick up an evading USAAF pilot, Lt R. Murphy, who had been shot down near Bourges.

Lysander sorties continued to be flown by No. 148 Squadron, which completed another six flights from Corsica – packed at the time with Allied aircraft preparing for the landing in the south of France – including two OSS operations. The very last Lysander pick-up in occupied France was flown by Peter Vaughan-Fowler to a field near Pont de Vaux on the River Sâone, close to the Swiss border, on the night of 10/11 August. Only one agent was collected, but because of the importance of the operation it had to be flown on a moonless night.

The emphasis was now on mass container and supply drops to the Resistance as the Allies prepared to open a second front in France. During the month of August a detachment of No. 624 Squadron's Stirlings, along with a flight of Halifaxes from No. 148 Squadron, moved to Fairford in Gloucestershire to augment Tempsford squadrons, while another detachment was flying a series of operations to drop OSS Operational Groups (OG) into southern France from Bone in Algeria.

The Tempsford Hudson flight was also augmented by a detachment of No. 334 Wing's SD squadron, No. 267, to carry and pick up agents in France. Operating from Cecina in northern Italy, one of the squadron's Dakotas, flown by South African Flg Off Rostron, flew three sorties to a grass-and-lavender field near Apt under the watchful eye of 'Mac' McCairns, now working for A12c and acting as second pilot. The first attempt, on the evening of 8 August, was aborted owing to bad weather over the landing ground. The following night Rostron managed to set the Dakota down on the rain-soaked field with fifteen passengers aboard to be greeted by thirty-one people, most of whom were evading US airmen.

However, owing to the state of the field, the useful length of which was reduced by the height of the lavender, only twenty-three could be carried with safety and it was arranged that the Dakota would return the next night to collect the remaining airmen. On 11 August a third Operation 'Spitfire' was mounted but the landing ground had been discovered by the Germans, who had shot the farmer who owned the field, along with members of his family, and had destroyed their farmhouse. There was no sign of the missing US airmen. The mission was abandoned.

The following night a B-24 of the 885th based at Blida dropped a total of eighteen OSS agents, including US Marine Capts Peter Ortiz and Francis Coolridge, and 67,000lb of supplies to the Resistance near Annecy in the south. A total of sixteen Jedburghs were also dropped into southern France during August; among the team's twelve OSS agents were Capt Aaron Bank and Lt John H. Hemingway. Along with many other OSS Jedburgh officers, Aaron Bank had been briefed in London alongside his SOE counterparts at Baker Street and had trained with them at Milton Hall, near Peterborough. He was part of a team codenamed 'Packard' that was dropped with an OSS radio operator and a French officer into the Massif Central region to train local Resistance groups in guerrilla warfare.

Jack Hemingway was the son of the writer who had championed the Republican cause during the Spanish Civil War, Ernest Hemingway, but he was less adept as a covert soldier than his OSS colleague. Dropped with his fishing rod, as he was an expert fly fisherman, Hemingway stood out from the locals and was soon stopped at a German checkpoint. Although he spoke excellent French, he was unable to convince the Germans that his radio mast was another fishing rod. He was promptly arrested and sent for interrogation. By a stroke of good fortune, Hemingway recognised the German officer questioning him; the man's girlfriend was a woman called 'Tiddy' who had, by a remarkable coincidence, been Jack's nurse when he lived with his family in Paris before the war. Hemingway was soon sharing a bottle of schnapps with him before being sent to Germany. As Jack arrived at a PoW camp at Ludwigsburg, near Stuttgart, on 24 August, his father was 'liberating' the Ritz Hotel in Paris with an OSS colonel, David K. Bruce. Bruce, head of SI and SO at OSS Station, London, had landed on a Normandy beach on D-Day with his boss, Wild Bill Donovan, only six weeks earlier.

After the Vercors disaster Francis Cammaerts had moved his operations to the Hautes-Alpes region, while Christine Granville was back on the Italian frontier making contact with the eastern European border guards. On the morning of 13 August Cammaerts was in a Red Cross car with British SOE agent Xan Fielding, who had recently dropped into Seyne-les-Alpes from Algiers, and French agent Commandant Sorensen. The driver of the car, which had a special pass enabling it to be driven during curfews, was Claude Renoir, son of the artist and film director who the previous year had directed a film in Hollywood about the French Resistance called *This Land Is Mine*, starring Charles Laughton.

They were on the outskirts of Digne when an Allied air raid bought them to a halt. Hearing the all-clear, they approached the village, only to be stopped by a German roadblock. When they persuaded the local Gestapo officer that they had hitched a lift in the car, Renoir was waved through but without his passengers. The three agents were arrested only when they could not give a plausible explanation as to why they were all carry a large amount of cash — with consecutive serial numbers. The Germans suspected them of being black-market racketeers and threw them into Digne prison. After only a cursory interrogation at the Gestapo headquarters, the three men were condemned to be shot without the Germans discovering their real identities.

As soon as she had word of their capture, Granville tried to mount a rescue, but local Resistance leaders decided the risk was too great. She then contacted an Alsatian gendarme who was acting as a liaison officer between the French prefecture and the Gestapo. Christine told Albert Schenck that the Allies were about to land in the south of France and that he would be identified as a collaborator by the Resistance when they arrived in the area. It would therefore be in his best interest to help secure the release of Cammaerts and his fellow prisoners. Schenck said that a Belgian interpreter working for the Gestapo, Max Waem, might be able to arrange it. He promised to contact him and set up a meeting. When no word of a meeting came she called on Schenck once again, just as news of the Allied landings was filtering through. Granville told him that by the end of the day Digne would be surrounded and his life would be in great danger. Within a couple of hours Schenck had arranged for Christine to meet Waem at his flat. Here Granville told the suspicious Belgian that she was a British agent, Cammaerts's wife and, for good luck, Gen Montgomery's niece. She was also made it clear that she was in direct radio contact with the Allied forces and that they were asking for details of anyone associated with the Gestapo. Waem agreed to help, but only if he was protected from the French Resistance and not imprisoned by the Allies. Granville agreed to his terms on behalf of the British government.

When Waem left to make arrangements for the agents' release, Schenck demanded a ransom of two million francs, which he said would be split between himself and Waem. Granville managed to get a radio message through to the SOE mission in Algiers, and 24 hours later the money was dropped to the Seyne DZ. Waem kept his promise, having told the Digne prison guards that he had come to escort Cammaerts, Fielding and Soresen to Gestapo headquarters for further interrogation. As soon as they were clear of the town he drove them to a rendezvous with Granville. After he had taken off his Gestapo uniform and hidden it in a ditch, Waem surrendered to the agents to await the Allies. Granville left almost immediately to continue her mission of persuading Polish and Ukrainian border guards to defect to the approaching Allies.

On 15 August Operation 'Dragoon', the Allied landings in the south of France, had been launched by General Patch's US Seventh Army. Leading part of the landing force was one of Tempsford's early customers, Gen Jean de Lattre de Tassigny, who led his Second Corps to liberate Toulon and Marseilles. It was during this period of fast-moving front lines and much confusion that an 885th BS B-24 actually made a night landing at Toulouse aerodrome, carrying two American doctors, two nurses and a large quantity of medical equipment – before the Germans had even pulled out of the base.

As British, US and Commonwealth troops led the charge through France, Soviet armies had pushed the Germans back to the River Vistula, and the Polish Home Army in Warsaw rose in an attempt to rid the city of its brutal occupiers. Encouraged by messages of support from Moscow Radio, Operation 'Tempest' was launched on 1 August. However, with British and American governments focused on the liberation of occupied western Europe, they were not in a position to provide direct military support to the uprising. The only way to support the partisan army was from the air, and so starting on the night of 5 August 1944 No. 148 (SD) Squadron and No. 1586 (Polish) Flight began dropping arms, ammunition and medical supplies under the supervision of Wg Cdr Roman Rudkowski.

The Polish crew of Liberator III of No. 301 (SD) Squadron at Trigno in Italy during the 1944 Warsaw uprising; note the Polish insignia and 'angel riding a container' artwork on the nose. *(ww2 images)*

No. 1586 Flight used the Polish-designed Type H container, which was lighter than the standard C-type used by most of the SD squadrons. Made up of five sheet-metal drums held together by two steel rods plus two extra containers, one acting as a shock absorber and the other holding the static line, they were not as strong as the British containers and were liable to disintegrate on impact with the ground.

Shrouded in smoke and surrounded by hundreds of flak batteries, Warsaw was a dangerous place for the low-flying Halifaxes and Liberators. Few drop zones were clearly marked and radio communications with the Polish Home Army were almost non-existent. By the end of the first night of operations four Halifaxes were missing, along with No. 148 Squadron's 'A' and 'B' Flight commanders; a fifth aircraft crash-landed on its return to Bari.

Liberators of Nos 31 and 34 Squadrons SAAF at Foggia and No. 178 Squadron based at Amendola supplemented the SD units, while aircrew from No. 300 (Polish) Squadron were drafted in to replace missing SD aircrews. In four days of operations between 13 and 16 August eighty Allied bombers attempted to reach Warsaw, but only fifteen managed to make contact with the partisans and drop their containers, most of which fell into German hands. Fifteen aircraft failed to return from the 1,800-mile round trip and another three were written off in landing accidents.

The losses continued to mount and by the time the Polish Air Force's pre-war commander, Air Cdre Ludomil Rayski, flew No. 1586 Flight's Liberator B III KH101/'H' over Warsaw to see the situation for himself on the night of 23/24 August, it was clear that the campaign could not be sustained. With the Soviets warning No. 334 Wing that any RAF or SAAF SD aircraft would be fired on if they attempted emergency landings in Soviet-held territory during the uprising, and with the loss of some 200 SD aircrew in only three weeks, the operation was cancelled by the end of the month.

The RAF SD squadrons had dropped more than 1,000 Sten guns, 19,000 grenades and some 2 million rounds of ammunition to the besieged Home Army fighters, but for every ton of supplies dropped over Warsaw, an RAF

No. 148 (SD) Squadron crews pose with members of the Russian Mission assigned to No. 334 Wing at Bari under the nose of one of its Halifax II Series IA aircraft, with drop-mission markings on the nose. *(Bruce Robertson)*

bomber was lost. Although close to the outskirts of the Polish capital, Soviet forces did nothing to help the uprising, or the RAF airlift, until it was clear that Operation Tempest was doomed to failure.

On 18 September 110 Eighth Air Force B-17s, flown from Soviet bases and escorted by 70 P-51 Mustang fighters, dropped 1,320 containers to the Polish Home Army; most of them fell into German hands. By this time Soviet GVF Po-2s and R-5s had begun night supply flights over Warsaw to the remnants of the partisan army, but by then it was a case of too little, too late. On 2 October the Polish Home Army commander-in-chief, Gen Bor-Komorowski, surrendered to the Germans and was interned in Colditz.

As the Allies tasted victory over what was left of the Axis in the west, the Soviet Union was planning to redraw the map of eastern Europe following Germany's defeat. In order to strengthen its hand in the Balkans, two Soviet units were sent to Bari and put at the disposal of the Balkan Air Force. During August ten GVF PS-84s, escorted by twelve Yak-9D fighters, arrived at the Italian base with eighty Soviet officers and airmen under the command of Col Socolov. They had flown via Habbaniya, Iraq, Cairo West and Lake Scutari in Albania – having left Moscow on 10 July led by a Soviet Air Force Douglas A-20 Boston that acted as a navigational leader – to become the only Soviet unit to be placed under Western command during the Second World War. They joined the two PS-84s already in Italy and flew their first mission into Yugoslavia on 22 August, when they picked up 135 members of Tito's Jugoslav Army of National Liberation (JANL) from an airstrip near Niksic, 50 miles north-east of Dubrovnik. Although part of No. 334 Wing, the Soviet unit was prone to carrying out freelance missions, some of which were flown without Allied permission. On 25 July a PS-84 had dropped two Soviet envoys to the headquarters of the Greek communist ELAS partisans who were planning to take over the country when the Germans withdrew.

The USAAF Special Duties squadrons were now being reorganised and were expanding their network of target areas. On 13 August the Carpetbaggers BG at Harrington was redesignated the 492nd Bomb Group (Heavy) and its four Bomb Squadrons were renumbered as the 856th, 857th, 858th and 859th, commanded by Capt Rodman A. St Clair, Maj Jack M. Dickerson, Capt Robert L. Boone and Maj McManus, respectively. Two weeks later Col Heflin handed over command of the group to Col Robert W. Fish. During August a detachment of six of the Group's Liberators, now B-24Hs, at Leuchars was dedicated to dropping and supplying agents in Norway, but because of bad weather and the threat of Luftwaffe night fighters only thirty-seven of sixty-five attempted missions were successful.

B-24J 42-51211 *Miss Fils* takes off from Harrington on a Carpetbagger mission. *(Harrington Museum)*

The following month, this group was tasked with supporting resistance fighters in Belgium and Denmark, but by the end of the month a decision had been made to switch the role of three of its squadrons to that of night bombing, leaving only the 859th BS to continue to fly covert operations. Between January and September the 801st/492nd BG flew 2,263 supply missions to occupied Europe, dropping 662 'Joes', 18,500 containers, 8,050 'nickels', more than 10,000 packages and 26 homing pigeons.

In the meantime, the overwhelming success of Operation Dragoon led to another and even more devastating cull of SOE agents captured in France. On 12 September, the day after the Allied Normandy and Riviera invasion forces met up at Dijon, more than fifty were executed. Madeleine Damerment, Eliane Plewman and Noor Inyat Khan were shot at Dachau concentration camp, while at Buchenwald Robert Benoist was hanged along with thirty-six Allied officers. It was to Buchenwald concentration camp that Wg Cdr Yeo-Thomas had been sent after his brutal interrogation at Avenue Foch, but with the collusion of a

B-24H *Scrappy* at the Harrington disposal fitted with a modified navigator's position in the nose in place of the gun turret. *(Harrington Museum)*

guard he had managed to escape before the 12 September murders. The instigator of these atrocities was the Austrian chief of the RHSA, Ernst Kaltenbrunner, who also oversaw operations of the Luftwaffe's KG 200.

Amongst the luckier SOE agents who were overrun by the advancing Allied forces during September were Francis Cammaerts and Christine Granville. Following Granville's courageous ploy to save the three SOE agents from execution, Schenck had been caught and killed by the Resistance, while Waem had been flown via Algiers to Cairo, where he disappeared – as did the two-million-franc ransom. One hundred miles to the north of Digne, Gordon Nornable, who had been wounded while fighting with *maquis* in the Ain, spent two weeks in September organising an airlift to return the agents of Richard Heslop's Marksman circuit to Britain. No. 161 Squadron Hudsons and Harrington C-47s took part in the airlift, which became known as 'Xavier's Air Express Service', 'Xavier' being Heslop's fieldname; it was mounted from a former Luftwaffe airfield at Ambérieu-en-Bugey.

As the Allied advanced pushed its way north, No. 138 Squadron made its first daylight drop of stores containers to members of the Belgian Resistance from 10 to 21 September with sixteen Stirlings and Halifaxes. The operations continued over the 10-day period, during which time none of the Squadron's aircraft was lost to enemy action.

The Allies were now poised to liberate the Netherlands. All active SOE networks in the country had long since been obliterated, with resistance being restricted to small, uncoordinated cells that published underground newspapers and assisted evading Allied airmen shot down over Holland. Prior to D-Day no OSS agents had been dropped into Holland, although its one-man Netherlands

Section in London was about to change that situation. Lt Jan Lavage, the American-born son of Dutch émigrés, was planning Operation 'Melanie': small teams to enter Holland and make contact with the disparate Resistance groups and transmit intelligence obtained from these sources, while trying to recruit new agents and extend the Dutch networks into Germany. The operation, supported by the Dutch government-in-exile, began with the first OSS team being inserted overland via Normandy.

Unfortunately Holland was about to become the scene of another intelligence disaster, one that may have cost thousands of Allied lives. In early September FM Montgomery conceived an operation to outflank the German's 'West Wall' defensive line by forcing a narrow corridor through Holland and establishing a bridgehead across the River Rhine into northern Germany's industrial heart, the Ruhr valley.

Operation 'Market Garden' was launched on 17 September, with hundreds of British and American transport aircraft and gliders lifting the 1st British Airborne Division and the 1st Polish Brigade Group to seize seven canal and river bridges in the Arnhem area. At the same time, the British 30th Armoured Corps was racing toward the bridgeheads to link up with the airborne troops and cross into Germany. However, the American Melanie mission was given no prior notice of Operation Market Garden, despite having established vital links with Dutch Resistance cells in the area and, by using the excellent Dutch telephone network, being in touch with the OSS SI office in Paris using its TR-4 wireless telegraph radio link. The team even had no contact with the US 82nd and 101st Airborne Divisions that were tasked with securing the bridges at Nijmegen, Eindhoven and Grave. Making matters worse was the fact that the OSS/SOE Jedburghs deployed with each Allied airborne division during Market Garden, with the primary task of obtaining tactical intelligence from Resistance groups, were also not aware of the Melanie mission or the intelligence it had gathered.

One of the most successful Jedburghs was dropped at Nijmegen from a C-47 with the 82nd Airborne Division. English SOE agent Robert Harcourt and OSS officer Arie Bestebeurtje, son of the head of Unilever, did manage to make useful contacts with the Dutch Resistance, but with only four Jedburghs to cover the whole of the airborne assault their value was severely limited. Jedburgh Team 'Claude', attached to the British 1st Airborne Division, had to rely on a junior Dutch OSS officer, Lt Knottenbelt, to vet all Resistance contacts before any intelligence could be passed to divisional command. Team Claude had also lost its only radio during the initial drop and its inability to communicate with Team 'Edward', dropped with the Polish Parachute Brigade by a C-47 of the 52nd Troop Carrier Wing, prevented a clear assessment of the situation in the Arnhem sector.

One of the reasons that the Dutch Resistance was not alerted to the Arnhem drop was because British intelligence erroneously believed that the Germans had penetrated their networks. If it had used local knowledge of the area, Montgomery's force would have been alerted to the presence of two German panzer divisions in the sector protecting the bridges. The outcome of the 10-day Operation Market Garden was almost 7,000 British and Polish paratroops killed, wounded or captured, and the Allied push into Germany seriously delayed.

In the Mediterranean theatre, the 885th Bomb Squadron (Heavy) was relocated to Brindisi to join No. 148 (SD) Squadron, tasked to support Italian partisans. In early October No. 148 gained another stepping stone in its drive to support Yugoslav partisans when a detachment of its Halifaxes moved to Araxos in southern Greece, sharing the recently captured airfield with Balkan Air Force Hurricane IVs of No. 6 Squadron. This had been made possible with the help of the other Balkan Air Force SD unit, No. 267 Squadron.

Civilians, evacuated from Yugoslavia during German attacks on partisan positions in late 1944, arrive at Bari on a No. 267 Squadron Dakota. *(ww2 images)*

It had become clear that as Germany's hold on Greece weakened, the main partisan groups would face each other in a struggle for control of the country. Greece was on the verge of civil war. In order to forestall any civil strife it was vital for an Allied force to gain control of Athens as soon as possible. Standing in their way were the German-held coastal defences and radar station on the island of Kythera, which protected the sea lanes leading to Athen's main port of Pireus. On 10 September No. 267 Squadron's pilot Mike O'Donovan and his regular navigator Jack Strain took off from Bari in Dakota III KG511 to drop an eight-man Royal Marine Commando team on the southern end of Kythera, to act as the eyes of the main Foxforce which landed on the island a week later.

Although there was now little threat to the SD flights over Italy from enemy fighters, two unfortunate losses during this period involved American aircraft. On 22 October No. 148 Squadron's Lysander T1456 was shot down en route to Austria during a daylight operation from northern Italy by a USAAF P-51, despite high cover provided by No. 3 (RAAF) Squadron Mustangs; the pilot, Flg Off Raynes, and the two SOE agents on board were killed. This was particularly devastating for the Lysander flight, coming only weeks after Flg Off Manning and his new wife Diana Portman, a member of FANY, were killed when the American aircraft, in which they had hitched a ride back to his base after a brief honeymoon in Florence, crashed on take-off.

Attrition of the SD Lysanders, a type that made its first flight in 1936, was now causing concern and various replacements were evaluated. One of the most promising was the Fairey Barracuda, the first monoplane torpedo-bomber to enter service with the Royal Navy. A successor to the 'Stringbag', as the Swordfish was known, which had been used briefly for SD operations in Malta, the three-seat Barracuda's large flap area and sturdy, widely-spaced undercarriage, designed for carrier operations, gave it excellent short take-off and landing characteristics. In 1944 several Barracuda IIs, powered by single 1,640hp Rolls-Royce Merlin engines that gave them a speed of over 200mph and a maximum range of 1,100 miles, were modified as paratroop transports. They were fitted with two underwing containers, each capable of carrying two paratroopers – or agents – while their equipment could be carried in the under-fuselage torpedo bay. Seated, or rather, crouched in tandem, the two passengers would be in radio touch with the pilot, who would activate a trap door to drop them over a DZ. This variant of the Barracuda was subjected to extensive trials at the Airborne Forces Experimental Establishment at Beaulieu, but was not adopted by the RAF SD squadrons.

The Luftwaffe's KG 200 had also been experimenting with similar personnel transport pods. Designed by the Forschungsgruppe Graf Zeppelin (GFZ), the

Royal Navy Fairey Barracuda II P9795, fitted with two-man pods under the wing, was tested in 1944 as a potential Lysander replacement for delivering agents behind enemy lines. *(Author's collection)*

German pods were mounted above the wing of the carrier aircraft with a trap door beyond the trailing edge of the wing. Four agents could be carried in each lightweight plywood pod which, not surprisingly, resembled a small airship. First tested on a Klemm Kl 35 trainer and later on a Junkers Ju 87D Stuka dive bomber, smaller one-man versions were built for installation on the wings of Bf 109 or Fw 190 fighters. Like its British counterpart the experimental programme, codenamed Doppelreiter (Double-rider), was not adopted for KG 200 operations.

By mid-1944 KG 200 had expanded in numbers and scope. Three more USAAF B-17s had been acquired, along with the first of five B-24s. Two B-17Fs, one of which was 41-30713 named *Phyllis Marie* of the 390th Bomb Group, had been captured undamaged in France in March, while a B-17G had crash-landed in Schleswig at the same time. A month later a second B-17G was forced down intact in Denmark and the fleet of captured Fortresses appeared on the KG 200 inventory as Do 200s. The Gruppe's first Liberator, B-24D 41-23859 *Blonde Bomber II*, had accidentally landed at Pachino in Sicily instead of

Malta in February 1943 and was tested at Rechlin before entering service with KG 200. Another Liberator, B-24H of the 449th BG, named *Sunshine*, had landed in error at Venegono airfield in Italy in April 1944.

One of the most ambitious operations assigned to the clandestine unit was to assist in the assassination of the Soviet leader, Josef Stalin, in Moscow on the anniversary of the October Revolution. One of a series of operations behind the lines on the Eastern Front, codenamed 'Zeppelin', it was instigated by RSHA chief Ernst Kaltenbrunner and planned by Oberstleutnant Reinhard Gehlen's office. It involved flying two Russian agents and a motorcycle sidecar combination to within 40 miles of Moscow. They were then to make contact with a group of dissident Russians, gain access to the Kremlin and kill the commander-in-chief of the USSR's armed forces with grenades and gunfire. After a team of Russian-speaking agents had been dropped by KG 200 to reconnoitre suitable landing sites and weather patterns for the operation in July, Unteroffizier Bruno Davids and his five-man crew flew an Arado Ar 232A to an

One of three USAAF B-24 Liberators used by 1/KG 200, 42-78106 coded NF-FL was destroyed at Hildesheim by retreating Luftwaffe personnel in May 1945. *(Richard Chapman)*

airfield near Riga in Latvia to pick up the two agents. They were flown to a forest clearing near Velikiye-Luki, but a heavy landing on a moonless night damaged the undercarriage and jammed the cargo door. As they were unable to unload the motor-cycle combination, the operation was abandoned and the agents were flown to Zareby in Poland, where the Arado's undercarriage collapsed. Assigned to 2 Staffel, the Ar 232 could have been designed with clandestine flights in mind. It was in fact designed as a potential replacement for the venerable Ju 52.

The twin-engined design featured a pod-and-boom fuselage with a rear loading door, and a tricycle undercarriage with eleven pairs of small main wheels for operating on unmade airstrips. Dubbed the Tausendfussler, or millipede, the Ar 232A could carry a 4-ton load and was armed with a 13mm MG 131 machine-gun in the nose, another at the rear of the fuselage pod, and a 20mm MG 181 cannon in a power-operated dorsal turret. Owing to shortages of BMW 801MA engines the twin-engined version was abandoned after only two prototypes had flown, one of which was used by KG 200. A total of twenty Ar 232Bs, each powered by four BMW-Bramo engines, had been produced by 1944: ten were assigned to the 'Black' unit for operations in Norway, Finland and the Soviet Union. Iceland was also subject to a series of clandestine visits by the KG 200 Tausendfussler.

The Zeppelin operation to Moscow had only been postponed, and so at dawn on 5 September a KG 200 Ar 232B headed for a stretch of the Smolensk-to-Moscow highway, a distance of 370 miles from Riga. The Arado, piloted by Oberfeldwebel Vierus, came under anti-aircraft fire while searching for the forest clearing and was forced to land at an alternative site at Karmanovo, some 90 miles from Moscow. The aircraft hit a tree on landing, ripped out one of its BMW-Bramo 323 radial engines and damaged the tailplane. The crew and agents, along with the Russian Type M-72 motorcycle combination, were unharmed but the aircraft had to be abandoned. Unknown to them all, one of the reconnoitre teams had been captured by the Soviets and the Arado was shadowed as soon as it entered Russian airspace. The Soviet major – one of Gehlen's best agents – and his girlfriend were soon picked up at a checkpoint outside Moscow while the crew, none of whom spoke Russian, radioed that they were trying to return on foot. With no Russian documents they were soon picked up, but there was no word of their ultimate fate.

Within days of the ill-fated Zeppelin operation, KG 200 was to lose one of its most experienced pilots. Oberleutnant Dümcke was killed on 19 September when his Ju 188D hit a high-tension line in Italy. At the end of August he had been appointed the commanding officer of KG 200's Kommando Carmen at

Bergamo. While the Luftwaffe unit suffered mounting losses, the Allies had dropped the first American-trained agent into Germany from England. On the night of 2/3 September OSS German agent Jupp Kappius parachuted into Germany from a Carpetbagger B-24 on a blind drop. Wanted by the Gestapo since leaving Germany in 1937, there was no reception committee to greet Kappius and nothing was heard of him after the drop. SOE was not convinced that the time was right to begin dropping agents into a still-defiant population that was not yet ready to capitulate. It wanted to avoid another Dutch fiasco.

However, No. 161 Squadron was to fly its first Hudson drop into Germany on the night of 7/8 September with an all-Canadian crew led by Flg Off Bob Ferris, but the operation was aborted when one of the two agents refused to jump at a DZ near the Rhine. On 3 October the operation was repeated and the flight's commander, Sqn Ldr Reg Wilkinson, flew the squadron's first successful operation into Germany, dropping two agents.

By this time the last Hudson pick-ups in France had been completed, fifty-two agents having been flown in and seventy-seven out since the beginning of the year. The Deputy Director of Intelligence (DDI) at the Air Ministry had reduced No. 161 Squadron's Lysander Flight from thirteen to three, used mainly for liaison and communications, and the first Stirling IVs began replacing the Halifaxes of 'B' Flight. Both the Tempsford squadrons began increasing their operations to Norway and Denmark. On the night of 19/20 September No. 138 Squadron dispatched ten Stirlings to Denmark and four to Norway. Typical of these operations was one flown by a Halifax captained by Sqn Ldr George Watson of No. 138 squadron to Flekkefjord in southern Norway to drop arms and supplies to the *Milorg*, the Norwegian resistance organisation: a round trip of over 1,600 miles. However, losses mounted on these long operations as the weather worsened with the onset of winter.

While the Allies continued their relentless advances, the German High Command was desperately seeking new and innovative methods of reversing its recent defeats on the both the Eastern and Western Fronts. With the arrival of a new Kommandore at the end of October, the Luftwaffe's KG 200 was further expanded. Oberstleutnant Werner Baumbach had been a charismatic bomber ace during the Battle of Britain, and had served with distinction on the Eastern Front flying Ju 88s of KG 30. At the same time a new unit was added to Kampfgeschwader 200 when KG 66 was reformed as 2 Gruppe, commanded by Hauptmann Horst Rubat and equipped with radar-jamming Ju 52s and He IIIs and Mistel composite aircraft and based at Bury. The Mistel comprised an unmanned Ju 88 fitted with an 8,400lb explosive warhead in the nose, and a controller aircraft either a Bf 109 or Fw 190 fighter – mounted on top piggyback style. After locking onto a target, the control aircraft released the bomber component at a range of a mile.

For 1 Gruppe pilots, the preferred short-to-medium range type for agent dropping was the Junkers Ju 188, a fast, twin-engined, four-seat medium bomber with a range of 1,200 miles. However only a handful of the type had been delivered, and even those had no room for passengers in the cramped crew cabin. Agents had to be carried under the wings in Personenabwurfgeräte (PAG), or Personnel Drop Devices, 13-foot-long, double-skinned, plywood tubes three and half feet in diameter, designed to carry three agents and their equipment. Developed by KG 200's parachute specialist, Leutnant Paulus, the PAG featured a domed nose designed to crumple on landing, inside which was a length of coiled rubber tubing, inflated at low pressure. The three occupants lay on small canvas hammocks while in flight, and four parachutes were fitted into

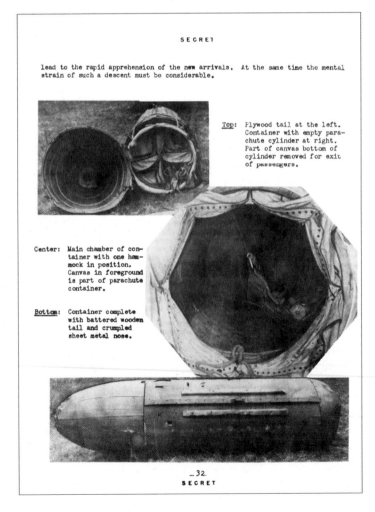

SECRET

lead to the rapid apprehension of the new arrivals. At the same time the mental strain of such a descent must be considerable.

Top: Plywood tail at the left. Container with empty parachute cylinder at right. Part of canvas bottom of cylinder removed for exit of passengers.

Center: Main chamber of container with one hammock in position. Canvas in foreground is part of parachute container.

Bottom: Container complete with battered wooden tail and crumpled sheet metal nose.

_32
SECRET

Left: The Personenabwurfgeräte (PAG), a three-man dropping container developed for KG 200 and carried on the underwing bomb racks of its Ju 188s. *(Bruce Robertson)*

Right: The crew prepare to board a KG 200 Junkers Ju 188 medium bomber that was used to drop Abwehr agents behind Allied lines in 1944–5. *(ww2 images)*

the rear section of the pod. Although the device had the advantage of landing up to six agents and their equipment within a very small area, the risks to the agents were considerable.

However, Hauptmann Peter Stahl flew a number of successful missions from Frankfurt with a PAG-carrying Ju 188 in the autumn of 1944. The first was a night flight to Armagnac in the south of France to drop a PAG carrying three agents and another loaded with equipment, a distance of 1,200 miles. Another five-hour mission flown on the night of 23/24 November covered three separate drops in three different countries. The first was a supply drop to Holland, the next a V-Lente drop in Belgium and the last a three-man PAG 60 miles north-west of Paris in France.

The workhorse of the long-range Staffel, the Junkers Ju 290, was also in demand during this period. Operation 'Rennstrecke' ('Running Distance') was the first stage in a rescue operation of 2,000 soldiers trapped 60 miles from Minsk, 300 miles behind Soviet lines. A Ju 290 was dispatched from Berlin-Finow to drop military personnel to make contact with the force's commanding officer, Oberst Scherhorn. This was followed up by a series of supply drops to the men, from He 111s and the Ju 290 flying from Stolp-Reitz near the Baltic, which it was hoped would sustain them through the harsh Russian winter. KG 200 was planning to pick up the survivors when the weather improved in the new year.

Another Ju 290A-5, coded A3+HB and flown by Hauptmann Heinz Braun and a crew of six, took off from Wiener Neustadt in Austria on 27 November to attempt KG 200's longest clandestine mission to date. The four-engined Junkers was carrying five Iraqi agents and two tons of supplies to supporters of Rashid Ali, the Axis sympathiser deposed by the British in 1941; he was located near Mosul in Iraq, a distance of 1,850 miles away. Cruising at 185mph at 12,000 feet, it headed south-east over Hungary, Yugoslavia, Greece and Syria, with the crew finding the DZ by astro-navigation. Following a successful drop in the Mosul area, Braun retraced his tracks and headed towards the Mediterranean. After 13 hours in the air the Ju 290 landed at Rhodes, still in German hands, to refuel with petrol ferried to the island by one of KG 200's B-24 Liberators. Braun also picked up thirty injured soldiers from the Rhodes garrison to prevent them from falling into Allied hands. During its take-off run, the flight engineer reported an undercarriage hydraulic leak and the take-off was aborted. This happened a second time before the Ju 290 succeeded in becoming airborne just as dawn was breaking. Two hours later, over the cloud-covered Alps, an in-flight electrical fire shut down most of the instruments. However, the crew managed to complete the flight and land safely, despite being fired at by 'friendly' flak as they crossed the Austrian border.

During November, three more Luftwaffe Ju 290A-5 maritime aircraft were converted into passenger/cargo transports, but not directly for KG 200. They were assigned to DLH to fly a regular service between Germany and Portugal via Spain, to carry German nationals and quantities of much-needed strategic materials supplied by the Spanish government. Despite growing pressure from the Allies to restrict German flights to Spain, Franco's government insisted that it was honouring commercial agreements, some of which dated back to the Spanish Civil War, and it had to bear in mind that DLH had a 25 per cent financial holding in the Spanish state airline, Iberia.

The Ju 290s, which replaced three modified Ju 88s allegedly in the passenger transport role, could carry up to 4 tons of cargo including military equipment, vehicle and aircraft spare parts, and raw materials such as wolfram. All scheduled flights between the two countries were required to use specified airway K22, but many unscheduled flights to Spain failed to keep to the specified routes. The DLH service was a perfect cover for clandestine flights to and from Spain by KG 200 Ju 290s.

Although Belgrade had been liberated by Soviet troops and JANL forces on 20 October, demand on the Balkan SD units remained as high as ever. One mission that reflected the conflict between the Yugoslavia's rival partisan groups was an OSS operation by a 64th TCG C-47 to pick up Lt Col Robert McDowell and his staff on 1 November from an airstrip prepared by Mihailovic's Chetniks at Doboj, near Tuzla. Despite the Allies, decision to support Tito's JANL, the Americans had hedged their bets and the OSS had sent an intelligence team codenamed 'Ranger', led by McDowell, to Draza Mihailovic's headquarters at Pranjani in August. Although General Donovan maintained that the team's eventual destination was to have been Austria, the Ranger team remained with the Chetnik leader and even met with German go-betweens, promising Mihailovic direct contact with the American President, before being recalled.

On the evening of 4 November No. 1586 Flight Liberator KH151/'S', flown by Flg Off Kleydor, dropped two SOE agents over Judenburg in Austria, and two more into northern Yugoslavia. On the same night three No. 267 Squadron Dakotas landed twenty SOE agents and partisans at a Yugoslav airstrip called 'Piccadilly Rose' and were picking up fifty-six wounded partisans when a Luftwaffe Ju 52 unexpectedly landed on the strip, its crew becoming the partisan's captives.

No. 1586 (Polish) flight at Bari was renumbered No. 301 Squadron on 7 November; with Flt Lt Krzywicki flew one of the unit's first operations when four SOE agents and Maj Mackers, head of a clandestine warfare course at OSS 43 Station, were dropped into Poland from Liberator KG994/'R'. A few days

A line-up of No. 267 (SD) Squadron Dakotas at Bari with USAAF 64th TCG C-47s and the 885th BS (H) B-24s in the background, all of which were involved in partisan support in Italy and Yugoslavia. *(Bruce Robertson)*

later the Soviet PS-84 unit and its Yak escorts departed from Bari heading for Zemun, near Belgrade, where it would remain for the rest of the war. During October 1944 the unit had flown 125 sorties and evacuated a total of 855 partisans from Yugoslavia.

Norway and Germany were now the main targets for the British-based SD squadrons, with four operations being flown into Germany by No. 161 Squadron Hudsons on the night of 26 November. Canadian Flg Off Bob Ferris dropped one agent, while Flt Lt Buster Webb and Flg Off Harold Ibbott each dropped two. The Hudson flight commander, Reg Wilkinson, dropped a Polish-German SOE agent south of Erfurt on his second operation to Germany, but was caught by a Luftwaffe night fighter over Belgium near Houffalise. Hudson 'L'-Love crashed in flames, killing the pilot and his two crew.

To cope with the demand for stores from the Norwegian Milorg groups, another Stirling squadron was withdrawn from the main bomber force. No. 295 Squadron, based at RAF Rivenhall in Essex, began SD operations in October, and a mission flown on 2 November illustrates the hazards of flying such operations in the depths of an Arctic winter. Eight of the squadron's Stirling IVs loaded with containers took off from Rivenhall and set course for Egersund, a well-used corridor for SD flights into Norway. After overflying Egersund the aircraft headed for Oslo in rapidly deteriorating weather, the DZs being near Eksund, some 80 miles north of the capital. In fact the weather was so bad that all but one of the Stirlings aborted the mission and returned to England.

The remaining aircraft was LK171, flown by the station commander, Gp Capt Wilfred Surplice, and his crew of five. Also on board was Lt Michael Hicks, an

Army liaison officer acting as dispatcher. When the navigator, Sqn Ldr Ken Bolton, informed the pilot that they were approaching their DZ at Numedal, the aircraft descended to 2,000ft, but there was no sign of a break in the cloud. With high ground in the vicinity, Surplice aborted the drop and climbed away, with ice building rapidly on the Stirling's wings. He was unable to climb above 10,000 feet and the containers were dropped to lighten the aircraft, which was almost at the point of stalling. Wrestling to keep the Stirling in the air, the pilot ordered his crew to bale out.

All but the pilot managed to jump safely before LK171 smashed into the 4,500ft-high Skarfjell with Surplice still at the controls. The rest of the crew landed without injury in thick snow, although two were soon caught by the Germans and handed over to the Gestapo for lengthy interrogations before being sent to Stalag Luft 1 in Germany. The remaining four were discovered hiding in a hut by a member of the Resistance, which smuggled them onto a small boat to Sweden after nearly a month on the run. After surrendering to the Swedish police, navigator Ken Bolton, radio operator WO Robert Dalton, tail gunner Plt Off Robert 'Red' Chapin and Lt Hicks were sent to Stockholm and on 2 January 1945 were put on board a BOAC Lodestar bound for Scotland.

While the Stirling survivors were heading for the Swedish border, Lt Hartmann and his No. 333 (Norwegian) Squadron crew also had a lucky escape while flying Catalina FP333/'B' from Woodhaven to Kirkenes in northern Norway, close to the Soviet border, during the night of 6/7 December. After the flying boat was damaged landing in heavy seas, Hartmann diverted to Lierhamis in Finland to make temporary repairs, before obtaining permission to fly to the Soviet flying-boat base at Grasnaya near Murmansk where, over the next six weeks, the hull was reskinned before flying back to Scotland.

A year that began with the loss of Pick Pickard, closely followed by that of Guy Lockhart, ended with news of the death of yet another larger-than-life character of the Special Duties fraternity. Wg Cdr Alan Sticky Murphy was killed on the night of 2/3 December over Holland in a No. 23 Squadron Mosquito VI while flying on a 'Serrate' operation, using a radar counter-measures device that homed into the radar used by German night fighters.

It was now clear that the war in Europe would not 'be over by Christmas' and that Tempsford was destined to remain in the front line of SD operations for some time to come. However, it would be without one of its longest-serving and most distinguished officers. Mouse Fielden had been injured in a car accident and was replaced as station commander on 20 December by Australian Gp Capt E.J. Palmer, after continuous service since the airfield had opened in April 1942.

CHAPTER 8

The Flames Reach Berlin

During the long dark nights of the fifth winter of the Second World War, the Tempsford squadrons concentrated their efforts on supplying the Norwegian Resistance. Few of the original Special Duties aircrew – many of whom had learned to fly before September 1939 and had done at least one tour on fighter or bomber squadrons before they were posted to Tempsford – still served with the 'moon' squadrons. They had been replaced by a new breed of young airmen who were more likely to have trained overseas as part of the British Commonwealth Air Training Plan (BCATP), with a Special Duties squadron as their first posting.

Flt Sgt 'Buck' Buckingham was typical of the latest intake, although his early career in the service was not. The son of a railway goods manager from St Albans, Roy Buckingham left school at 16 and was in a reserved occupation working for a chronometer manufacturer when he volunteered to join the RAF. He was accepted for flying training in January 1942, aged 17, and when he went solo after six hours in a Tiger Moth, Buck was sent to Naval Air Station Grosse Ile, Michigan, on the shores of Lake Erie, under the American Towers training scheme. Although handling the US Navy's heavy-handling N3N biplane trainer was easily mastered, Roy found its customs and discipline more difficult to accept.

I don't think the Americans liked training the 'Brits' very much. How you addressed officers, when and where you ate, how you stowed your kit: these were all completely different from anything we had experienced in the RAF, and nothing was explained to you until you were on a charge for failing to get it right. Even the phonetic alphabet was completely different and had to be relearnt. The locals were friendly enough. Me and a mate saved up for a full Christmas dinner – steak, wine, the works, and when the restaurant manager learned we were 'Brits', he tore up the bill. But the instructors were something else.

In the harsh Michigan winter, training continued until one day I was flying some distance away from the airfield when a snowstorm blotted out the horizon. My instructor ordered me to return to Grosse Ile. I said, you tell me what direction its in and I'll fly you there. The next day I was 'washed out' of the course for insubordination. I thought my flying days were over. However, when I was sent to the RAF headquarters in Canada, they said we gets lots of 'wash outs'. Don't worry, you can carry on flying – but not as a pilot. I chose to be a bomb aimer as it was the shortest course!

Having completed his training at Mount Hope RCAF Station, Roy Bucking-ham was posted to a Wellington Operational Training Unit (OTU) at RAF Westcott on his return to England. It was after surviving a crash-landing near the end of his course that Buck was asked to volunteer for Special Duties.

I'd no idea what 'Special Duties' were, but it sounded interesting and in June 1944 I was on my way to Tempsford. After learning the ropes, I flew on a couple of Halifax operations over France before joining a new Stirling crew with No. 138 Squadron, then commanded by Wg Cdr Burnett.
    Over the winter of 1944–5 most of the sorties we flew were to Denmark and Norway, mostly in bad weather. I worked closely with the nav, Flt Sgt 'Wally' Westwood when planning the course to a DZ, and acted as the eyes of

No. 138 Squadron Stirling IV LK283/'S' at Tempsford in 1944, with one of the Squadron's Halifaxes in the background. *(Andy Thomas)*

the pilot, Flg Off 'Heck' Shaw, a New Zealander, after crossing the enemy coast. I had to watch out for landmarks, flak batteries and when near the DZ, the signal lights from the reception committee. I also looked after the 'Joes' along with the dispatcher who was normally the mid-upper gunner. On one occasion we had to bring our 'Joe', a young lady, back with us to the forward base at Kinloss in Scotland after the 'Joe' hatch had frozen solid over a DZ in Denmark.

It was my duty with Bill Clarkson, the dispatcher, to make sure that no one talked to the agent while we were away from base. We had to stick close to her even in bed – we were all fully clothed – and when she went to the toilet, the door remained unlocked. We were standing outside the women's toilet when a senior WAAF officer wanted to go in. We barred her way and she demanded to speak to our commanding officer. We gave her the number and when she got through, her face went bright red when he told her in no uncertain terms that she should leave us to do our duty.

All the crews were left to their own devices when it came to plotting a course to the DZs. After several operations to Norway, I was able to identify the code letters flashed by lighthouses along the coast to German shipping passing by. They proved to be a very useful guide to us, especially when the weather clammed up overland. In winter the DZs were more often than not remote frozen lakes which were easy to spot on a moonlit night. However, one operation to a region of central southern Norway known as the Oster Dahlan was a bit dicey.

We were heading for some lakes along a valley at 500 feet above ground level with high mountains towering above us on both sides when we hit a severe frontal system. We couldn't turn to avoid it and it took the combined efforts of 'Heck' and me, both hanging on the controls, to climb out of the situation. We were lucky. On another operation, we were one of fourteen Stirlings heading for Norway that night when we saw Flt Lt McGregor's aircraft hit by flak. It exploded and fell into the sea, killing all the crew.

While it was now clear that the Allies were close to forcing the Germans out of the countries they had overrun in 1940, there was no sign that Hitler was about to accept defeat. Only two weeks before Christmas 1944, German forces had launched a surprise attack in the Ardennes. In what would become known as the Battle of the Bulge, secretly assembled German reserve forces made substantial early gains while the Allied air forces were grounded by fog over the area. Part of their success was Operation 'Greif', a daring raid by SS troops dressed in US uniforms. They were dropped behind Allied lines by KG 200 aircraft and were led by one of Hitler's most successful irregular soldiers.

Oberstleutnant Otto Skorzeny, head of the Jagdverbande, an SS sabotage and clandestine operations unit, was a giant of a man who sported the badge of a Prussian warrior, a duelling scar on his cheek. He first came to prominence in September 1943, when he led a covert, glider-borne force of ninety troops which landed on the Gran Sasso plateau in the Italian Abruzzi mountains to abduct Mussolini. He flew the disgraced Italian leader out of his Abruzzi mountain prison in a Fieseler Fi 156 Storch, a single-engined aircraft with an even better STOL performance than the Lysander. Almost immediately, Skorzeny was ordered to assemble a hand-picked assassination team near Vinnitsa, in German-occupied Ukraine. Operation 'Long Pounce' was the codename for one of the most audacious German missions of the Second World War: the assassination of the three Allied leaders Winston Churchill, Franklin D. Roosevelt and Joseph Stalin when all three attended the Teheran Conference in November 1943. The hit-team comprised twenty anti-communist Russians selected from German prisoner-of-war camps, led by ten German SS officers. At the beginning of November they were flown 1,500 miles in a Ju 290 aircraft and dropped into Kurdistan. Here the plot began to unravel.

The Luftwaffe's equivalent of the RAF's Lysander was the two-seat Fieseler Fi 156 Storch, used by both KG 200 and Otto Skorzeny's commandos. *(MAP)*

Some of the Russians had posed as anti-communists only to gain their release from PoW camps, and they were soon able to make contact with a large contingent of Soviet security forces sent to guard Stalin at the conference. All but six of the team were rounded up by Soviet and Persian forces before the conference had even begun. Those who slipped through the net, all of them Germans and led by SS-Sturmbannführer Rudolf von Holten-Pflug, managed to escape from the city and hide for nearly three months among mountain Bedouins, before being captured and executed by Soviet troops. Operation Long Pounce was over.

Almost a year later, undeterred by the failure of the Teheran operation, 'Scarface' Skorzeny kidnapped the son of the Hungarian Regent, Adm Miklos Horthy, when his father began negotiations with the Soviets, and forced the father to abdicate in an operation codenamed 'Mickey Mouse'. By early January 1945 the German offensive in the Ardennes had been checked, but not before No. 138 Squadron had repeated its successful D-day ploy of dropping dummy parachutists behind enemy lines, playing Skorzeny at his own game.

Although Skorzeny was never part of KG 200, he had been involved with one of the ever-expanding unit's new experimental Gruppen. Formed on 10 January at Berlin-Staakan, under the command of Maj Helmut Viedebantt, 3 Gruppe was concerned with trials of aircraft fitted with anti-shipping weapons such as the BT 1400 Bomben-Torpedo. The ultra-secret 4 Gruppe, formed on the same day at Prenzlau, was the culmination of a project that did not have the whole-hearted support of Kampfgeschwader Kommodore Werner Baumbach.

The brainchild of Luftwaffe staff officer Hauptmann Heinrich Lange, the chief of the Institute of Medical Aeronautics at Rechlin, Dr Theo Benzinger, and Germany's leading female test pilot, Flugkapitän Hanna Reitsch, the project was the development of manned flying bombs – in essence, suicide aircraft. Designed to be used against Allied shipping and other high-priority targets, the system would be based on the Me 328A, an inexpensive, high-performance, ground-attack aircraft powered by two pulse-jets. Adapted for suicide tactics, the Me 328 would be carried aloft on the back of a Do 217E bomber and released 50 miles from its target. However, after initial tests at Horsching in Austria proved unsatisfactory, Oberstleutnant Otto Skorzeny, another supporter of the project, suggested using a manned version of the V-1 that could carry a 2,000lb warhead. Already in mass production, the V-1 was easily modified for manned flight by removing a fuel tank and the auto-pilot to make way for a pilot. However two test pilots were killed flying the Fi 103 Reichenberg, and even Hanna Reitsch had to bale out before her aircraft broke up in mid-air.

In the meantime, 1 Gruppe continued to expand into what some Luftwaffe commanders were calling 'an air force within an air force'. By 10 January the Kampfgeschwader had more than 200 aircraft on strength, almost half being various transport types from France, Italy, the Soviet Union and the United States as well as Germany. These included Dutch-built Do 24K flying boats based in Norway and Denmark, as well as the Italian Savoia-Marchetti SM.79H Sparviero and Piaggio P.108Cs, all of which would be in great demand in the coming months.

An armistice between Finland and the Soviet Union at the end of 1944 had been a blow to the Germans who were forced to retreat into northern Norway, opening the way for USAAF operations in neutral Sweden. Having previously permitted B-24s to pick up US and Norwegian nationals from Stockholm in March 1944, the Swedish authorities were persuaded by the Norwegian government-in-exile to allow USAAF aircraft to use Swedish bases for another clandestine operation. They were to carry Norwegian military supplies, and personnel who had taken refuge in Sweden, back into Norway to form a new Free Norwegian force to pursue the retreating Germans.

At the beginning of the year, ten C-47s based at Metfield in England flew to Stockholm's Bromma airport en route to the Swedish Air Force fighter base at

USAAF C-47A at Kallax airfield in neutral Sweden ready to fly military personnel and supplies into Norway during Operation Ball, which began in January 1945. *(Bo Widfeldt)*

Kallax-Luleå, close to the Arctic Circle. In command of the detachment was Norwegian-born USAAF pilot Col Bernt Balchen, and on 12 January Operation 'Ball' began when the C-47s flew to Höibuktmoen, near Kirkenes in northern Norway, with a mobile hospital and returned the next day with a Norwegian officer travelling under cover. Although the Soviets had agreed to support the operation by providing weather reports and limited maintenance facilities, they had vetoed any attempt to carry troops out of Norway into Sweden. Höibuk-moen had recently been vacated by the Germans, who had destroyed most of the airfield's buildings although the runways, covered in a layer of hard-packed snow, remained serviceable.

Radio reports from the Soviets were spasmodic, but the Americans made good use of their Eureka/Rebecca systems and Sugar-phones. Many of the flights, which would continue until the end of the war, entered Finnish airspace illegally, but none was intercepted. However, one of the Norwegian 'police' battalions flown in during the operation strayed into a German minefield. More than twenty soldiers were killed and many more injured. Medical personnel and supplies were dropped by the C-47s and some of the injured were airlifted by ski-equipped Swedish Air Force Fi 156 Storches to an airfield at Kiruna near the Arctic Circle, the centre of the Sweden's ball-bearing industry.

Another USAAF SD unit, the 859th BS (H), now commanded by Col Bob Fish, flew its Liberators out of Harrington to join the 885th BS (H) at Brindisi in January as part of a newly formed 15th Special Group (Provisional) commanded by Col MacClosky. The 859th's B-24s were tasked with dropping supplies and personnel to friendly agencies in northern Italy, while the B-17s and B-24s of the 885th would operate over the Balkans. During February the 15th SG (P) flew 486 sorties, dropping 34 agents and over 400 tons of weapons and supplies. Within a 10-day period of clear weather conditions, the squadrons flew 135 sorties in support of the Committee of National Liberation of Upper Italy (CLNAI) partisan groups in the Po and Alpine Valleys.

An 885th B-24 flown by Capt Partridge dropped supplies to a group of OSS and SOE agents and partisans trapped by heavy snowfalls near the Brenner Pass on the night of 14/15 February. On 24 March the special group was renumbered the 2641st SG (P) and moved north to Rosignano, near Rome. At the same time the RAF's No. 267 Squadron was conducting its last SD operations from Bari, Italy before preparing to join South East Asia Command to operate alongside No. 357 (SD) Squadron in Burma.

As the Allies tightened their noose around Germany, it provoked orders from Berlin to begin another frenzy of executions at the concentration camps not yet liberated. On 26 January SOE agents Violette Szabo and Lilian Rolfe, who had both arrived in France on the same day in April 1944, along with Denise Bloch, the Chestnut circuit wireless operator, were all executed at Ravensbrück and their bodies burned. A few days later, Cammaerts's courier Cecily Lefort was gassed at Jugendlager while Charles Grover, another of the former Bugatti racing drivers who belonged to the ill-fated Chestnut circuit, was shot at the Sachsenhausen concentration camp on 18 March.

Some were more fortunate. SOE wireless operator Eileen Didi Nearne made a courageous escape from Markleberg and another FANY recruit, Odette Sansom, survived Ravensbrück under sentence of death – as did her colleague, Yvonne Baseden – until the Americans overran the camp. Daughter of a British First World War pilot and a French mother, Yvonne had joined the WAAF before being recruited by SOE. Trained as a wireless operator, the 22-year-old para-chuted into France on 18 March 1944 to work with the Scholar circuit in the Dôle region. She was captured three months later after being caught out during a daylight bombing raid on Dijon and was sent to Ravensbrück, from where she was liberated by the Swedish Red Cross nine months later.

The new year saw all of the European-based RAF SD squadrons dropping agents into Germany. On the night of 20/21 January No. 148 Squadron Halifax

Containers aimed at Tito's partisan army dropping from an 885th BS B-24 over remote snowfields in central Yugoslavia during the winter of 1944–5. *(ww2 images)*

Flg Off Attenborrow with his No. 148 Squadron Lysander IIIA (SD) at Calvi, having evacuated a seriously wounded OSS officer serving with the Italian partisans. *(Bruce Robertson)*

JW958/'A' flew a single SIS agent from Lyons to Germany, and two weeks later its sister SD unit at Brindisi, No. 301 Squadron, dropped three SOE agents near Judenburg from Halifax LL465/'J' flown by Flt Lt Blaszak. The Polish squadron flew its last Balkans SD operation on 25 February before it was transferred to Transport Command and moved to England.

No. 334 Wing's only remaining SD squadron, No. 148, continued operations over Yugoslavia and northern Italy with one of its Lysanders, flown by Neil Attenborrow, picking up Flt Lt Ball on 8 February – a No. 73 Squadron pilot who had force-landed his Spitfire IX near Bihac in Yugoslavia. The following month the squadron dropped SOE agent Manfred Czernin back into Italy from a Halifax to a DZ near Bergamo airfield, from where one of the captured B-24s of the KG 200 Kommando Carmen detachment had been operated.

Paola Del Din, the Italian agent Czermin had recruited the previous year, had completed her parachute training at San Vito di Normanni near Brindisi airfield, and was assigned as a courier to the Bigelow mission in northern Italy. She was then forced to spend a frustrating three months waiting for the opportunity to return to her birthplace, because of shortage of aircraft, bad weather and aborted sorties. On the night of 9 April 1945 the young agent, whom her training officer had likened to a sixteen-year-old schoolgirl, finally boarded a 64th TCG C-47 at Rosignano near Pisa for the 250-mile flight to a DZ some 50 miles north of Udine, near the Austrian border. For the next four weeks Paola was involved in the fierce fighting between the local partisan groups and Cossack troops fighting for the Germans, for which she was awarded the same *Medaglia d'Oro al Valor Militare* that her brother had received posthumously.

As Allied troops carried across the Adriatic liberated the Dalmatian islands along the Yugoslav coast and headed north to the Italian border, many partisans and their families were trapped between the opposing forces. A massive airlift began on 25 March, when almost 2,000 people were flown out of Piccadilly Hope A airstrip near Griblje, between Fiume and Zagreb, by twelve 51st TCS C-47s escorted by Balkan Air Force Spitfires.

Tito's partisans continued to provide a vital lifeline for evading Allied airmen shot down over Yugoslavia, taking great risks while doing so. Flt Lt Lyn Bridge was the navigator of a No. 37 Squadron Liberator based at Foggia in southern Italy. Returning from a bombing raid on Graz in Austria on the night of Easter Sunday, 1 April, his aircraft was shot down by a Ju 88 near Vinica, 20 miles north of Zagreb. Bridge and four of the crew were able to bale out of the stricken bomber, but the remaining five men on board, including its New Zealander pilot Flt Lt Vern Cave, were killed in the crash. Soon after he landed at the edge of a forest, Bridge met up with the bomb-aimer, Plt Off Snowy

Innes. The two airmen walked into the nearest village, hoping that the natives would be friendly. They were.

The next day, the pair of RAF airmen were greeted by a local band of heavily armed partisans. They were unaware that an aircraft had crashed in the area, but promised to search for it and any other survivors. They had, however, sent word to their headquarters which in turn contacted the local RAF liaison officer, Flt Lt Mac MacPherson who, accompanied by his Alsatian dog, roared into the village in a jeep to pick up the two airmen. He told them that another group of partisans had got to the Liberator's crash site before the Germans and had recovered the bodies. Two of its gunners, Flt Lt Cliff Wing and Sgt Ginger Cummings, had also been found, badly wounded but alive. MacPherson drove Bridge and Innes to a remote cottage in the hills, where two RAF wireless operators had news that all the survivors were to be picked up from a nearby airstrip the following day. While waiting overnight in the cottage, MacPherson told Bridge that when he was dropped into Yugoslavia he often took his dog with him. It had its own harness and parachute. Mac would push the dog out first and jump out after him. Apparently the dog was quite unconcerned, and went on wagging its tail all the way down.

The next morning they arrived at the airstrip to find the two gunners swathed in bandages, and with them three American aircrew who had been with the partisans for almost a year after being shot down over Austria. A C-47 touched down as an RAF Spitfire circled overhead. Out of the aircraft stepped two high-ranking Yugoslav officers, one of whom was believed to be Tito himself, but the Allied airmen had no time to confirm this. They were soon landing at Bari, where the wounded were loaded onto ambulances and Bridge and Innes were debriefed by intelligence officers.

As the German SS troops fought a series of ferocious rearguard actions during their retreat north, destroying everything in their wake, aircraft of the USAAF 2641st Special Group (Provisional) and No. 148 Squadron began to switch their covert supply operations to Czechoslovakia from the end of March. This decision coincided with the beginning of Operation 'Sunrise', secret negotiations with the SS Commander in Italy, Gen Karl Wolff, and Allen Dulles, Chief of OSS Station Bern in Switzerland. After a series of clandestine visits to Switzerland, Wolff, who led the fight against the Italian partisans, released an OSS agent and an Italian partisan leader as a sign of good faith, and issued his demands for a surrender through a Czech OSS radio operator spirited into German headquarters. These included safe passage for his family, who were allowed out of Germany and sent abroad; despite objections from Stalin, a surrender was agreed on 23 April. At the cessation of hostilities in Italy and the Balkans on 2 May

1945 No. 334 Wing squadrons had flown a total of 11,632 SD sorties into Yugoslavia, 2,652 into Italy and 2,064 into Greece.

Ironically, only weeks earlier and unbeknown to General Wolff, Ernst Kaltenbrunner, the head of the notorious RHSA and the man responsible for the death of so many captured SOE agents, had also made contact with Allen Dulles. Through Dr Wilhelm Höttl, a shadowy figure who worked for Germany's security chief General Schellenberg and was involved with OSS's failed Ranger team attached to Mihailovic, peace feelers were proposed. Although not rejected out of hand by OSS chief William J. Donovan in Washington, Kaltenbrunner was to be given no offer of immunity.

As hostilities in north-west Europe continued, the SD units based in England were almost entirely involved in flying operations to Norway, Denmark and Germany. The Tempsford squadrons had been joined by several other Stirling units dropping supplies to the Norwegian Resistance, and losses continued to mount. On the night of 22 February Stirling LK566 of No. 190 Squadron from Great Dunmow was shot down near Holt, and Stirling LK119/'Y' of No. 161 Squadron crashed near Heggland, killing its crew of eight. It was one of nine RAF aircraft that fell to German night fighters in the early hours of 1 April. Stirlings of No. 161 Squadron flew their last SD operations to Norway on the night of 2/3 May, by which time at least thirty Allied SD aircraft had been lost on Norwegian missions since 1942. The RAF had flown over 700 sorties, dropping nearly 200 agents and more than 9,000 containers to the Resistance.

SD operations to Denmark continued, also at great cost. On 4 March a Stirling flown by No. 161 Squadron's new commanding officer, Wg Cdr Mickey Brogan, was lost with its crew during a supply-drop operation to Denmark. It was only two weeks since he had replaced Wg Cdr George Watson, a former No. 138 Squadron flight commander, who had also failed to return from a mission: Operation 'Croc', a Hudson sortie to Denmark on the night of 21 February, just four weeks after his promotion to the post.

The B-24 Liberators of 859th BS (H) had left Harrington, but it was not the end of SD operations from Station 179. A new unit equipped with the Douglas A-26C Invader, a fast, twin-engined medium bomber, was investigating the suit-ability of the new aircraft for dropping agents into Germany. During February an 856th BS B-26C, 44-39524, was tested at the Airborne Forces Experimental Establishment at Beaulieu by Capt Walker. The bomber, similar in size and performance to the KG 200 Ju 188 and having a maximum speed of over 350mph at sea level and a range of 1,400 miles, also suffered from the same problem – lack of space. With its crew of four, the only place available for an agent was the same as that used in the BOAC Mosquitoes – the bomb bay.

A small compartment large enough for two 'Joes' was made in the forward section of the bay and was fitted with a plywood floor, hinged on one side and secured on the other by catches which could be released by a cable leading to the navigator's position in the glazed nose. The agents, who had to lie on their parachute back-pack, which was attached to a static line, were equipped with German money, forged papers, a silk map, concentrated food packs, a Luger pistol and a 'Joan/Eleanor' radio set. This communications system was developed by two US radio technicians, Lt Cdr Stephen Simpson and Dewitt R. Goddard of the Radio Corporation of America (RCA); the codenames referred to their respective wife and girlfriend.

Operating on 260 MHz, a frequency then free of enemy surveillance stations, the agent's Joan set had a range of 20 miles. Messages in plain language could be sent to an operator squeezed into a USAAF Mosquito PR XVI of the 654th Reconnaissance Squadron at Watton, equipped with an Eleanor set flying Ascension-type profiles at high altitude. Stripped of all but essential equipment, the modified Invaders were fitted with Loran and 'Gee' navigation equipment and a radio altimeter to enable the pilot to fly with precision at the optimum drop altitude of 300 feet.

Pressure was mounting for the USAAF to begin OSS drops into Germany, which for the previous six months had been undertaken by the slow and vulnerable Hudson of No. 161 Squadron. While five B-26Cs were being modified, pilots assigned to the 492nd Bomb Group's 856th Bomb Squadron commanded by Col Rodman A. St Clair were busy converting to the new type, writing off more than one in the process. Harrington's new base commander, Col Hudson H. Upham, who had no experience of SD operations, was keen to prove that the squadron was ready to fly a mission into Germany, while Col Fish, his second-in-command at the base, was not convinced that it was fully prepared.

He had flown an 856th BS B-24 fitted with H2X radar to the group's temporary forward base at Dijon on 17 March for a reconnaissance mission over southern Germany the following night to evaluate flak defences in region. On 19 March orders were received to fly Operation 'Chisel', the first A-26C mission into Germany, codenamed 'Red Stocking', but it was promptly cancelled. Twice during the day the order was reinstated, but neither the crew nor the aircraft was fully prepared when they finally took off from Harrington at 1145 hours. Flown by Lt Oliver H. Emmel, navigator Maj John Walsh and gunner Staff Sgt Frank Brummer, accompanied by the group's highly experienced navigation officer, Maj Edward Tresemer, the B-26C was carrying a single agent to a DZ near Dummer Lake in southern Germany. There was no Mosquito available to cover the mission and bad weather was forecast over the DZ. There was to be no

USAAF Mosquito PR XVIs of the 654th Reconnaissance Squadron were assigned to Red Stocking Operations in 1945 as airborne radio relays with agents on the ground. *(Bruce Robertson)*

confirmation that the agent was successfully dropped, or of what happened to the B-26 and its crew when they failed to return. Months later the aircraft was discovered, along with the remains of its crew, on a moor near Bramsche.

The night after the doomed Red Stocking mission, a total of eight Stirlings and five Hudsons of No. 161 Squadron, now commanded by Wg Cdr Len Ratcliff, took off from Tempsford for operations behind enemy lines. All the Hudsons headed for Germany. The leading pair, flown by Flt Lt Buster Webb who dropped a German agent codenamed Colehill near Berlin, and Plt Off Ronald Morris who dropped an SIS agent, both returned safely. Unfortunately Bob Ferris and his all-Canadian crew in O-Oboe had been shot down over France, possibly by an Allied fighter, after dropping an SOE agent near Remagen; and 'L'-Love was lost with Chris Ragan, another Canadian, his crew and an SOE agent on Operation 'Walnut' before it reached its German DZ.

Hudson 'N'-Nan was carrying three Belgian SOE agents on their second mission to occupied Europe, one which had been previously aborted twice due to bad weather. Flt Lt Terence Helfer and three crew were attacked by a night fighter, possibly American, over the Belgian village of Maulesmühle at 0045 hours on 21 March. When the Hudson burst into flames Helfer, who was the only member of the crew wearing a parachute over 'friendly' territory, managed to jump from the aircraft before it crashed, killing all six still on board.

Before these losses decimated No. 161 Squadron's Hudson flight, its sister unit No 138 (SD) Squadron had departed from Tempsford for the final time. Its crews had withdrawn the last of their tired Stirlings and moved to RAF Tuddenham on 9 March to convert to Lancaster bombers with No. 39 Group. During four years of Special Duties operations the squadron had carried 995 Allied agents into occupied Europe, dropped some 29,000 containers and almost 10,000 packages. But the price had been high: 70 aircraft and nearly 300 aircrew had been lost.

Despite the failure of the first Red Stocking mission, 856th Bomb Squadron B-26Cs led by Captain Walker flew three OSS agents to a DZ 30 miles from Berlin on the night of 9/10 April, accompanied by the Mosquito relay aircraft now assigned to the squadron. Four Mosquito PR XVIs, new off the production line at Hatfield, were fitted with 200-gallon long-range tanks under the wings, to enable them to fly as far as Brindisi if required. A radio operator, carried in addition to the normal crew of pilot and navigator, was required to crouch in a small recess cut into the bomb bay; he was equipped with a heated flight suit and an intercom link. He gained access to his cramped position through a small hatch cut into the starboard side of the rear fuselage. Five of the first nine Red Stocking missions were successfully completed without further loss and with the Mosquitoes managing to pick up most of the agent's transmissions as soon as they landed.

The 856th BS had also been earmarked for Operation 'Iron Cross', an ambitious OSS mission to assassinate Adolf Hitler at his mountain redoubt near Berchtesgaden. Capt Aaron Bank, whose Jedburgh team had led a successful campaign of ambush and sabotage in France the previous year, was ordered to scour US-run PoW camps to recruit Germans who had good reasons to hate the Nazi regime, and Hitler in particular. By early 1945 Bank had selected 175 ex-PoWs, most of them ardent communists, to form a phoney German infantry force in Alsace. Those selected were trained to parachute into confined DZs and were briefed on Hitler's known habits and predicted movements. However, the speed of the Allied advance into Germany trapped Hitler in Berlin before Bank's team could attempt the mission. Following the cancellation of Operation Iron Cross on 12 March, Aaron Bank volunteered to join OSS Detachment 101 in the Far East.

While Ernst Kaltenbrunner, RHSA chief and KG 200's task-master, was making contact with the OSS in Switzerland, the Kampfgeschwader was under great pressure as its sphere of operations shrank with every Allied gain. It had lost all its outstations, with the exception of Austria and Denmark, by this time as well as an ever-increasing number of its aircraft. On 10 February one of its B-17G Fortresses operated by Kommando Olga exploded soon after take-off at Echterdingen, killing Oberfeldwebel Knappenschneider, six of his eight crew and ten members of the Vichy French government, including the Comte de Bony de Lavergne. Another Kommando Olga B-17F, *Mr Five by Five*, was shot down by a USAAF Beaufighter night fighter as it headed towards Strasbourg on the night of 2/3 March after dropping nine agents near Dijon. Three of its crew baled out and survived. A successful mission was carried out by one of the surviving Olga B-17s on the night of 19 March. Operation Karneval was flown by Leutnant Pohl, who flew from Hildesheim to drop one agent on the outskirts of Brussels and six near Waals on the Belgium/German border. These agents were in fact SS commandos whose mission was to assassinate the Mayor of nearby Aachen, who had just been appointed by the occupying US forces. They succeeded in their task.

Having conceded that it was too late to achieve any workable plan for the deloyment of Leonides Staffel – although 175 Reichenberg IVs, the manned version of the V-1, had been completed at Dannenburg – Werner Baumbach was replaced on 6 March by Maj Adolf von Hernier. Most of the Reichenbergs were scrapped and information on Germany's Kamikaze programme was suppressed.

However, as the situation worsened on the Eastern Front, two Gruppen were ordered into action against Soviet forces in East Prussia. Their targets were bridges over the Rivers Oder, Neisse and Vistula, and on 6 March an He 111H-12 of 3 Gruppe scored a direct hit on the Oder bridges at Görlitz with a Henschel Hs 293 guided glider-bomb. Two days later II/KG 200 Misteln were deployed to attack the same targets.

Almost a hundred Mistel S 2 Ju 88/Fw 190 composites, known in KG 200 as Beethoven 2s, had been completed by February and a training programme for Operation 'Eisenhammer' was under way at five airfields in the Merseberg area before they were overrun by the Soviets. They were dispersed to Oranienburg and Rechlin-Lärz in Germany and Prague-Ruzyne in Czechoslovakia. Four Misteln, accompanied by five KG 200 Ju 188s, attacked the same Oder bridges at Görlitz on 9 March; two of them were damaged for the loss of one Mistel, flown by Feldwebel Lukaschek, and a Ju 188. On the night of 25/26 March Misteln and Ju 188s again attacked the Oder bridges and others over the Vistula, and preparations were made for 50 Misteln to attack Soviet power stations close to Moscow and Gorki three nights later. However, this operation was called off at the last minute and the Mistels continued to concentrate on the destruction of vital bridges. Six succeeded in damaging a railway bridge at Steinau on 31 March, putting it out of action for some days, while two Ju 88 and two Ju 188s attacked the nearby railway station. During the following week more raids were mounted against the Vistula bridges and some across the Rhine. Losses continued to mount. KG 200 was being bled of some of its best pilots

KG 200 Mistel S 2 comprising an Fw 190F-8/Ju 88G-1 composite at Merseburg in 1945.
(Barry Wheeler)

and the principal Mistel base at Rechlin-Lärz had been put out of action by
USAAF bombers.

In desperation, another of KG 200's diverse fleet was selected for highly
secret Mistel-style operations codenamed 'Aktion 24'. At the beginning of April
several Do 24 flying boats were prepared for their one-way mission, the
destruction of railway bridges over the Vistula. They were to be fully laden with
explosives and flown by a pilot, navigator and Jagdverbande soldier, and were to
land on the Vistula behind the Soviet lines in Poland upriver, close to the
bridges. The pilot and co-pilot would then get ashore by dinghy, while the
soldier was supposed to guide the floating bomb towards the bridge.

Few had much confidence in the mission's potential success. There was every
chance of the flying boats being shot down on the long flight to their targets,
and hardly any chance of getting safely away from the aircraft after landing. In
the event, the Aktion 24 Dorniers were discovered at their temporary base on
the Müritz See at Rechlin, and by 10 April three of the Do 24s had been
destroyed by USAAF P-51s and B-24s. Operation Aktion 24 was cancelled.

KG 200's last serviceable B-24, former 41-28779, was hit by German flak, force-landed in a field near Quedlinburg and was burned by its crew after the nose wheel collapsed during attempted take-off. *(NEMB)*

Other bases were being evacuated, and it was during a low-level flight between Hildesheim and Bavaria on the night of 6 April to avoid advancing US forces that the KG 200 B-24H Liberator A3+PB *Sunshine* was shot down by German flak at Aschersleben, near Halle. The same fate befell its B-24D KO+XA as it fled from Wackerlaben on 13 April to avoid the Soviet advance. Flown by Oberfeldwebel Rauchfuss and carrying twenty-nine KG 200 personnel in broad daylight, the Liberator was hit in the wings and fuselage, killing one of the passengers and causing the pilot to make an emergency landing in a field. After the Liberator had been patched up Rauchfuss attempted to take off from the muddy field, but the nose wheel collapsed and the B-24 had to be burned by its crew, who fired flare pistols into the fuel tanks. B-24H A3+KB also suffered a nose-wheel collapse while taxiing at an airfield near Salzburg in Austria, and was abandoned. A few days later it was reclaimed by American troops when they overran the airfield. *Blonde Bomber*, 1/KG 200's B-24D, was also abandoned at Rechlin-Lärz after being badly damaged by Eighth Air Force bombers during April.

While many of KG 200's air and ground crews had virtually been dismissed and told to fend for themselves – most made for British and American front lines – the Kampfgeschwader was still planning an airlift of German units trapped behind Soviet lines. Operation Rennstrecke had continued over the winter months, with supply drops being made from Riga by He 111s to the trapped force near Minsk which included some of Otto Skorzeny's Jagdverbande

A KG 200 Dornier Do 24 abandoned at Schleswig at the end of the war had been earmarked for the aborted Operation Aktion 24. *(Richard Chapman)*

units. On 20 April two KG 200 Arado Ar 232Bs, one of which was flown by Unteroffizier Bruno Davids, who had flown the first aborted mission to assassinate Stalin the previous July, took off from Flensburg on the Danish border – to where many of the unit's aircraft had been moved – in an attempt to rescue some of the surviving troops, but the operation was aborted due to bad weather en route. It was later revealed that all the German troops had been captured by January, but the Soviets had continued to request supply drops using captured radios.

Apart from those in Denmark the only KG 200 base still operating outside Germany was Prague-Rusyne, close to the Rudy Letov plant at Letnany where a Ju 290 assembly line had been established in 1943. A development of the Ju 290 was produced at the end of 1944, the six-engined Ju 390 GH+UK, and was one of several long-range types evaluated by KG 200 to fly non-stop missions to Japan or South America. The other long-range type evaluated was the giant Blohm und Voss Bv 238, a six-engined flying boat with a wingspan of almost 200 feet developed from the Bv 222 Viking maritime reconnaissance aircraft, the transport variant of which saw limited use on operations from Norway to the Soviet Union. The Bv 238 was designed to carry a 40-ton payload over a maximum range of 6,000 miles, but development was abandoned in 1945 after the prototype was destroyed by USAAF P-51 Mustangs on Lake Schaal, near Kiel.

However, early in April two Bv 222 Vikings of Lufttransportstaffel See 222, based at Travemünde on the Baltic Coast near Lübeck, were prepared for a long flight north. Although KG 200 was not officially involved in the operation, large quantities of equipment began to arrive at the docks: skis, tents, sledges and supplies of condensed food. The unit was told to expect up to thirty of the most senior surviving Third Reich officials. The Vikings would pick them up from an inlet north of Kiel, where the remnants of the German High Command were gathering. The plan was to fly them on to Greenland, a Danish territory. However, as soon as the Vikings were almost ready for the operation they were strafed by USAAF P-51 Mustangs on 8 April. One of the flying boat's navigators, Hauptmann Ernst Koenig, remembered the raid. 'By April 1945 we had just three Bv 222s left at Travemünde and now two were completely destroyed as they sat in the water. We had another in the workshop and that, too, was made ready. It required a lot of work, but it was done and once again the stores arrived for loading on board.' Many of its possible high-ranking passengers were now surrounded in Berlin with little prospect of reaching Travemünde, which in any case was in danger of being overrun by advancing British and Soviet forces.

One last-ditch attack by KG 200 Misteln took place on the afternoon of 27 April when seven of them led by Ju 188s, attempted to destroy a bridge over the Oder that had been captured by Soviet troops. Led by Leutnant Eckard Dittmann, they were met by a furious barrage of anti-aircraft fire as they approached the target near Küstrin. Dittmann's Mistel was hit, but he managed to release his Ju 88 and flew his Fw 190 back to an airfield at Werneuchen on the north-east outskirts of Berlin. Only one other Fw 190 pilot survived the attack and the bridge remained standing.

Following Hitler's suicide on 30 April, a Luftwaffe Bv 138 flying boat was ordered to fly from its base in Copenhagen to Lake Havel in Berlin, by then surrounded by Soviet forces, to pick up two important government couriers rumoured to be carrying a copy of his last will. However contact could not be made so the pilot, Oberstleutnant Klemusch, flew ten wounded soldiers out of Berlin under heavy Soviet shellfire. For Ernst Koenig and his fellow-Bv 222 crew members at Travemünde, the waiting was over. 'We were called on the base on 2 May. Our commanding officer, Hauptmann Mayerling, called us together. He told us his responsibilities had ended as the war was over, gave us our papers and sent us all home. Then we destroyed the final flying boat with explosives.'

Elsewhere, as fuel ran out, communications all but ceased and airfields were overrun, KG 200 was disbanded and its crews released from duty. Since June 1944 more than 600 agents, including five women, had been dropped behind enemy lines by aircraft of 1 Gruppe/KG 200. Although there were widespread

Luftwaffe Bv 222 flying boats were prepared to evacuate members of the German High Command from the Baltic to Greenland in April 1945, but were destroyed by their crew at Travemünde at the end of the war. *(MAP)*

reports of high-ranking Nazi officials and vast amounts of cash and valuables smuggled out of Germany by KG 200 as the Third Reich crumbled, in reality very few of its aircraft were capable of flying anywhere. One exception was a Ju 290A that was flown to Spain at the end of April by Hauptmann Braun and his crew. It was reported that this aircraft was Hitler's personal transport, a Ju 290A-0 converted in August 1944 to a 50-seat VIP transport designated Ju 290A-6, and not a KG 200 aircraft, but this has never confirmed. The exact purpose of this flight, and who or what it was carrying at the time, was never fully explained. What is known, however, is that the flight was carried out while the authorities argued over the release of another Ju 290A that had made an emergency landing at Barcelona two weeks earlier.

The DLH Ju 290A-5 D-AITR had flown from Berlin to Barcelona's Muntadas Airport via Munich along the K22 corridor on the night of 5/6 April. Its pilot, Flugkapitän Sluzalek and his crew of five, encountered heavy fog as they approached the Spanish airport and after two aborted approaches he decided to land on a short secondary runway, coming to a halt in a ploughed field with a damaged undercarriage. Again, the exact purpose at this flight remained a mystery, although a number of passengers were seen to leave the stricken aircraft before the Spanish authorities arrived on the scene. The crew was flown back to Berlin on a DLH Fw 200 Condor on 14 April, by which time the Spanish government had decided to cancel all flights between Germany and Spain with effect from 21 April. Although the Junkers was repaired by German DLH mechanics stationed in Spain, its departure was blocked and the aircraft interned. After the war it was purchased by a private owner who sold it on to the Spanish Air Force, with which it served until the mid-1950s.

During the last four weeks of hostilities in Europe No. 161 Squadron's Hudsons had flown another twelve operations to drop twenty-three agents into Germany and two more into Holland, the last operation being flown on the night of 24 April by a new Canadian pilot, Flg Off J.L. Nicholson. A few days later Capt Per Hysing-Dahl, RNAF dropped the last agent into Norway from his Stirling; and on the night of 2/3 May the veteran Norwegian Special Duties pilot returned to Norway to drop the last containers of the war by the RAF's 'moon' squadrons.

Twenty-four hours before the end of hostilities in Europe the squadron's new commanding officer, Wg Cdr Len Ratcliff, accompanied Capt Hysing-Dahl in a Hudson to Trondheim in his native Norway to take the surrender of the 50,000-strong German garrison; a few hundred members of the Resistance assisted.

Following VE-Day on 8 May, the squadron was tasked with repatriating Allied prisoners-of-war to England, and ironically it was while fulfilling this task that it suffered its last loss. Having picked up two former PoWs at Lüneberg, a Hudson flew on to Brussels to collect some more but crashed on landing, killing its three crew and two passengers. On 5 June No. 161 (Special Duties) Squadron was disbanded; it had flown 13,500 SD sorties from Tempsford and Tangmere to occupied Europe, landed 324 agents, picked up 593 and parachuted another 1,500. It had also made more than 500 Operation 'Ascension' contacts.

In fact the last clandestine flight to be flown from Tempsford was to transport a team of six British Technical Intelligence officers, including Col William Cook and Colin Campbell, to Lichtenau on the night of 11/12 June. American troops had overrun the secret German rocket test and assembly complex at Nordhausen, some 30 miles to the west of Leipzig. The British scientists had just six days to obtain as many technical data and rocket-motor components as they could before the Soviets advanced to a demarcation line across Germany that had been agreed with the Western Allies, and that would seal off the area.

With Germany's unconditional surrender, and with the occupied countries liberated from the Nazi yoke, clandestine operations in Europe, for which so many had given their lives, were now at an end – but not yet so in the Far East.

CHAPTER 9

The Setting Sun

Japan's catastrophic attack on Pearl Harbor on the morning of 7 December 1941 had underlined the United States' complete lack of a credible intelligence system. President Roosevelt had watched events unfold in Europe, with Hitler's lightning occupation of much of the continent, while Japan continued its brutal domination of China and Manchuria. And still no unified foreign intelligence service had been established.

Soon after Germany attacked the Soviet Union on 22 June 1941, Hitler's Abwehr agents learned that Japan was planning war against Britain and the United States and that this information had been intercepted by the US Office of Naval Intelligence. The USONI had broken Japan's diplomatic code, known as *Magic*, as messages were sent between the Japanese embassy in Berlin and Tokyo via a powerful transmitter in the Madrid embassy. In August 1941 SIS agent Dusko Popov had flown to America with vital information about Japanese plans to attack the United States, gleaned from his Abwehr contact in Lisbon, but thanks to FBI chief J. Edgar Hoover and British double agent Guy Liddell his information was treated as unreliable and never passed on to US defence chiefs.

Britain was no better prepared for the Japanese attack than was the United States. Although an SOE Far East Section had been established in Hong Kong in 1940 under the directorship of brothers John and Tony Keswick, *taipans* of the powerful Far East trading company Jardine Matheson, they had had to make a hasty retreat to the British enclave in Shanghai when Hong Kong and Singapore fell to the Japanese at the beginning of 1942. Here they were surrounded by the Japanese, cut off from any outside communications or support and rendered virtually useless as an intelligence source. SOE in South East Asia had to start again from scratch.

Two new British covert organisations and an Australian one were formed in April 1942: SOE Force 136 and the SIS Inter-Services Liaison Dept (ISLD); both had their headquarters at Meerut in India. An Allied Intelligence Bureau (AIB) was established to collate data from the different agencies. The first US military unit created specifically for conducting unconventional warfare operations behind enemy lines – Detachment 101, formed at the same time in New Delhi – was initially tasked with sabotage operations at the Japanese air base at Myitkyina in Burma. Fighter aircraft from the base were shooting down US transports flying the vital 'Hump' route over the Kumon mountains supplying General Stilwell's Chinese divisions in the north. While these units were recruiting and training agents, the first SD flights were taking place in the Far East.

Following the fall of Singapore earlier in the year and Japan's seizure of the Dutch East Indies and New Guinea, the Australian Coast Watching Organisation (CWO) was established. Manned by expatriate Australian civilians and military personnel who decided to remain in hiding on the many remote islands in the region when they were overrun, they were initially the only Allied contact from behind enemy lines in the first months of war in the Far East.

The only practical way to supply these CWO agents was by air, but communications were sporadic at best and the probability of discovery by the Japanese was high. The danger in which these Australians operated was soon brought home to all concerned in chilling fashion. Responding to a short radio message, Plt Off Norman 'Robbie' Robertson of No. 11 Squadron RAAF flew Catalina A24-22 on 28 May from Horn Island, off Australia's northern tip, across the Coral Sea to a position near Port Moresby in New Guinea, to drop supplies to CWO agent Sub-Lt C.L. Page, RNVR. Unfortunately the arrival of the flying boat had been reported to the Japanese, who subsequently captured the hapless CWO agent and executed him a month later.

The day after the Australian squadron's operation another Catalina unit, the RAF's No. 240 Squadron, departed Lough Erne in Northern Ireland to begin the long flight to another island in the Far East. By the end of June its Catalina IIA flying boats had arrived at Red Hills Lake at Madras, on the south-east coast of India, to fly SD operations for Force 136. Earlier three of its aircraft were detached to Koggala in Ceylon (Sri Lanka) to join two other RAF Catalinas, the only survivors from Nos 202 and 205 Squadrons that had managed to reach the base after the fall of Singapore in February. With the Japanese poised to invade Ceylon, their task was to supply a secret emergency Royal Navy base at Abbu Atoll, a remote coral island in the Maldives some 600 miles from the island. At the end of March the sole No. 202 Squadron captain, Australian Flt Lt D.H. 'Toby' Hildyard, flew his Catalina to Nancowry in the Nicobar Islands, to destroy British installations and supplies and evacuate twenty-three personnel before the Japanese overran the island. A Dutch Catalina and its exhausted crew, led by Lt Hamers, which had arrived at Koggala from the Netherlands East Indies, was also earmarked for the hazardous Abbu Atoll missions.

No. 240 Squadron Catalina IIA AM269/'K', based at Red Hills Lake near Madras in India, flew clandestine flights to Burma and Thailand from mid-1942. *(ww2 images)*

Further to the east, Catalina A24-26 of No. 11 Squadron RAAF, flown by Flt Lts Athol 'Attie' Wearne and Gordon Priest, carried a USAAF doctor from Cairns to eastern New Guinea on the evening of 14 August to pick up injured survivors of a B-26 crew rescued by members of the CWO. The Coast Watchers jungle camp overlooking Porlock Harbour was only a few miles east of the Japanese-held town of Gona, and when the flying boat touched down and taxied towards the shore there was a very real possibility of alerting the enemy. It took some considerable time to transfer the injured airmen to the aircraft by canoe before the Catalina was able to take off and head for Townsville in Australia. Another of the squadron's Catalinas flew a covert mission from Cairns on 3 September, when three Australian and two American agents were inserted onto Ontang Java, a small atoll in the Solomon Islands.

Only weeks later Attie Wearne had the misfortune to lose a leg to a shark while swimming near his base at Cairns. After emergency surgery and lengthy rehabilitation he was fitted with an aluminium leg that came with a useful optional extra attached – a bottle opener. He was able to return to active service to become one of the RAAF's most experienced Catalina captains, completing three tours and finishing the war as commanding officer of No. 20 (RAAF) Squadron.

During this period in the south-west Pacific theatre, the Americans began launching a series of operations to control the central Solomons and eastern New Guinea. Two of the RAAF's most experienced flying boat captains – Sqn Ldr Dick Cohen, who had flown the first official clandestine flight of the war, flying Lord Gort to Morocco, and Norm Robertson – were lent to the USAAF to fly with the lead formation of the first US bomber attack on Rabaul in New Guinea.

Norm Robinson and his crew also flew a number of operations to support Allied agents in the region. In February 1943 his No. 11 Squadron RAAF Catalina A24-25 was detached to Darwin, from where it transported an Australian Imperial Force (AIF) party and 3 tons of supplies to the Aroe Islands. The same squadron was back in enemy territory on 24 March when Sqn Ldr Reg Burrage and Flg Off John Ryan took off from Port Moresby in Papua in Catalina A24-17 at 1750 hours for a night landing at Open Bay, near Rabaul. Their mission was to rescue three surviving aircrew of a USAAF B-26 shot down 10 months earlier who had been found and hidden by John Stokie, a member of the CWO, and his native trackers. Food, torches and codes had been dropped to the group and a prearranged signal was seen as the Catalina approached the Ea Ea shoreline at 0130 hours. Flare floats were then dropped to form a flarepath and the flying boat touched down safely. By 0245 the three airmen, John Stokie and three of his native assistants were aboard and the flying boat was taking off along the improvised flarepath. They landed back at Port Moresby after the successful completion of the 14-hour mission. Reg Burrage was awarded an immediate DFC.

On 30 April the Allies suffered their first loss on Special Duties operations in the south-west Pacific theatre when B-24 Liberator 42-40352 of the 321st Bomb Squadron/90th Bomb Group, flown by Lieutenant Chovance and dropping stores to a CWO group in New Guinea, crashed near Bena-Bena. Nine of the crew died in the crash, while three survivors were later killed and reportedly eaten by local cannibals.

A second loss, this time a Catalina of No. 11 Squadron RAAF, occurred at the end of May. Flt Lt Bill Clark and Observer Flg Off Clifford were flying Catalina A24-43 on a night supply drop over Bougainville in the Solomons when the flying boat hit a hillside. Clark and two of his crew were killed, but Australian Coast Watchers and local islanders rescued four survivors. However, while waiting to be evacuated by submarine, the CWO camp was unexpectedly attacked on 16 June by Japanese troops. All but eight of the group escaped into the jungle, but amongst those captured was one of the Catalina's crew, Flg Off Cliff Dunn. None of them survived the war. Later in the year, the American submarine USS *Guardfish* evacuated eighty Allied personnel from the island, including two of the flying boat's crew, Cpl Hugh Wettenhall and Sgt Fred Thompson.

A former Netherlands East Indies (NEI) Naval Air Service officer, Cdr A.J. de Bruijn, was later flown out of the Wissel Lakes in Dutch New Guinea to Australia by a NEI Navy Dornier Do 24 flying boat, to form a Dutch SD unit at Rathmines in New South Wales. Manned by NEI crews, the unit was equipped with a former NEI NAS Dornier Do 24K, X-24, the last survivor of five that left Java in March 1942, and Catalina Y-45. During the first two months of 1943 Lt Aernaut flew several intelligence operations with the new unit to deliver agents and stores to the Merauke area of Dutch New Guinea. Aernaut's flight engineer, Henk 'Harry' Gryzen, had flown with KLM's Dutch East Indies subsidiary KNILM before he was conscripted into the NEI Naval Air Service when the Japanese attacked.

Netherlands East Indies Flight Dornier Do 24K X-24 based at Rathmines in New South Wales was used for clandestine flights to New Guinea and the NEI in 1942–3. *(Brett Freeman)*

During April Lts H.A. Valk and Henk van Hasselo flew Catalina Y-45 from Rathmines on a 10-day long intelligence operation, ranging from Merauke and the Wissel Lakes to Tanah Merah in Malaya. On 18 April a No. 20 Squadron RAAF Catalina landed at Johann Albrecht Harbour in Dutch New Britain to pick up Coast Watchers Capts Harris and McCarthy and party of local agents.

Prior to the Allied offensive in the South Pacific codenamed Operation 'Cartwheel', the NEI Rear Adm Koenrood visited Cdr de Bruijn on 23 May at his covert flying-boat base at the Wissel Lakes and advised him to leave. He refused, but on 1 June the Dutch unit's two Catalinas, Y-45 and Y-87, were ordered to be flown to Ceylon – undertaking the first non-stop flight across the Indian Ocean from Australia – to become part of No. 321 (Dutch) Squadron based at China Bay. The Dornier X-24 was transferred to No. 41 Squadron RAAF and given the serial number A49-6. On the same day No. 1576 (SD) Flight with Liberators was established at Dum Dum, near Calcutta in India, to support SOE Force 136.

Intelligence on Japanese activities in New Guinea continued to be a priority for the Americans and Australians, and many covert operations carrying agents and stores to the Sepik and Yellow rivers were flown under constant threat of enemy attack. Three US Navy PBYs belonging to VP-101 flew a series of missions in early July from Port Moresby to Yiribbi on the Sepik river, which by then was virtually surrounded by the Japanese.

Lt Walter Hartley was one of the flying-boat captains.

We had completed the five-hour flight across the high mountains and dense jungles of New Guinea to let down to the Sepic river with no sight of the enemy. Our purpose was to carry Aussie commandos, native police and supplies. The native police had previously been taken to Australia where they were shown the build-up of aircraft, landing craft, tanks, men, etc. After that, no one had to instruct these guys to tell what they had seen, and impress the other natives as to how strong the Allied forces were.

While taxiing to the mooring on the Sepik, Hartley's PBY struck a large submerged tree branch which penetrated the bow, shattering the bomb aimer's Perspex and destroying the bombsight. As water poured into the bow compartment, Hartley ordered the crew to sit on the tailplane while ammunition box covers and a mattress were jammed into the hole, and the unloading of supplies and passengers was quickly completed.

We secured the nose of the plane as best we could and took off with about 2 feet of water in the cockpit. With 100-foot tall jungle trees to climb over in a very nose-heavy aircraft, I pushed everything to the firewall and just made it. We now had to dispose of the water. A bilge pump was produced; it would have taken 10 hours to remove the water with that gizmo, so I shot a .45 automatic slug into the bilge. The water drained right out.

'Cat' 08227 landed safely at Port Moresby.

These covert operations continued until December, with VPB-11 joining VP-101 in September 1943. Six PBYs of the new unit, led by Lt Cdr C.M. Campbell, were called on to evacuate Australian commandos from the upper reaches of the Sepik river as Japanese forces closed in at the end of the year. Over a 5-day period from 16 December the flying boats flew seventeen sorties from 0500 to 1400 hours every day, bringing out 219 Australians, their equipment and several New Guineans. For almost 12 hours during this period the PBY of Lt Tom Ragsdale had been sitting on the river in broad daylight while his crewmen struggled to repair a damaged starter motor. All the American flying boats eventually returned safely to their base at Samarai on the southern tip of New Guinea.

During December 1943 the OSS expanded its activities in the Far East when Wild Bill Donovan visited Detachment 101 Headquarters in Assam. Accompanied by its first commanding officer, Capt Carl Eifler, Donovan insisted on flying into Japanese-held Burma in a two-seat Piper L-4 'Grasshopper' to interrogate Japanese prisoners personally. He also sent Eifler to Washington to brief the authorities on the situation, replacing him with Col William R. Peers. With the Axis powers facing the possibility of defeat in Europe, the tempo of clandestine flights in all theatres was set to become an important part of the Allies' strategic operations.

In the Pacific theatre American flying boats were used for long-range air–sea rescue operations into Japanese-controlled waters, codenamed 'Dumbo' missions. One of the most daring of these was flown by Lt Nathan Gordon, a US Navy PBY-5A pilot assigned to VPB-34 at Samarai. He had been called out on 19 February 1944 to search for survivors of USAAF B-25s shot down over Kavieng Harbour at New Ireland, in the Bismarck Sea. All the bomber crews had parachuted into the water and Gordon's 'Cat', named Arkansas Traveler, had to taxi around the harbour four times picking up survivors. He had shut down his engines, started them up again and taken off on two occasions before all were safely aboard, picking up the last of them only 500 yards from a Japanese gun battery on the harbour wall. Gordon eventually managed to haul the overweight flying boat, carrying twenty-five men and a lot of water in the bilges, into the air without being hit by the gunners and return safely to base, a feat for which he was later awarded the Congressional Medal of Honor; he was the only US flying-boat captain to be so honoured.

One of the busiest RAF flying-boat bases outside Great Britain was at Koggala in Ceylon, where Catalinas of Nos 205, 240 and 413 Squadrons and Sunderlands of No. 230 Squadron were based. Located near Ceylon's southern-most tip, the village of Koggala on the shores of a lake of the same name was requisitioned early in 1941 as the site of an airfield and seaplane base from which to defend Ceylon. Its inhabitants were given 24 hours to evacuate and surrender their property to the Royal Air Force.

In March 1944 two No. 230 Squadron Sunderland III flying boats, nicknamed 'Gert' and 'Daisy' after two music hall-stars of the day, were deployed from Koggala to Assam to evacuate wounded Chindits. Over a 32-day period they flew from the monsoon-swollen Brahmaputra river to Lake Indawgyi in Burma, behind Japanese lines, to evacuate 537 wounded and exhausted soldiers, survivors of Gen Orde Wingate's Long Range Penetration Group, named 'Chindits' after the mythical beast *Chinthe*.

Our Popsie, a No. 240 Squadron Catalina IV at Red Hills Lake in 1945, served with detachments at China Bay, Koggala and the Abbu Atoll. *(ww2 images)*

Col P. Cochrane's American Air Commandos had dropped Wingate's second Chindit attack force, in an operation codenamed 'Thursday', into Burma on 5 March. USAAF C-47s and Waco CG-4A gliders of 'Cochrane's Circus' took off from Assam bound for an area north-west of Bhamo codenamed 'Broadway'. Unfortunately only half the force landed without damage, but worse was to come. Their leader, 41-year-old Orde Wingate, had boarded a USAAF B-25 in India on 24 March and was on his way to join his men when it crashed in the jungle near the Burmese border. There were no survivors. With the loss of their unconventional and truculent leader, whom Churchill described as a 'man of genius who might have become a man of destiny', his Chindits were left for the second year running to separate into small groups and fight their way out of trouble as best they could.

In early 1944 the Far East Liaison Office (FELO), the cover for SOE's 'D' Section of the AIB tasked with propaganda to encourage escape and rescue, was formed, supported by the various SD units now operating from land and sea bases in India. On 1 February these had been augmented when No. 1576 Flight was renumbered No. 357 Squadron, commanded by Sqn Ldr J.R. Moore. Six Liberator IIIs and three Hudson IIIs were assigned to 'A' Flight, based at Digri with detachments at Dum Dum and China Bay, and three Catalina flying boats equipped 'B' Flight at Red Hills Lake. Only six weeks later 'B' Flight was expanded to become No. 628 (SD) Squadron with six Catalina IBs on strength, all fitted with long-range fuel tanks.

The long-range SD Consolidated Liberator III, built by the same company as the Catalina, was capable of dropping four agents at a time, each weighing 200lb with kit, from 800 feet at an optimum speed of 140mph. Unlike those operating into occupied Europe from Tempsford, No. 357 Squadron's Hudsons were used almost exclusively for dropping agents and supplies, and not for pick-ups. Two agents, or 750lb of cargo could be carried and dropped at a speed of 120mph. Unfortunately one of the Hudsons was lost within the first month of SD flights. During Operation 'Buffer', a series of supply drops to SOE agents in Burma, Hudson AM949 crashed near Bhamo on 12 March, killing one of the crew. The surviving crew member was badly injured and No. 357 Squadron's Medical Officer, Flt Lt George Graham, was dropped from a Liberator the following day to give him urgently needed medical attention. Both were able to hack their way through the dense jungle back to Allied lines with the help of local tribesmen.

On the night of 2 May a No. 628 Squadron Catalina flown by Plt Off Les Brooks dropped two agents off the coast of Thailand, near Bangkok. Following an SOS from the agents a week later the flying boat returned to pick them up, but only one made the rendezvous. The Australian navigator on Operation 'Balmoral', and many other long-range SD flights to the area, was Flt Sgt George Drummond, who had to make do with nineteenth-century maritime charts as his main aid to pinpoint navigation. The resourceful Drummond would subsequently be mentioned in dispatches twice and receive a commendation from the South East Asia Allied Supreme Commander, Adm Louis Mountbatten, in recognition of his clandestine flights, as would another of No. 628 Squadron's Australian aircrew. Flg Off John O'Meara had qualified as an airman pilot in 1942, having formerly been a teacher at Swan Hill High School, Victoria, where one of his pupils was a certain George Drummond.

Another unit with a strong Australian connection was the US Army's 25th Liaison Squadron (LS), commanded by Col Frank Barlett, which had been sent to Australia before its 'A' Flight was deployed to Saidor as the Allies fought their way along the east coast of New Guinea in early 1944. Many of its pilots had been washed out of combat pilot training and had been 'retreaded' to fly the rugged two-seater Stinson L-5 as sergeant pilots. Little was expected of them when they arrived in theatre.

Tasked with air evacuation of downed aircrew from airstrips hacked out of the jungle, they also flew night interdiction sorties – dropping small bombs and empty bottles on the sleeping enemy – and flew agents behind enemy lines. Their powerful, high-wing, light aircraft had excellent short take-off and landing (STOL) perfomance and reliability. They were fitted with identification friend-or-foe (IFF) lights in the belly which were used to send predetermined light signals to those on the ground during night operations. Although the L-5 was designed to carry only one passenger, it was capable of carrying a useful load in large cargo pouches attached to shackles under the wings. These could carry weapons, ammunition, food, field tools or medical supplies to be either airdropped to forces operating behind enemy lines or downed pilots, or delivered after landing.

While searching for a downed P-47 pilot the unit, then known as the 'Guinea Short Lines', received an intelligence report on 25 May telling them that escaped PoWs had been observed in the nearby Ramu Valley. Suspecting a trap, two L-5s flown by Sgts James Henkle and Lyle Gleason were escorted to the area by a fighter squadron flying high cover. This time they were able to locate the fighter pilot, who had begun clearing a landing strip for the L-5s. Over the next few days supplies were dropped to the P-47 pilot while he continued to hack out a clearing large enough for the L-5s to land on. At the same time, the party of escapees had been spotted: some thirty Indian Sikh PoWs who had been brought to New Guinea by the Japanese as slave labour. After setting up a message pick-up rig by running a line between two trees, it was discovered that they had valuable information about the strength and location of Japanese troops in the area. As the L-5s dropped food, water and medical supplies to the Indians and guided them toward the now completed jungle airstrip, it was decided to attempt to fly them all out to safety. After Sgt Henkle had picked up the downed pilot, the L-5s returned to fly one, or sometimes two, at a time to evacuate twenty-three of the surviving Indians back to Saidor.

Not long after this feat 'A' Flight, which had adopted the Australian kangaroo as its logo and painted it on the nose of its L-5s, was asked to ferry a raiding party of fifty Australian commandos and their equipment behind enemy lines to attack a Japanese radio position at Wantoat. After silencing the radio and most of the guards, four Japanese were taken prisoner. Each of the captives was placed on the lap of an Australian commando who held a knife at his neck in the rear seat of an L-5. There were no attempts to escape!

With both SOE and OSS expanding their clandestine operations in south-east Asia the demand for air support increased, and with it, operational problems surfaced. Although Gen Cochrane's Air Commando units had more than 100 aircraft assigned to them, ranging from L-5s to P-51 Mustang fighters and B-25 Mitchell medium bombers, most of its C-47 transports were dedicated to the support of regular American ground forces. The OSS Detachment 101 would have to rely on No. 357 Squadron to carry out most of its stores and personnel drops.

Although there were conflicts between the two Allied agencies over the insertion of agents into Indo-China and Thailand, it was day-to-day operational problems that affected the squadron. These included the incompatibility of its radio fit with that of the USAAF base at Kunming during operations into China. The RAF used low-frequency wireless/telephone (W/T) at long range, while the USAAF used radio/telephone (R/T), with a different frequency. Following his command of No. 161 (SD) Squadron, Lewis Hodges had been posted to the RAF Staff College for a rest. However, he was not happy without action and asked for another command. He was offered No. 357 (SD) Squadron in Jessore, India, with a drop in rank from group captain to wing commander.

I was happy to drop rank as I could be back in the air and not head the way of many by flying a desk. The unit in India had been initially equipped with the Hudson and then they were given the American Liberator bomber. After my experience with the Hudsons and Halifaxes of No. 161, I was quite happy to take this mixed bag over. Technically it was under the South East Asia Command (SEAC) but, like its counterparts in Europe, No. 357

Squadron acted in conjunction with the SOE and the ISLD. Unlike Europe, the territory over which we flew was totally different from that of France and the Low Countries. It was dense jungle, with many more Japanese troops in evidence on the ground, although anti-aircraft fire was rare as was enemy air activity.

Hodges arrived late in 1944 to take over the Liberator VIs and Dakota IIIs that were replacing the Hudson. Also formed at the end of 1944 was No. 358 (SD) Squadron under the command of Wg Cdr P.G. Farr. Hodges relates that his Liberators had been extensively modified for the SD role.

They were fitted with additional fuel tanks in the fuselage, which meant that the payload suffered on a long flight. One aircraft, I remember, flew a 22-hour sortie. But generally the flights were between 8 and 9 hours, although I did fly some longer ones.

On these long missions to Burma, Thailand and China, the Liberators burned a heavy fuel load, typically 16,000lbs while carrying only a 2,000lb payload, flying at low level over enemy-occupied territory where there was no possibility of landing to refuel. The Hudson had made some landings behind enemy lines earlier in the year but was later replaced by the versatile Dakota, which could land on strips carved out of the jungle by the local resistance groups or by Allied troops working behind the enemy lines, including the remnants of Wingate's Chindits. Navigation was always a problem, as the maps issued to RAF aircrews were often outdated and inaccurate and the radar homing devices were not as advanced as those used in Europe. Added to this, the terrain and weather were certainly more hostile than those of Europe. Heat and humidity took their toll on both aircraft and aircrew. Tropical storms, monsoon rain and severe turbulence made low-level flying all the more hazardous, reducing visibility to such an extent that the remote drop zones were often completely obscured by low cloud.

Contact with agents was the same as used in France: small torch-lights flashing an identification letter, while personnel on the ground lit small fires at the DZ that could be seen by the approaching aircraft. The aircraft flew at low level, where temperatures were always at their highest, causing the aircrews to be constantly bathed in sweat; generally when there was a moon. They flew to predetermined times so that the reception committee could be ready to receive stores and human cargo. It was no easy task after a 10-hour flight using only dead reckoning, often in bad weather and over featureless jungle or ocean.

Sqn Ldr Lewis Hodges, third from left, with his crew in front of No. 357 (SD) Squadron Liberator IV at Jessore in India in 1945. *(Lewis Hodges)*

Stores were packed into the standard container and air-dropped from the bomb bays of the Liberator or out of the large cargo door of the Dakota; different techniques were worked out by the aircrews and the dispatcher to suit height and terrain. Weather was the major factor in these uncertain climes. Early on, the aircraft remained grounded during the monsoon season, but later they would continue to be flown even during the wettest periods to support the ground troops, who were battling for survival behind enemy lines in the mud and rain. Often the DZs were hard to spot, especially when they were small gaps cut out of thick jungle on the sides of hills.

There were also tensions between the SOE Force 136, headed by Colin MacKenzie, and OSS Detachment 101 commanded by William Peers – particularly in the China–Burma–India theatre of operations. The Americans preferred to use local agents recruited from anti-colonial or nationalist factions including the communists, and a certain amount of subterfuge had to be employed by the old colonials, particularly Britain and France.

Typical was one of the first operations that No. 357 Squadron flew from Kunming in south-east China on 4 September. Flt Lt Bill Cost and the crew of Liberator BZ847 flew into the American base with six French agents on board, all dressed in RAF uniforms. By the time the aircraft took off again bound for Indo-China the agents had changed into Free French Foreign Legion uniforms. Two nights later the squadron dropped two Thai SOE agents on the outskirts of Bangkok, where the pro-Japanese government had just been overthrown by Allied sympathisers in the police and navy.

The OSS felt that the British were limiting their operations in Thailand, as well as in Malaya and the Netherlands East Indies, and was determined to establish its own airborne support for Detachment 101 and to no longer have to rely on favours from the hard-pressed RAF SD squadrons. Douglas C-47 Skytrains were in short supply and Col Cochrane was still loath to release any of his for the clandestine transport of a few agents. One type that was readily available was the Stinson L-5. Able to operate from short airstrips hacked out of the jungle by native tribesmen, the L-5 was ideal for covert missions behind the lines; its only drawback was that it could carry only one passenger – or two at a pinch – in the tandem seat behind the pilot. OSS officer Lt Philip S. Weld of Detachment 101 was flown to one such airstrip at Hpungkan-Tingsa in Burma,

Two of No. 357 (SD) Squadron's Liberator IVs at Jessore being prepared for a clandestine supply drop over Burma in early 1945. *(Andy Thomas)*

60 miles south of Myitkyina, in an L-5 on 15 October. His mission was to take command of a group of Chingpaw tribesmen, but within days Weld and the tribesmen were retreating further into the jungle pursued by Japanese forces. After calling for a number of stores drops to their remote camp, all of which were unsuccessful, Lt Weld was forced to trek overland, to reach Allied lines after nearly three months in the field.

Further to the west No. 628 Squadron Catalinas continued to fly a series of long-distance SD operations to the occupied Andaman Islands in the Bay of Bengal, including two flown by Flt Lt B. Daymond and Jack O'Meara. On the first one they had to evade a Japanese convoy to land agents at Chance Island. Daymond's 'Cat' stayed on the water for two hours, covered by O'Meara circling above, while the agents checked out the bay before going ashore. Eventually the two flying boats returned to Red Hills after an elapsed time of 26 hours.

On a subsequent operation Daymond's Catalina hit a submerged object that ripped a hole in the hull while making a night landing off Bentinck Island. With great presence of mind, he was able to take off again before the flying boat flooded and to circle the island, while his crew plugged the hole with mattresses and spare clothing, before he could land safely, offload the agents and return to Red Hills. Daymond was to fly three more operations during October, flying more than 100 hours, most of them over enemy territory.

Master navigator George Drummond had flown eleven SD missions during the month, including one on 28 October. His Catalina flew from China Bay on Operation 'Oatmeal' to land four agents and their equipment on the Perhertian Islands, off Kota Bharu on the east coast of Malaya, when a Japanese patrol boat appeared, causing the mission to be aborted after 30 hours in the air. Two days later Flt Lt McKeond and WO Brooks returned to the Islands with Capt Ibrahim bin Ismail and three Malay NCOs on Operation 'Oatmeal II'. Although the agents were betrayed by informers, Ismail managed to persuade his Japanese captors that they were willing to act as double agents, and for the next six months they transmitted and received spurious messages to and from Force 136 headquarters.

Flg Off Armand Etienne, a Russian-born 'Black Cat' pilot serving with No. 43 (RAAF) Squadron, flew 900 miles from Bowen, Queensland into enemy territory on 24 October to rescue another Catalina crew. They had been forced down on the sea off Makassar in the Celebes after being hit by anti-aircraft fire during a mine-laying operation the previous night. The downed No. 42 (RAAF) Squadron crew had managed to taxi away from the enemy coast while covered by a long-range USAAF P-61 Black Widow night fighter, and at dawn Etienne's Catalina A24-59 arrived overhead and landed alongside the stricken

Australian Black Cat Catalina IVB A24-63 *Dabster* of No. 43 Squadron RAAF, which carried out aircrew rescue operations behind enemy lines and spoof raids during 1944/5. *(Brett Freeman)*

flying boat. After the crew and their equipment had been transferred to the Black Cat, the abandoned A24-100 was sunk by gunfire from the P-61.

Although the main role of the US Navy and RAAF Black Cats was to locate and intercept nocturnal enemy shipping in the Pacific, on what were known as 'Mike Searches' by the Americans and 'Milk Runs' by the Australians, some of No. 43 Squadron Catalinas also carried out spoof raids, dropping 'window' to confuse Japanese air defences during mining operations in the waters around the Philippines.

At the beginning of December in the Burma–China–India theatre Dakota KJ921/'H' of No. 375 Squadron flew the first RAF pick-up operation into Burma from Jessore. Its pilot, Australian Flt Lt Terence 'Pat' O'Brien, had survived a tour on Coastal Command Blenheims before being seconded to the Army in India. Almost by chance he had found himself in the co-pilot's seat of a Waco glider on Wingate's second Chindit operation and had spent four months fighting his way out of the jungle with the help of local tribesmen and OSS agents. One of the latter, codenamed Edgar, was Capt Oliver Milton, a British-born soldier who had been dropped behind the lines in 1942 tasked with rescuing USAAF airmen shot down while flying the formidable mountain ranges between India and China known as the Hump.

The US Navy's VPB-34 was also actively involved in rescuing downed airmen, as illustrated by a long-range mission flown over the Philippines by its charismatic commanding officer on 10 December. Lt-Cdr Vadm Viktorovich 'Vad' Utgoff, affectionately known as the Mad Russian, was the son of a Russian count, Viktor Viktorovich Utgoff, who had been a seaplane ace with the Imperial Russian Navy in the First World War. After the Revolution, he had emigrated to the United States with his good friend Igor Sikorsky, the pioneer flying-boat designer whose company built the first Trans-Pacific PanAm Clippers in the 1930s. So the young Vad Utgoff had flying boats in his blood.

Escorted by eight US Marine Corps F4U Corsairs, Utgoff's PBY flew from the recently taken base at Leyte Gulf to Luzon, the most northerly island of the Philippines and still deep in Japanese-held territory. He landed at an isolated bay and ten evading airmen and escaped PoWs were ferried out to the flying boat by the Filipino villagers who had hidden them from the Japanese. As he climbed away from the bay, Utgoff sighted a Japanese patrol boat heading for the village and asked the Corsairs to intervene. The enemy vessel was sunk by the fighters' 0.5in machine-gun fire.

At the beginning of 1945 the strength of the Allied special operations organisations had reached its peak. Some 12,000 men and women worked for SOE, almost a quarter of whom were trained as agents. They included some 500 FANYs who worked as wireless operators and cipher experts keeping contact with agents in the field. Although, unlike some of their colleagues in Europe, none was sent into the field herself, they manned some of the most remote outposts in the Allied theatre. Eight of them had even flown the Hump to Kunming, the important Allied railhead leading to the Chinese government's wartime capital at Chungking.

OSS had almost exactly the same number on its staff at 40 locations around the world, including 2,000 at Field Station London. At this time 45 per cent of its operations were directed to its Far East Theatre of Operations (FETO), with less than 20 per cent devoted to the European theatre, including Germany.

During January No. 357 Squadron flew a total of 105 SD operations including its longest to date, from Chittagong to South Lahore, flown by Flg Off John Churchill on 25 January, in an airborne time of 21 hours 55 minutes. The squadron's last Hudson operation was flown in January when Flt Lt King mounted a mission from Kunming in China to pick up a single Free French agent from Indo-China, which was still under a pro-Japanese, Vichy-style administration.

No. 357 (SD) Squadron's Dakota Flight with its Australian flight commander, Sqn Ldr Terence O'Brien, a veteran of Wingate's second Chindit operation, in the centre. *(Lewis Hodges)*

OSS Detachment 404, attached to SEAC Headquarters at Kandy in Ceylon, was responsible for operations in Thailand, previously considered an SOE stronghold. However, on 25 January an OSS mission was flown to the Gulf of Thailand by a No. 628 Squadron Catalina to make contact with pro-Allied members of the Thai government. One of the three agents assigned to Operation 'Sequence', Richard Greenlee, who had been brought up in Thailand as the son of a US missionary, was picked up again by the same flying boat on 4 February on the first leg of a journey to Washington to brief his superiors on the outcome of his meetings.

Six weeks later he returned to Thailand on another RAF Catalina as part of an OSS operation codenamed 'Siren'. He would remain in the country while yet another No. 628 Squadron flying boat picked up his two colleagues, one of whom was suffering from a nervous breakdown, and an evading pilot, Lt W.D. McGarry, who had been a PoW for more than two years. William 'Black Mac' McGarry had joined the American Volunteer Group (AVG), known as the Flying Tigers and based at Kunming, six months before Pearl Harbor and had scored ten victories when his P-40 was shot down by anti-aircraft fire while attacking a Japanese air base at Chiang Mai in Thailand on 24 March

1942. Captured by the Thai forces, he was handed over to the Japanese who, after a short interrogation, handed McGarry back to his captors. He escaped from an internment camp in May 1944 and had lived on the run with the help of friendly villagers for almost a year before making contact with the OSS mission.

Operation Siren had been mounted by the OSS as a token of appreciation for McGarry's old boss, Gen Claire Chennault, who had formed the Flying Tigers in 1940. He now commanded the US 14th Army Air Force in China and frequently provided some of his overburdened fleet of transports to support OSS operations. Between February and April several OSS agents were inserted along the south coast of China between Hainan and Hongkong as part of Operation Akron, flown by armed USAAF C-47s that were now being released for use by Detachment 101. Following the invasion of the Philippines USAAF Catalinas also began to undertake clandestine support operations, dropping agents and stores to native resistance fighters over a wide area in the South Pacific. On 19 March two OSS agents, four downed US Navy aircrew and a Catholic priest were plucked from the south coast of China by a USAAF 2nd Emergency Rescue Squadron (ERS) OA-10A Catalina based at Morotai. On another mission by the 2nd ERS Lt Shandelmeir landed on the coast of Naburos Island to pick up five evading airmen and deliver weapons, ammunition and leaflets to the tribesmen who had located them.

No. 112 ASR Flight RAAF, based at Darwin, was another Catalina unit specialising in long-range rescues of Allied aircrew in Japanese-held waters and was involved in one of the most demanding air-sea rescues of the Far East campaign. It took place on 6 April 1945 when ten RAAF Mitchells and four Liberators attacked a Japanese troop convoy, escorted by the light cruiser *Isuzu*, off Koepang in the Netherlands East Indies. Japanese Zero fighters shot down two of the Liberators, with eleven members of the crews taking to their parachutes. Catalina A24-54, flown by Flt Lt Bullman, alighted in the area and had picked up four of the survivors when it too came under attack from another Zero, setting the flying boat on fire. It sank within minutes and the survivors of this attack had hardly enough time to scramble onto a five-man dinghy dropped by one of the circling Liberators.

A second No. 112 ASR Flight Catalina, A24-58, was sent to the scene with Flt Lt Robin Corrie at the controls. He was able to land near the dinghy to pull all the airmen aboard, including Bullman, and was searching for two others when two Japanese twin-engined Nakajima J1N Irvings attacked with cannon fire. The blister-gunner of A24-58 responded while Corrie made an emergency take-off with water cascading through the open blisters. Pursued by the Irvings the overweight Catalina twisted and turned only a few feet above the sea, and it was only when the covering Liberator threatened the Japanese fighters that Corrie was able to make a laboured climb to 3,500 feet and the safety of a cloud bank. The flying boat, escorted by the Liberator, eventually arrived safely at Darwin and although another search was mounted for the missing aircrew, none was found.

From the beginning of the new year, No. 357 Squadron's Dakota flight commander, Sqn Ldr Terence 'Pat' O'Brien, was putting his knowledge of Burmese landing strips to good use. On the night of 26 February he flew one of the flight's longest sorties, during which he was airborne for 16 hours 15 minutes when Dakota KJ921/'H' flew from Myitkyina in Burma to drop six French agents over Indo-China on Operation 'Satiristi'. A few days later O'Brien dropped food and supplies provided by the Force 136 commander in Calcutta to a Kachin village at Sinthe, whose headman had earlier been murdered by the Japanese for harbouring him during his long trek out of Burma the previous year.

On 23 March he conducted the first pick-up operation in Indo-China when he landed behind Japanese lines at Dun Bien. Of the two French agents who climbed aboard the Dakota during Operation 'Opponent', one was Col André Dewavrin, codenamed Passy, head of de Gaulle's secret intelligence service, the Bureau Central de Renseignements et d'Action (BCRA). He had flown into France with Yeo-Thomas on No. 161 Squadron Lysanders in 1943.

One of O'Brien's colleagues on the Liberator Flight, Flt Lt Tommy Lee, dropped three SOE agents over Jason Bay in Malaya on the night of 26/27 March, but after suffering an engine failure over the DZ Liberator KH391/'Y' had to be nursed back to its base in India on three engines, a distance of nearly 1,500 miles, having been airborne for 22 hours 45 minutes.

During the month of March No. 357 Squadron's Liberators flew another 67 SD operations, losing two aircraft. Its commanding officer Lewis Hodges recalled, 'We did lose an aircraft, KJ921/"H", on Operation "Globe" near Canton in the Province of Kwantung, China. Flg Off Hunter and his crew lost their lives on this operation, when their aircraft crashed into the island of Hailing in the South China Sea, just off the mainland.' It was one of 115 sorties that the squadron flew that month, with No. 358 Squadron flying 149.

A new Australian SD unit was established at RAAF Laverton on 15 February: No. 200 (SD) Flight, commanded by Sqn Ldr L.H. Pockley DFC and equipped with six B-24M Liberators. On 24 March Pockley flew from MacGuire Field on Mindoro in the Philippines to drop four OSS agents to a DZ on the west coast of Batu Lawi in Borneo. On his second run over the DZ Pockley dropped his 'Storepedoes', as the Australians called the standard SD supply containers,

Chinese troops with containers dropped by a No. 357 (SD) Squadron Liberator near Canton during Operation 'Glove' in February 1945; it crashed into the Island of Hailing on its return. *(Lewis Hodges)*

but during the return flight to the Philippines Liberator A72-191 was shot down while attacking a Japanese patrol boat and crashed into the sea. Pockley and his crew of ten were lost along with SOE liaison officer Maj Bill Ellis, who had been the resident parachute expert with No. 624 Squadron at Brindisi in 1944. He had also supervised the first drop tests at Blida from the Squadron's SD Stirling IVs.

The new Australian unit had worked alongside No. 113 ASR Flight RAAF, based at Cairns but operating out of Tarakan Island in Borneo. Its ace rescue pilot, Flt Lt Wally Mills, flew a series of operations during April from the Rajang River to pick up AIB groups from Brunei Bay in Sarawak, and Balikpapan and Jonahmerah in Borneo. On 30 June Mills landed on the Rajang River in Sarawak with an AIB party, and remained on the water for two hours before taking off again to fly to Leiput on the Barum River to locate a second AIB group. When they were located, two Japanese soldiers they had captured were handed over to the crew who flew them back to Labuan in Sarawak.

By this time, OSS Detachment 101 claimed to have expanded its guerrilla force to over 10,000 in the China–Burma–India theatre, under Col Peers. In

THE SETTING SUN 225

addition to a number of American-staffed intelligence bases in Burma, such as that of Capt Oliver Milton, 162 native agents had been inserted by land, sea and air by March 1944. Many of the OSS guerrilla fighters in Burma were Kachin hill tribesmen such as Lazum Tang, an English-educated Kachin officer who led a force of several hundred men operating in the border area, and had helped the retreating Chindits the previous year.

On 26 March the Minister of War of the Japanese-established 'independent' Burmese government, General Aung San, was flown out of a secret OSS-built airstrip by Stinson L-5 and taken to British 14th Army headquarters, where General Slim persuaded him to change sides. A week later Aung San and his commander-in-chief, Gen Ne Win, led their forces into the Irrawaddy Delta, launching a fierce guerrilla war against their Japanese rulers, while British forces defeated the Japanese at Mandalay and headed towards the capital, Rangoon.

As the Allied advance gathered momentum in Burma the Americans took a more pro-active stance in support of covert warfare in the former British colony. On 5 May Detachment 101 troops captured the Burmese coastal town of Sandoway, an operation that involved another Air Commando Stinson L-5 flown by a Lt Condict, who landed a total of five American OSS agents to lead the local guerrilla forces.

Early in 1945 Lt Wilmot G. Rhodes demonstrated a top-secret special-operations device to the US–British Joint Staff at Jessore. Rhodes was a flight commander at the US Army Liaison Pilot School at Fort Sill, Oklahoma, when he was assigned to the OSS to assist with the development of the Brodie System, a device to enable light aircraft to operate without a landing strip. Conceived by Capt James H. Brodie of the USAAF Transportation Corps, the system enabled a light aircraft rigged with an overhead hook to land by snagging a six-foot-wide sling, hanging from a 600-foot-long elevated cable slung between two 65ft tubular steel gantries, and rolling to a braked halt only 50 feet along the cable. The aircraft was then lowered to the ground. To take off, the aircraft was winched up to the sling, where the hook was put into the stirrup. A travel release, consisting of a long holdback line and spring-loaded trip, prevented the aircraft from beginning a run until the engine was at full power. A pull on the lanyard attached to the trip lever disconnected the aircraft from the holdback. An emergency release functioned if the aircraft had not been released from the trolley before the end of the cable. Without wind, an average light aircraft took off from the cable in 400 feet; with wind it was off in 200 feet. And it worked!

The Brodie system could provide a good landing and take-off site in thick jungle, on rocky terrain, marshes, soft sand, or anywhere where constructing an airstrip was difficult or impractical. It was perfect for forward military positions or behind enemy lines. From the air it was almost impossible to spot, and even more difficult to destroy. The whole system, including the tools and tackle, weighed less than 7,000lbs and could be transported along with its nine-man crew by a C-47, and parachuted into a location. The rig could be assembled and ready for operations within 12 hours.

Having successfully demonstrated the system to Pentagon Army Staff, who approved the programme's continuation, Lt Rhodes travelled to India with two enlisted Brodie specialists and carried out a series of demonstrations using an L-5 at Jessore airfield before bemused members of No. 357 (SD) Squadron. The purpose of the exercise was to determine if the Brodie system could assist Merrill's Marauders in the Burma campaign, as well as inserting and extracting OSS and Force 136 agents in the region. In the event, the Allies' swift advance into Burma during 1945 meant that enough usable airstrips became available for forward observation and special duties operations. The Brodie system was, however, used to great effect during the battles for Saipan and Okinawa when fitted to the US Navy Landing Ships Tank (LST), again using the ubiquitous L-5.

By mid-1945, the OSS also viewed the former French dependency of Indo-China as a target for its activities. Operation 'Gorilla' involved the blind drop of a five-man OSS mission led by Maj John W. Summers on 24 April. After running into a Japanese patrol three days later, they met up with a force of some 100 Vichy French troops who had turned on their 'protective' Japanese masters. The OSS troops soon became involved in another firefight with the enemy, during which two of Operation Gorilla's officers were killed and Maj John W. Summers was wounded. Sgt Donald S. Spears, who was the only remaining able-bodied OSS trooper, then supervised the building of an airstrip at Keng-Tung with the assistance of local tribesmen and managed to make radio contact with the OSS mission at Kunming. On 2 May an L-5 arrived at the airstrip with Lt Sullivan bringing in Capt Patti to replace Maj Summers, who was flown out from the airstrip to Szemao en route for Kunming nine days later.

OSS officer Capt Aaron Bank had requested a transfer to Detachment 101 and by early June, following Hitler's suicide on 30 April before his team could assassinate the Führer, had been also parachuted blind into Indo-China as the Japanese moved against the Vichy French administration. He quickly made contact with the Communist resistance leader Ho Chi Minh, who had been released from jail in China at the insistence of the OSS. When Banks met the Viet Minh leader, the latter was attempting to get US aid to help keep Indo-China free from French rule when the war ended.

Bank attended a meeting between Ho and the Japanese puppet emperor, Bao Dai, who had recently been overthrown and was now allying himself to the Viet

Minh cause. Banks and other OSS officers recommended that Ho Chi Minh be given the United States' full support, in the same way that it was given to Tito's communist JANL in 1944. But their requests were largely unheeded and Ho Chi Minh remained in his Tonkin stronghold, building a guerrilla force that would be directed more at the returning French than the retreating Japanese.

While Indo-China would remain a bone of contention between the Allies the campaign in Burma was altogether more focused, with additional assets being deployed to support the guerrilla forces behind the lines. In January No. 357 (SD) Squadron had been assigned a single Stinson L-5B, known in the RAF as the Sentinel II, one of sixty supplied under the Lend-Lease programme. Operating from Akyab and Kyaukpyu on Ramree Island during the Allied reconquest of Burma, the Sentinel's STOL qualities were appreciated, although its limited carrying capacity left the squadron seeking a replacement. This came in the shape of Lewis Hodges' old aircraft, the dependable SD Lysander, the first of which was deployed to the Far East in June to replace the Sentinel, flying short sorties to difficult locations in Burma, landing agents and stores and evacuating the wounded.

Manned by old SD hands from Tempsford, 'C' Flight's commander was Flt Lt George Turner and its first sortie to Meiwang was flown by Peter Arkell on 3 May 1945. The 'Black' Lysander's ground crews had adopted the British 14th Army emblem, which was painted under the cockpits along with an unofficial spider symbol that appeared in the centre of the blue-and-white SEAC fuselage roundel.

Two of the Lysanders flew four Force 136 agents on 5 May to an abandoned Japanese airfield outside Rangoon that proved to be ideal for the short-take-off and landing aircraft, as its runway was pitted with bomb craters following sustained Allied attacks, making it almost impossible for use by faster or larger aircraft. The Lysanders flew a total of forty sorties during May, to pick up thirty-seven people and deliver four tons of supplies. Apart from the SD veterans, the Lysander flight was also manned by new pilots from widely varying backgrounds. Prince Varanand was a member of the Thai royal family serving with the RAF, but was not considered experienced enough to carry out any pick-up operations from behind Japanese lines. Flt Sgt Gordon Scott was a recently qualified Hurricane pilot who had given up waiting for a posting to a Typhoon Operational Training Unit (OTU) in England when the war in Europe ended, and had volunteered for Special Duties as the only way to see action before the end of the Pacific war.

Although the Lysanders were in little danger from enemy fighters, the SD Liberators were more at risk. On the night of 12 May No. 358 Squadron

Special Duties Lysander IIIA V9289 of No. 357 (SD) Squadron at Mingaladon in Burma in 1945, with the squadron's Liberators and Dakotas in the background. *(Bruce Robertson)*

Liberator KH350/'T', flown by Flt Sgt Mathews, was attacked by three Japanese A6M2-N Rufes, a floatplane variant of the Zero fighter, while flying to a Malayan DZ. The accurate shooting of the Liberator's mid-upper gunner scared off the fighters, and although one continued to shadow the Liberator, Mathews lost it by entering a thick cloudbank. Only ten days later Mathews was again attacked by fighters – this time no fewer than eight Imperial Japanese Army Ki-43 Oscars of the 77th Sentai – near a DZ on the Salween River, 100 miles north-east of Rangoon, while flying another Liberator, EW274/'F'. Again he managed to lose them in thick cloud, in which the pilot hid for such a long time that the operation had to be aborted.

Not so lucky was No. 200 Flight Liberator EW174/'P', flown by Canadian pilot Flg Off H.V. Smith on an operation on 29 May to drop three OSS agents into Thailand. It was attacked by nine Oscars near Alor Star in Malaya and although the rear gunner managed to shoot down one of the Japanese fighters, four of the crew were killed in the attack and Smith was forced to crash-land the crippled aircraft into a jungle clearing on the Thai border. Two more men were killed in the crash, including OSS agent Edward Napieralski, and another four were badly injured. With the help of local tribesmen, the pilot and his rear gunner Flt Sgt Copley managed to escape and make contact with an OSS group, the others being taken to a Bangkok internment camp by the Thai police.

Earlier in the year a second Australian SD unit was formed at RAAF Laverton, No. 201 (SD) Flight, with three Liberators being allotted to it by June, but it never progressed beyond the training stage. Some of its aircrew were later posted to No. 200 (SD) Flight which had been expanded to form No. 8 Squadron RAAF at the end of May, equipped with six B-24M Liberators and an Anson 'hack'. It would fly a total of twenty-two SD missions during its first full month of operations.

Typical of the 'Joes' dropped behind the lines into Thailand by the SD squadrons was Sydney Hudson. Commissioned in the Royal Fusiliers at the beginning of the war, Hudson was invited to join SOE in 1942. Fluent in French, having lived in Switzerland for three years where his father was an ICI distributor, he became an 'F' Section agent and was parachuted into Clermont-Ferrand from a Polish-crewed Halifax in September 1942. He was soon captured, but managed to escape to Spain with the help of fellow SOE agents Anne-Marie Walters and George Starr.

Two months after arriving back in Britain in February 1944 he was dropped from a Hudson south of Issoudun with two other agents, George Jones and

A No. 8 Squadron RAAF Liberator IV flying over Burma near the Indian border in August 1945. *(Andy Thomas)*

Muriel Byck. He remained in France until it was overrun by Allied troops after D-Day. Early in 1945 Hudson sailed for India to join the Thai Section of Force 136, and in late May was preparing for his third drop behind enemy lines in three years, along with the Thai Prince Varanard who was a serving RAF officer and known only as 'Nicky'.

> We took off from Jessore at night in a four-engined bomber and by the time dawn broke, we were well clear of the Burma–Thailand border. We flew on for perhaps an hour, then the dispatcher connected our parachutes and we felt the plane circle. He took the cover off the hole in the floor and we saw we were passing over thick forest. Suddenly there came a clearing. The dispatcher shouted 'Go!'
>
> Then the familiar steeling of nerves, the drop, the buffeting of the slipstream, the jerk of the 'chute opening and the sensation of floating down. I could see we were in a large open space with quite a few people around it. I landed easily enough and, as my parachute training demanded, immediately began to fold my 'chute. A rather thickset Thai man of about 30 years of age, in British tropical uniform and wearing captain's shoulder badges, came up to me.
>
> In excellent English he said, 'Never mind about that. Let's get off the ground quick.' He escorted me, also 'Nicky' who had landed nearby, to a large hut made of bamboo. 'It was better to get you off the ground,' he explained. 'There were quite a few locals watching and there aren't many European faces around these days!'

They had landed near an airfield at Khonsan, where an elderly Royal Thai Air Force Potez XXV biplane that had been captured from the French was put at their disposal. Their task was to search for suitable landing strips that could be used by No. 357 Squadron's Dakotas. Although Thailand was ostensibly a satellite state of Japan, a sophisticated resistance movement was being run from the RTAF headquarters in Bangkok. Allied agents were flown around the country in elderly Fairchild 24Js and Japanese two-seat Tachikawa Ki 36 communications aircraft, codenamed Ida, as well as in the Potez biplanes.

Hudson had selected a strip at Naarn near the Laos border where agents could be flown in and rescued downed Allied airmen flown out. He was picked up from the site by a Dakota on 19 June and flown back to Jessore. While in Thailand he had been joined by another SOE officer, Maj David Smiley, who with a British sergeant and two Thai agents was dropped on 31 May from a No. 357 Squadron Dakota, also to reconnoitre airstrips suitable for SD operations.

Smiley, who had headed SOE reception parties in Albania two years earlier while serving under Julian Amery, the SOE's Liaison Officer to the Albanian resistance movement, was in the habit of carrying a booby-trapped briefcase containing his documents when on operations behind the lines. On this occasion it accidentally exploded when he landed heavily, injuring his arm. On board the Dakota that picked him up from Naarn at the end of June was Sydney Hudson, who was returning from Jessore for another stint in Thailand.

For some unaccountable reason the British Air Ministry chose the start of the monsoon season to drop its own bombshell for the hard-pressed SD aircrews. It decreed that as from the end of May 1945, the length of a full RAF tour for Special Duties aircrew in the Far East would be increased from 300 hours to 400 hours, a decision that showed little insight into the conditions they faced while carrying out their everyday operations. The only reason given was that as many sorties were of more than 12 hours' duration, it would only take 33 sorties to complete an operational tour, whereas Bomber Command Pathfinder pilots in Europe had been required to complete 45 sorties.

Someone who was well aware of the challenges faced by SD crews was another Tempsford old boy, Hugh Verity, who had been posted to Headquarters Air Command, South East Asia, at Kandy after VE-Day to supervise SD operations. It was his old friend Lewis Hodges who made the first landing of an Allied aircraft in Japanese-occupied Thailand, when Dakota KJ919/'F' touched down at Kyankpyn on 1 June. The No. 357 Squadron aircraft was carrying two OSS officers and supplies, and fifteen people were picked up from the strip to be flown back to Jessore. Pat O'Brien also picked up a similar number from an airstrip in the pro-Japanese Shan State of Central Burma. These flights occurred during Operation 'Parterre-Muslin' when the Allies were advancing into Burma on all fronts, fighting an ever-determined enemy to the finish.

Two of the survivors of the No. 200 Flight Liberator shot down on 29 May were picked up from an airstrip at Phukhieo in northern Thailand on 14 June. Flt Lt Lewis had flown a No. 357 Squadron Dakota to Tounon on the Sittang river in Burma to collect an OSS agent, before flying on to Thailand to pick up the Liberator's pilot and rear-gunner plus an evading US pilot, an escaped Australian PoW and three OSS agents. Only days later one of its Liberators came close to disaster on an operation to Indo-China, where the Vichy French administration had recently been ousted by the Japanese. Flt Sgt D.J.F. McCulloch staged through the liberated Burmese Island of Akyab in the Bay of Bengal to drop six of De Gaulle's BCRA secret-service agents. Despite a runaway propeller after take-off, which required the engine to be shut down, the Liberator arrived over the DZ within five minutes of its ETA, and returned safely, its three engines keeping them airborne for 27 hours to complete the 4,300-mile flight.

The legendary reliability of the 1,200hp Pratt and Whitney Twin Wasp engines that powered the Liberator, Catalina, Dakota and Hudson SD aircraft used in the Far East enabled many crews to return to safety when the odds seemed stacked against them. Sqn Ldr Wearne tested the Twin Wasp to its limits when he had to retrieve a Catalina that had made an emergency landing short of its base at Darwin, following a rare engine failure. As there were no facilities for an engine change in the area, Attie Wearne decided to fly it home on one engine – but could it take off on one engine? Having removed the propeller from the broken engine and removed all extraneous equipment, he and his crew were about to find out.

Unfortunately, there was very little wind and the bay was very calm. These features, together with the heat, made things more difficult than would be the case if a decent breeze was blowing and a good chop on the surface was available. As a result the take-off run took 4 minutes. The aircraft seemed to just not want to stay up on the step, no matter how hard I worked. Eventually enough speed was gained and we came unstuck much to the relief of all concerned, especially the flight engineer who was very worried about the excessive temperature of the remaining engine. Once airborne, the aircraft performed admirably and we arrived back at Darwin without incident, after a four-hour flight. Although overheated for more than the maximum time advised, no apparent damage was done to the engine.

While the engines kept turning, the fuel they consumed was critical on many of the long-distance SD operations. No. 358 Squadron Liberator EV925/'B', flown by Flg Off Outram on a sortie to Indo-China, developed a serious fuel leak and was then attacked by three Oscars as it neared the DZ on 30 June. The fighters were successfully fought off, despite the twin .50in machine guns in the rear turret being the Liberator's only defensive armament. After hiding in clouds for nearly two hours, Outram finally dropped the six French agents some way from their designated DZ. Running short of fuel, he managed to put the Liberator down on a short advance airstrip used by Mosquito fighter bombers at Hmawbi, some 30 miles from the Burmese capital Rangoon.

As OSS demand for their services increased, the RAF SD units were relieved when they were finally supplemented in June by a USAAF Air Transport Command squadron of C-47 Skytrains. They were made available to OSS Detachment 404 for SD operations into Thailand, the first being flown on the

Force 136 troops dragging supplies to the jungle from a No. 357 Squadron Dakota on an airstrip behind the Japanese lines in northern Burma. *(ww2 images)*

night of 25 June when two agents were dropped near Kanchanaburi, west of Bangkok and close to the Burmese border. Operations resumed during the moon period in late July, beginning with the parachuting of three agents into the Klong Pai area on July 21. By the end of the month the Skytrains had dropped another fifteen OSS agents into Thailand and nearly 100 tons of stores.

Across the South China Sea No. 8 Squadron Liberators flew five Operation 'Platypus' missions during July from Morotai to DZs in Borneo. However, communications failures with the Eureka/Rebecca equipment and S-Phones led to many of the stores containers missing their targets, although the Squadron had more success when dropping agents. Wg Cdr Read, the squadron's commanding officer, dropped another five-man AIB team two weeks later on the southern shore of Lake Milintang in Borneo. As he made his first run in to the DZ, Catalina A24-92 of No. 113 ASR Flight, with Flt Lt Eddie Allison at the controls, touched down on the same lake to pick up another group of agents but ran ashore, holing the hull. Having successfully dropped his agents, Read circled the damaged flying boat until a second No. 113 ASR Flight Catalina, flown by Flt Lt 'Chick' Chinnick, arrived on the lake carrying a high-powered bilge pump. After transferring all of its heavy equipment to the second Catalina, Allison was able to take off, while Chinnick picked up Dutch Army major and a wounded native and flew them to Morotai, escorted by Read's Liberator.

The ASR Flight flew several more SD missions during the following month to pick up ten agents and land five Canadian Chinese agents on the Rajang river, where Wg Cdr Read dropped a five-man army team, including Maj 'Shorteye' Wooler, from Liberator A72-187 on the night of 7 July. In response to emergency radio calls received on 3 August, Chick Chinnick flew Catalina A24-109 to Lake Milintang to pick up nineteen agents, including the five dropped by Read in July, and two wounded natives. Owing to strong currents, Chinnick had to water-taxi for more than 12 miles before finding a suitable stretch of water to take off from, getting airborne just minutes before the arrival of a Japanese patrol boat.

A supply drop from a No. 357 (SD) Squadron Dakota over a jungle clearing in Japanese-held Burma during Operation 'Carpenter' in 1945. *(Lewis Hodges)*

No. 358 Squadron's bad luck continued in July. Two Liberators were lost, one of which, KH365/'N' flown by Flying Officer Manning, crash-landed in a mangrove swamp near Dalhouse Point on the Sundarbano coast of Borneo after running out of fuel. The pilot and rear gunner were badly injured, but all of the crew were later picked up by a Catalina of No. 240 Squadron which flew them back to Calcutta.

As the Allied noose tightened around the Japanese home islands, Kamikaze operations against Allied warships became ever more desperate. This desperation was illustrated by the deployment of the MXY7 Ohka (Cherry Blossom), a single-seat, rocket-powered suicide attack aircraft inspired by KG 200's still-born Reichenberg project. The Ohka was carried to within 20 miles of its target by Mitsubishi G4M twin-engined long-range bombers. Allocated the Allied codename Betty, the bomber was also chosen for Operation 'Tsurugi' (Sword), one of the few clandestine missions to be planned by the Imperial Japanese Navy.

On the night of 24 May Japanese army commandos had been dropped from ten Ki-21 Sally heavy bombers to sabotage USAAF B-29 bombers based on Okinawa. Although most of the commando force was wiped out, the fact that several Superfortresses were damaged during the raid encouraged the launch of a much more ambitious operation. The plan was for 100 specially modified G4M2s, codenamed Rikko, from the 704, 705 and 706th Kokutai based at Misawa and other bases in northern Honshu, to carry a force of 600 army and navy commandos to B-29 bases in the Marianas, Guam and Tinian. Stripped of much of their defensive armament including the dorsal turret, the Rikkos would be crash-landed on the American airfields during a low-level attack by Yokosuka P1Y Ginga medium bombers.

The operation's objective was not only to destroy the B-29s, but also to hijack one of them and fly it to Japan. Japanese pilots had inspected a crashed Super-fortress at Nagoya and studied captured flight manuals. The English-speaking aircrews selected for the mission would all wear replica USAAF flying suits and ground crew fatigues. Operation Tsurugi was planned to take place in late July, but a raid on the Rikkos' base by US Navy fighter-bombers on 14/15 July damaged several aircraft, and it was postponed to the moon period between 19–23 August. However, another US raid on 9 August, the same day that an atomic bomb was dropped on the Japanese city of Nagasaki, destroyed more than thirty of the modified Rikkos and Operation Tsurugi was cancelled.

That same day, a Jedburgh team assigned to OSS Special Operations Detachment 202 in the China theatre severed a vital link between the Japanese armies of north and south China. The mile-long, double-track railway bridge that crossed the Hwang-Ho (Yellow) river near Kaifeng was the target of Mission Jackal, a band of Chinese guerrillas led by Jedburgh veterans Col Frank Mills and Maj Paul Cyr, who had been dropped into the area by a C-47 from Kunming. On 9 August Mission Jackal blew away two spans of the bridge just as a troop train carrying some 2,000 Japanese soldiers was passing over. Most of the bridge and the entire train fell into the Hwang-Ho river.

During the preparations for a Japanese withdrawal, No. 357 Squadron Dakotas continued to insert OSS Detachment 404 agents into Thailand, flying three intelligence specialists to Phukhiero on 10 August. Two of these agents were picked up by a Royal Thai Air Force aircraft and flown to Don Muang near the capital, Bangkok. They climbed out of the Thai plane in a hangar that was shared by the Japanese, before being driven to the Thai army barracks in the capital to negotiate with the pro-Allies government. In Burma the squadron's Lysanders were kept busy operating from Force 136 HQ's Panda airstrip at Myingyan and Hyena airstrip at Lipyekhi as photo-reconnaissance aircraft, mapping the area forward of the 14th Army advance and landing reconnaissance parties.

Several of No. 357 Squadron's Lysanders had been lost to enemy action or landing accidents, and three were written off at Meiktila during a freak monsoon storm, but by VJ-Day on 15 August the squadron still had six of the veteran aircraft on strength. During last-ditch attacks by the Japanese in Burma Lysander V9665, flown by Flt Sgt Castledine, landed two agents and stores at Hyena, but skidded off the muddy airstrip and damaged its propeller and undercarriage. A new propeller was later flown out and fitted on site by the hard-pressed ground crew, who were exposed to the monsoon downpours. By 13 August the Lysander was fit to be flown back to Jessore. This was a week after an atomic bomb had been dropped on Hiroshima, and two days after No. 358 Squadron Liberator KG877/'O' had crashed near Akyab Island on a routine supply-drop sortie. There were no survivors among the eight-man crew.

Lewis Hodges recalled that No. 357 Squadron's final sorties, following the unconditional surrender of Japan on 15 August, were supply drops to the PoW camps which the Japanese had abandoned in their retreat.

While the Lysanders landed at the camps with medical personnel and supplies, the Liberators and Dakotas parachuted food, water and clothing to the Allied prisoners. One of the Liberators, which had landed at a nearby airfield and embarked the seriously ill from one of the camps, crashed on take-off, killing five of the eleven on board. These accidents were thankfully rare and mostly the airborne evacuations and operations went smoothly.

It was also during this period that one of the surviving Lysanders was written off. On the day after the Japanese surrender, Peter Arkell's Lysander V9885 crashed on landing at Hyena airstrip carrying a dispatcher and a 500lb load of supplies. The aircraft overturned on the soft ground trapping both the crew, who had to be rescued by a troop of Gurkhas. The dispatcher, who had been trapped by the load in the rear cockpit, was shaken but not injured, while Arkell ended up with cuts, bruises, and a broken arm. When George Turner flew to the airstrip bringing the squadron's medical officer with him he also skidded off the muddy strip, damaging his Lysander's undercarriage. However, it did not prevent him from flying Arkell back to Jessore the following day after some panel beating by the overworked ground crew. During more than 400 sorties, the Lysander flight had landed 142 people and picked up 282 in less than four months of operations in Burma.

Nos 357 and 358 Squadrons lost a total of twenty-seven aircraft during 1944–5, only one of which is known to have been lost to enemy action. The OSS detachments in the Far East had mounted 122 insertion operations, sixteen to Burma, seventeen to Malaya, eight to the Netherlands East Indies, ten to the Andaman Islands and 71 to Thailand and Indo-China. Eighty-seven of the agents dropped, including one female, Elizabeth McIntosh, were US officers, fifteen of whom were killed in action behind the lines; another 147 were native to the region.

While the bravery of many agents, both men and women who risked and, in many cases, gave their lives on hazardous missions in enemy-occupied countries in Europe and the Far East has been well documented, the sacrifices made by those who flew the clandestine fights has remained something of a well-kept secret. To put the cost of supporting Churchill's undercover army of resistance fighters into perspective: for every SOE, SIS or OSS agent who lost his or her life in the field – more than 400 – at least one RAF or USAAF airman was killed while flying Special Duties operations.

Postscript

When SOE closed its doors at the end of 1945, much to the relief of the senior British intelligence agencies MI5 and SIS, many of its files were destroyed, lost, or simply buried by the authorities. There was little overt recognition from governments for what the organisation had achieved within its short life, and the public remained largely unaware of the significant part it played in the fight against the Axis powers. Its personnel moved on.

Some senior desk officers such as Sir Brooks Richard, who replaced Jacques de Guélis as head of SOE's French section in Algiers, and pilots Sir Robin Hooper and Sir David Hildyard entered the diplomatic service, ending their careers as British ambassadors, while others became successful business executives. A few, including the Norwegian Per Hysing-Dahl, entered politics. Many more former members of the French Resistance entered political life, three of them becoming presidents of the Republic. One of these was Vincent Auriol whose daughter-in-law, Jacqueline, was also a member of the Resistance. She had two young sons, and had narrowly evaded arrest on more than one occasion. After the war Jackie Auriol learned to fly, became one of France's leading test pilots and was the second woman to break the sound barrier. Many other French SOE and OSS agents simply tried to pick up their pre-war lives as lawyers, journalists, teachers or farmers.

Two of the alleged double agents had mixed fortunes. Mathilde-Lily Carré, 'The Cat', was deported to France, tried, sentenced to death and reprieved. After eight years in prison she was released and wrote her memoirs. The extrovert Henri Déricourt was also brought to trial in France but his former SOE colleagues, including Major Nicholas Bodington and Philippe Livry-Level, rallied to his defence. He was acquitted on all charges, although he later admitted taking money from the Germans in exchange for certain information supplied by SIS, thus making him a triple agent! He later moved to Indo-China to resume his career as an airline pilot, before mysteriously disappearing on a flight over Laos in 1962.

Many of the surviving SOE agents had had close contacts with Carré and Déricourt, possibly too close, and after the war some of them found it difficult to adjust to peacetime life. Wg Cdr Yeo-Thomas was awarded the Military Cross and the George Cross, and the Croix de Guerre with palm from Charles De Gaulle, for exceptional bravery, but the legacy of the appalling tortures he suffered at the hands of the Gestapo led to his early death in 1964. Odette Sansom was awarded the George Cross for the same reasons and married fellow SOE agent Peter Churchill after the war, but the marriage could not survive the relative monotony of domestic life.

The talented, headstrong Christine Granville was virtually abandoned by her SOE masters after her adventures in France and was left stranded in Cairo. She was awarded the George Cross and Order of the British Empire, but the War Office had been reluctant to recommend the awards as she was a Pole. Granville had to borrow money from friends in order to move to London. There she took up a variety of menial jobs, culminating in that of a stewardess on the liner *Winchester Castle* in 1951; but when her superior, Dennis Muldowney, became infatuated with her she was forced to leave, becoming a porter at the Reform Club in London. On 15 June 1952 Muldowney tracked her down at her hotel and stabbed the 37-year-old SOE heroine to death.

Of those who risked their lives flying agents into occupied Europe and east Asia, several remained in the post-war RAF, among them Sir Lewis Hodges, Sir Alan Boxer, Douglas Bell and Hugh Verity. AVM Sir Edward Fielden resumed his position as captain of the King's Flight, later the Queen's Flight, while Gp Capt Peter Vaughan-Taylor was appointed deputy captain of the Queen's Flight in 1963. Many more took up careers as civil airline captains – John Affleck, Bob Large and Henk van Hasselo – and Armand Etienne, who died in a Swissair accident in 1969. Even the defecting Luftwaffe Ju 88 pilot Heinrich Schmitt flew as a commercial pilot in Germany after the war, before emigrating to South America and disappearing from view. Coincidentally, KG 200's Dutch pilot Willem De Graaf also joined the ex-Nazi escape line to South America after a period of hiding in Germany, and all trace of him was also lost.

The OSS, which was terminated on 1 October 1945, spawned a new espionage organisation, the Central Intelligence Agency (CIA), formed in 1947 to fight the new Cold War between the former Eastern and Western allies; it was manned by many former OSS officers. No fewer than four of its directors spent their early careers with the Office of Strategic Services, one of the first being Allen Dulles. He was later followed in the office by Richard Helms, William J. Casey and William E. Colby, all of whom had served at OSS Station London, as had Arthur M. Schlesinger, who became Special Assistant to President John F. Kennedy in 1961. Colby had trained as a member of a Jedburgh team that was dropped into France in 1944, and into Norway the following year.

The first major post-war trial of strength between the East and West, Operation 'Vittles', brought together many elements of the wartime covert organisations to fly again behind enemy lines, in this case the Soviet Union's. Following the Soviet blockade of the Allied Western Zones of Occupation in Berlin in June 1948, the United States and Britain mounted a massive, seventeen-month-long airlift to the beleaguered capital. Responsibility for intelligence gathering during the initial stages of the airlift fell to a former OSS officer, Frank G. Wisner, then working for the CIA from a mansion in Berlin that had once belonged to Hitler's foreign minister, Joachim von Ribbentrop, who was executed in 1946.

By a strange twist of fate, Wisner's leading agent in post-war West Germany was Lt-Gen Reinhardt Gehlen – former OKH chief of intelligence in eastern Europe and the architect of the Zeppelin operations – who had established several vital espionage-gathering bureaux in East Berlin fronted by import and export agencies and a publicity company.

Among the first units to take part in the airlift was former No. 334 Wing veteran the 60th Troop Carrier Group, then based in West Germany as part of the newly formed United States Air Force (USAF). Among the twenty-one squadrons that supported Operation 'Plainfare', the RAF element of Operation Vittles, were No. 30 Squadron, which had carried out the first airlift to British forces behind enemy lines at Kut in 1916; and No. 47 Squadron, which had carried out the first SOE operation in Abyssinia in 1940. One of the first RAF aircraft to join the airlift, landing on Lake Havel in Berlin on 5 July 1948, was a Sunderland flying boat of No. 230 Squadron, the same unit that had rescued hundreds of Orde Wingate's Chindits from Japanese-occupied Burma in 1944.

Across the Atlantic Col Robert W. Fish, one of the original USAAF Carpetbagger pilots who had supervised the first successful Red Stocking operations over Germany, had also been recruited by the CIA to organise its first training schools in the United States, working in cooperation with the newly created USAF. He was joined by one of his former RAF colleagues, the Polish Wg Cdr Roman Rudkowski, who took the American rank of colonel when he joined the CIA as a liaison and recruiting officer for clandestine flight operations. He recruited a number of Polish air crew who had flown with the RAF's Special Duties squadrons to take part in the infiltration of agents into communist Albania in 1948, and the CIA air offensive in Indonesia a decade later, flying unmarked B-26 Invaders.

Former OSS officer Aaron Bank resumed his career with the US Army. When the US Department of the Army activated the 10th Special Forces Group (Airborne), its first unconventional warfare unit, at Fort Bragg in 1952, Col

Bank was in command. He became known as the Father of the Green Berets. During the bloody South East Asian conflicts in the 1960s his Green Berets would face the North Vietnamese Army under Ho Chi Minh, the resistance leader Bank first met in 1945.

For the survivors of the vanquished KG 200, there were mixed fortunes. The head of the RHSA, the organisation that sanctioned many of the Kampf-geschwader's operations, Ernst Kaltenbrunner, was sentenced to be hanged for war crimes at the 1946 Nuremberg Trials, where the aide to the chief prosecutor was former OSS chief Gen William J. Donovan. Another senior German secret-service officer brought to trial was SS-Gen Walther Schellenberg, who was sentenced to six years' imprisonment but released early on ill-health grounds. Otto 'Scarface' Skorzeny was also tried at Nuremberg and after being acquitted on all charges, retired to Spain.

KG 200's best-known commander, Werner Baumbach, fared less well. Arrested at Flensburg with many of his aircrews, he was brought to England in August 1945 and was subjected to lengthy interrogations about the activities of KG 200 and threatened with trial as a war criminal. However, he was eventually cleared and released in February 1946. Two years later Baumbach joined a group of former Luftwaffe colleagues in Argentina as part of a team of German scientists working on a secret project codenamed Operation 'Soberani'. Former members of Werner von Braun's V-2 design team, they were working on a radio-controlled flying bomb derived from the Henschel Hs 293 that had been used by KG 200 against the Oder bridges in the last month of the war, and it was now ready for flight testing.

The Argentinian Air Force aircraft selected to carry the prototype PAT-1 missile, ironically a British Avro Lancaster bomber, took off with a five-man German crew including Baumbach, although he was not the pilot, on 20 October 1953 for a routine test flight. While flying over Quilmes near Buenos Aires one of the Lancaster's Merlin engines caught fire and the aircraft crashed into the River Plate while attempting an emergency landing, killing three of the crew – including Werner Baumbach.

In the twenty-first century the spirit of the Special Duties airmen, established at such cost during the Second World War, lives on in the modern-day RAF, USAF and RAAF. In recent conflicts in the Balkans, the Far East and the Middle East, more and more emphasis has been placed on Special Forces operating behind enemy lines, and their insertion and support by air. Hercules of No. 47 Squadron RAF and No. 20 Squadron RAAF, and C-141 Starlifters of USAF's 7th Airlift Squadron remain dedicated to the task of upholding the simple, one-word motto of No. 138 (Special Duties) Squadron: 'Freedom'.

Bibliography

BOOKS

Bickers, Richard Townsend, *The First Great Air War*, Hodder & Stoughton, 1988

Binney, Marcus, *The Women who Lived for Danger*, Hodder, 2003

Chalou, George C., *The Secrets War*, National Archives and Records Administration, USA, 1992

Clark, Freddie, *Agents by Moonlight*, Tempus, 1999

Creed, Roscoe, *PBY – The Catalina Flying Boat*, United States Naval Institute, Annapolis, 1985

Collier, Richard, *Bridge across the Sky*, Macmillan, 1978

Cull, Brian, *Hurricanes over Malta*, Grub Street, 2002

Doyle, Paul, *Where the Lysanders Were*, Forward Airfield Research Publications, 1995

Foot, M.R.D., *SOE, The Special Operations Executive 1940–6*, Mandarin, 1967

Freeman, Brett, *Lake Boga at War*, Catalina Publications, Australia, 1995

Galea, Frederick R., *Call-Out*, Malta at War Publications, Malta, 2002

Glen, Alexander and Bowen, Leighton, *Target Danube*, The Book Guild, 2002

Hess, William N., *B-17 Flying Fortress Units of the MTO*, Osprey, 2003

Hill, G.A., *Go Spy the Land*, Cassell, 1931

Hudson, Sydney, *Undercover Operator*, Pen & Sword, 2003

Jackson, Robert, *The Secret Squadrons*, Robson Books, 1983

Jefford, C.G., *RAF Squadrons*, Airlife, 1998

Lamb, Charles, *War in a Stringbag*, Cassell, 1977

Lewis, Cecil, *Sagittarius Rising*, Peter Davis, 1936

Lloyd, Mark *The Guinness Book of Espionage*, Guinness Publishing, 1994

Lucas, Laddie, *Out of the Blue*, Hutchinson, 1985

McCall, Gibb, *Flight Most Secret*, William Kimber, 1981

McKee, Alexander, *The Friendless Sky*, Souvenir Press, 1962

Merrick, K.E., *Flights of the Forgotten*, Arms & Armour, Australia, 1989

Miller, Russell, *Behind the Lines*, Secker, 2003

O'Brien, Terence, *Out of the Blue*, William Collins, 1984

Persico, Joseph E., *Roosevelt's Secret War*, Random House, 2002

Reynolds, Quentin, *They Fought for the Sky*, Cassell, 1958

Smith, Richard, *On Special Missions*, Air War Classics, 2003

Stahl, P.W., *Geheimgeschwader KG 200*, Motorbuch-Verlag, 1979

Thomas, Geoffrey and Ketley, Barry, *KG 200*, Hikoki Publications, 2004

Tomlinson, Michael, *The Most Dangerous Moment*, William Kimber, 1976

Verity, Hugh, *We Landed by Midnight*, Ian Allan, 1982

Ward, Chris, *138 Squadron*, Squadron Profiles, 2001

Watson, Jeffrey, *Sidney Cotton – The Last Plane out of Berlin*, Hodder, 2002

MAGAZINES

Aeroplane, IPC

FlyPast, Key Publishing

Wingspan International, Wingspan International Publishing

Index